Remaking the Italian Economy

A volume in the series

Cornell Studies in Political Economy

EDITED BY PETER J. KATZENSTEIN

A full list of titles in the series appears at the end of the book.

Remaking the Italian Economy

RICHARD M. LOCKE

CORNELL UNIVERSITY PRESS

Ithaca and London

First published 1995 by Cornell University Press.
First printing, Cornell Paperbacks, 1997.

Printed in the United States of America

⊗ The paper in this book meets the minimum requirements of the American National Standard for Information Sciences—Permanence of Paper for Printed Library Materials, ANSI Z39.48-1984.

Library of Congress Cataloging-in-Publication Data

Locke, Richard M., 1959–
    Remaking the Italian economy / Richard M. Locke.
       p.   cm. — (Cornell studies in political economy)
    Includes bibliographical references and index.
    ISBN 0-8014-2891-2 (hc. : acid free paper). — ISBN 0-8014-8421-9 (paper: acid free paper)
       1. Italy—Economic policy. 2. Italy—Economic conditions—1976– . 3. Industrial relations—Italy. 4. Competition, International. I. Title. II. Series.
HC305.L64   1995
338.954—dc20   94-38366

Cloth printing   10   9   8   7   6   5   4   3   2   1
Paperback printing   10   9   8   7   6   5   4   3   2   1

To Juliana, Nathaniel, and
the memory of Walker

Contents

Preface

This book analyzes recent efforts to remake the Italian economy. I became fascinated with Italy because of its many contradictions and anomalies. On the one hand, Italy is seen as the "sick man" of Europe, because it suffers from just about every conceivable problem afflicting the advanced industrial democracies: unstable government, terrorism, massive social protest, stagflation, and a variety of macroeconomic imbalances. On the other hand, even a cursory examination of the comparative data reveals that Italy performs well on key political-economic dimensions: GDP growth, personal savings rates, labor productivity, investment in new equipment. In fact, Italy appears to be performing as well as, at times even better than, its supposedly more "stable" and "efficient" neighbors. How can we reconcile these two apparently contradictory images of the same country?

But Italy is more than an empirical puzzle. It doesn't fit nicely within the traditional categories of comparative political economy. Much of the literature focuses on what I call "national models" to explain divergent patterns of industrial development, decline, and adjustment. This approach stresses how individual nations with divergent political histories and varying positions in world markets develop different institutional arrangements to govern their economies. More than a description of institutional differences, this approach often assumes that certain national systems with particular organizational features are more efficient or stable than others and either prescribes the active replication of these "best (institutional) practices" or assumes their inevitable diffusion across national boundaries.

During the 1970s and 1980s, for example, alternative institutional arrangements associated with particular national models were advanced as the most appropriate means to reverse industrial decline and promote economic adjustment. The suggested models included etatist France and Japan with their highly technocratic state bureaucracies providing "administrative guidance" to leading economic sectors and firms; northern European, neocorporatist systems of centralized interest intermediation, peak-level bargaining, and consensual politics; even the United States, with its staunch defense of free markets and individual entrepreneurialism.

In this book I examine how Italy, a country without a coherent national model, or at least none that fits neatly into any of these categories, restructured its economy in the 1980s. Not only was Italy able to adjust to changing world markets as well as (and perhaps better than) its liberal, statist, and neocorporatist neighbors, but this adjustment took place notwithstanding several failed efforts aimed precisely at remaking Italy in the image of other national models.

Italy's political and economic elites, like many American and European social scientists writing in the 1970s and 1980s, came to perceive their nation's problems as stemming from the absence of a strong and coherent national model. Through a series of institutional reforms aimed at replicating practices found in other, apparently more successful nations, they sought to reconstitute the Italian economy. With few exceptions, however, almost all these efforts failed. They failed for a variety of reasons, not least because of the difficulties inherent in importing institutional practices developed (and embedded) in another national context, but especially because they fell victim to political infighting among Italy's key socioeconomic actors. Despite these political struggles and failed reform efforts, the Italian economy underwent a dramatic restructuring that resulted both in patterns of entrepreneurial vitality and in cases of industrial decline. I seek to explain this paradoxical mixture by arguing that the Italian economy should be viewed not as a coherent national system but rather as an incoherent composite of diverse subnational patterns that coexist (often uneasily) within the same national territory.

Industrial decline and entrepreneurial vitality are both present in the Italian economy, but they are situated in different localities characterized by different patterns of associationalism, intergroup relations, political representation, and economic governance. In other words,

the divergent patterns manifest within the Italian economy are produced by the different sociopolitical networks within which economic
actors like firms and unions are embedded. Divergent sociopolitical
networks create different mixes of resources and constraints that
shape the strategic choices for local economic actors. These sociopolitical networks not only structure information flows and relations among
local economic entities, but also provide local actors with different
linkages or channels of representation to national interest groups and
policymakers.

Thus, although Italian firms throughout the country faced similar
challenges (i.e., increased international competition) and analogous
public policies, they responded in a variety of ways. Both their understanding of the challenges they faced and their capacity to respond
were shaped by the particular features of their context.

In telling this unconventional tale of Italy, I am advancing an alternative approach to the study of comparative political economy. In
contrast to the dominant approach, which sees nation-states or national
systems as the basic unit of analysis and seeks to explain cross-national
variation in economic performance by focusing on particular institutional arrangements or patterns of state-society relations, my focus is
on the microlevel, on the strategic choices of the economic actors
themselves, in order to describe diverse patterns of industrial politics
within the same nation-state. Moreover, rather than view economic
behavior as the product of various structural factors (firm size, technological process, skill level), I stress the role of politics in shaping the
conceptions and strategies of local economic actors.

This book makes three basic points. First, the absence of strong,
centralized institutions and coherent national policies does not necessarily translate into a return to laissez-faire marketism. Beneath Italy's
facade of institutional chaos lies a dense network of regulation and
order. This regulation does not fit neatly into traditional categories.
It does not emanate from a strong, central government, and it takes on
different forms in different localities within the country. Nonetheless,
these multiple, localistic patterns of industrial regulation shaped the
reorganization of Italian industry in the 1980s.

Second, my story is not simply about Italy but concerns all advanced
industrial states as they struggle to govern their economies in an
increasingly international and interdependent world. Other national
governments appear to be losing macroeconomic control over their

economies, and today countries as diverse as Japan, Germany, Sweden, and the United States—national models Italians once sought to emulate—are beginning to resemble Italy in terms of institutional vulnerability and macroeconomic disorder. The Italian case may provide insight into the future evolution of state-economy relations in the advanced industrial states.

Third, the book elucidates the micropolitical determinants of industrial strategy and policy. It suggests that successful industrial strategies build on dense but egalitarian networks of associationalism, interest group organization, and local institutions which facilitate information-sharing and the pooling of scarce resources, mediate conflict, and generate trust among local economic actors. Firms and unions embedded in local economies characterized by such networks appear to adjust with greater facility to shifts in world markets than their counterparts in other regions with more limited or differently shaped sociopolitical infrastructures. This alternative understanding of industrial change has significant implications for future research and policy-making.

This book has taken longer to finish than I care to admit. Yet many people and institutions have helped me along the way. The book began at the Massachusetts Institute of Technology. My work was made easier by an ITT Fellow Doctoral Dissertation grant, a Social Science Research Council Dissertation grant, and an affiliation at the Center for European Studies at Harvard University. I began teaching at MIT in the spring of 1989. While I have been there, I have benefited greatly from extensive comments, prodding, and encouragement from Lucio Baccaro, Donald Blackmer, Zairo Cheibub, Joshua Cohen, Steve Eppinger, Rebecca Henderson, Ellen Immergut, Donald Lessard, Anthony Levitas, Jonah Levy, Steven Lewis, Lisa Lynch, Robert McKersie, Uday Mehta, Wanda Orlinkowski, Paul Osterman, Simona Piattoni, Charles Sabel, Richard Samuels, Serenella Sferza, Marcie Tyre, Karl Ulrich, Eleanor Westney, and Nicholas Ziegler. I also thank Karen Boyajian, Florin Toader, and Susan Wright for their help with manuscript preparation.

Many other friends and colleagues on both sides of the Atlantic have provided research advice and comments on earlier drafts. I thank Aris Accornero, Mario Agostinelli, Bianca Beccalli, Giuseppe Berta, Arnaldo Camuffo, Gian Piero Carpo, Arnold Cohen, Abby Collins,

Marco Giuliani, Peter Hall, Roger Haydon, Chris Howell, Harry Katz, Peter Katzenstein, Horst Kern, Peter Lange, Carol Mershon, Robert Putnam, Pippo Ranci, Marino Regini, Michele Salvati, David Soskice, Kathleen Thelen, Lowell Turner, and the late Maurizio Vannicelli.

I owe a particular debt to a group of friends who continued to listen and talk through ideas when everyone else tired and who patiently provided support during those moments when I feared that I had gotten it all wrong and that the book would never be finished. Thanks again to Suzanne Berger, Victoria Hattam, Gary Herrigel, Thomas Kochan, Michael Piore, Gloria Regonini, and Ano Saxenian.

Finally, I thank my mother, Franca Franzaroli, and brother, Leo, for their support; my wife, Jessica, for her patience and encouragement; and my children for teaching me the most important lessons in life. I dedicate this book to them.

Richard Locke

Cambridge, Massachusetts

Remaking the Italian Economy

CHAPTER ONE

Introduction:
Making Sense of Italy

> The need for a system of planning is, if anything, more acute in a
> country like Italy where the structure of large-scale industry weakens
> the play of market forces and the economic life of the country is
> largely determined by disparate decisions made in a series of uncon-
> nected centers of power, both in the public and the private sector.
> . . . The truth is that behind an administrative facade which bears
> many of the French labels and whose design has been deliberately
> modelled on French ideas, the Italian system of government is in
> practice among the least coordinated in Western Europe.
> —Andrew Shonfield, *Modern Capitalism*

Italy has historically appeared to be a nation with a "weak state" or,
at least, without a concerted political will capable of regulating the
economy. Its government is "weak" and "unstable," civil service "in-
competent," and political party system "polarized." Adjectives like
"backward," "corrupt," and "clientalistic" are regularly used (by foreign and native observers alike) to describe various features of Italy's
political economy.[1]

Recent events have reinforced this negative image. Since February
1992, for example, an ever widening scandal over bribes paid by
businesspeople to politicians in return for public works contracts has
shaken Italy. The estimated amounts involved are between 10 and 20
billion U.S. dollars. One fourth of the 630-member Parliament has
been implicated in the corruption scandal, as have several former

[1]See, for example, Banfield 1967; Cella 1989: 167–86; Chubb and Vannicelli 1988:
122–60; Graziano 1978: 290–326; Tullio-Altan 1976; and Sartori 1966: 137–76.

I

government ministers and the heads of most major political parties.[2] Irresponsible public spending and archaic fiscal policies have also resulted in an enormous government debt (exceeding 104 percent Gross Domestic Product [GDP]) which, in turn, contributed to the lira's collapse on international markets and its withdrawal from the European Exchange Rate Mechanism in the autumn of 1992.[3] Finally, open attacks on the state's authority by the Mafia and other organized crime syndicates, especially in the South, and the electoral defeat of the traditional governing political parties (e.g., Christian Democrats and Socialists) by new, regional parties (e.g., Lega Nord[4]) have together reinforced the image of Italy as weak and unstable.

Alongside these various political and economic crises, however, exists a second, more dynamic Italy. Although often obscured by the negative portrayals of the country, the existence of this second Italy is confirmed by a series of comparative statistics that indicate that Italy in the late 1980s outperformed most of its more efficient and stable neighbors in terms of growth of exports and GDP, labor productivity, firm profitability, investment in new machinery and equipment, and the accumulation of personal savings. Italy's economic performance undoubtedly declined in the early 1990s, due to the global recession and the country's domestic difficulties, but its economy is still far more vital than most popular accounts suggest. For example, in a variety of diverse sectors, including machine tools, automobiles, specialty steels, textiles and apparel, and ceramic tiles, Italian producers remain major exporters in world markets.[5]

---

[2] For more on this scandal, see Kramer 1992: 108–24; "The Tangle in Italy," *Economist*, February 20, 1992: 3–4; and articles by Alan Cowell in the *New York Times* (April 11, 19, 21, 1993). For more on the pervasiveness of political corruption in Italy, see Cazzola 1992; and della Porta 1992.

[3] For more on Italy's growing debt, see Della Sala 1988: 110–25. For an interesting analysis of the fall 1992 currency crisis, see Kevin Muehring et al., "Currency Chaos: The Inside Story," *International Investor*, October 1992.

[4] For more on the Lega, see Mannheimer 1991; and Woods 1992: 56–76.

[5] In the late 1980s, Italy's national champion in automobiles, Fiat, ranked second only to Volkswagen in number of autos produced in Europe. Since then, Fiat, along with other leading European automobile manufacturers (e.g., Volvo, Volkswagen), has experienced challenges to its competitiveness. Nonetheless in 1992, Fiat remained the sixth largest automobile manufacturer in the world. (See *Automotive News*, May 26, 1993: 3.) Italian producers hold about 10 percent world market share in textiles and apparel (see *International Trade and Statistics Yearbook*, 1991); 27 percent world market share (52 percent European market share) in ceramic tiles (see *Il Sole 24 Ore*, May 31, 1993: 3);

This book seeks to explain the apparent paradox behind these two contrasting images of Italy while at the same time advancing an alternative approach to the study of comparative political economy. In contrast to the dominant approach that sees nation-states or national systems as the basic unit of analysis and seeks to explain cross-national variation in economic performance by focusing on particular institutional arrangements or patterns of state-society relations, my alternative micropolitical analysis emphasizes the internal heterogeneity of national economies and the "embeddedness" of economic activity in local sociopolitical networks. In this alternative view, national political economies are not coherent systems but rather incoherent composites of diverse subnational patterns that coexist (often uneasily) within the same national territory.[6]

The micropolitical approach explains how within the same national economy one can identify *both* entrepreneurial dynamism *and* industrial decline. Although present within the same country, these divergent patterns are situated in very different local economies that are, in turn, characterized by alternative patterns of associationalism, intergroup relations, political representation, and economic governance. In Italy, firms and industries situated in localities with particular sociopolitical attributes (e.g., dense networks of well-developed associations and interest groups capable of aggregating diverse interests, mediating industrial conflict, and diffusing information) adjusted more successfully[7] to changing world markets than did other companies embedded in areas with different historical legacies and more limited local resources.

Viewing the Italian economy as a complex composite of diverse local systems helps us not only to reintegrate the two contrasting images of Italy, but also to understand some of the country's difficulties. Because the massive wave of industrial restructuring that swept across the Italian economy in the 1980s had such divergent conse-

---

over 11 percent world market share in machine tools (fourth largest producer, after Japan, Germany, and the United States; see *American Machinist,* February 1993: 33–77); and about 25 percent of the European market for specialty steels (number two spot, after Germany; see Balconi 1991: 473).

[6]This point was raised initially in a series of conversations with Gary Herrigel and is elaborated in his own work on Germany. See Herrigel 1995.

[7]In this book I embrace Peter Katzenstein's definition of "successful adjustment," which includes political as well as economic outcomes. See Katzenstein 1985: 29.

quences for the country's various subnational economies, socioeconomic disparities within Italian society increased in the late 1980s and early 1990s. For example, differences in income, employment, and the quality of social services between the developed North and the less developed South (and even among various regions of the South)—differences that appeared to be narrowing in the 1970s—actually increased in the 1980s.[8] Through various government-funded programs, the Italian state sought to compensate for these growing socioeconomic disparities and hold together the country's divergent subnational economic orders. Yet the costs of these programs have strained the Italian political economy and provoked a major fiscal/macroeconomic crisis and a wave of political mobilization by the Lega Nord aimed at dismembering the Italian state into a loose confederation of macropolitical regions.[9] By creating a more costly and uncertain business environment, these macroeconomic and political crises may threaten to undermine even the more successful Italian regional economies.

To the extent that other national governments also appear to have lost macroeconomic control over their economies,[10] and given that today countries as diverse as Sweden, Germany, and the United States—national systems Italians once sought to emulate—are beginning to resemble Italy in terms of institutional fragmentation and economic decentralization, the Italian case may provide more general lessons for students of comparative political economy.

The remainder of this chapter develops this argument about the way different local sociopolitical networks shape the strategic choices of economic actors in divergent ways. It is divided into three sections.

---

[8]For more on these trends, see CENSIS 1992. For more on differences within the South, see Piattoni, Diss. in progress.

[9]The Lega's proposal for a reconfiguration of the Italian state into a looser federation of regions is remarkably similar to what certain *Meridionalisti* (southern scholar-activists) at the turn of the last century advocated as well. These earlier federalists argued that increased local and regional autonomy was essential for the economic and civic development of the Italian South. For more on this, see Trigilia 1992. For more on the recurrent debates within Italian history over the degree of centralization vs. local autonomy in Italy, see various essays in De Rosa and Di Nolfo 1986.

Should the Lega actually achieve its goal and divide Italy into three macroregions, it may find itself facing many of the same problems currently confronting the present Italian government, given that the North is an extremely heterogenous area with divergent political histories and socioeconomic structures. For more on this, see Rusconi 1993.

[10]For a provocative essay on this issue, see Cassese 1992.

4

The first section examines the Italian case to highlight the contradictory trends manifest within it. The second part assesses various alternative explanations for the Italian case and then lays out in greater detail my own argument. The final section outlines the structure of the book and highlights the key findings of the subsequent chapters.

THE ITALIAN CASE

Like other European countries, Italy in the 1970s witnessed a significant deterioration in economic performance. Three critical and mutually reinforcing events marked these years: the domestic shock generated by the wave of strikes and worker militancy commonly referred to as the Hot Autumn of 1969 (Brandini 1975; Pizzorno, Reyneri, Regini, and Regalia 1978), the external shocks resulting from the collapse of the international monetary system, and the oil price crises of 1973 and 1978.

The consequences of the Hot Autumn for industrial output, profitability, productivity, and labor costs were substantial. Between 1970 and 1974 unit labor costs increased 64.15 percent (see Table 1.1), as opposed to annual increases of 8.5 percent between 1963 and 1969 (Rey 1982). Moreover, unions used their newfound power to eliminate overtime, regulate layoffs, restrict internal mobility, and slow down the pace of work. Together these shop floor changes dramatically reduced the length of the workweek—the number of hours worked per employee decreased 12 percent during the first half of the decade (Rey 1982)—which, in turn, significantly cut productivity growth (see Table 1.2). Following legislation in the early 1970s which severely limited the ability of employers to dismiss workers (Reyneri 1989: 135–36), Italy became the only major European country with stable employment in manufacturing notwithstanding the sharp decline in value added (OECD 1984: 25). Squeezed between higher wages, shorter workweeks, and more stringent labor regulation, firm profits dropped sharply (see Figure 1.1).[11]

Italy's competitiveness and foreign trade also deteriorated in the 1970s. During the first half of the decade, Italy's average annual

[11] For more on this profit squeeze and its impact on industrial strategies during this period, see Barca and Magnani 1989: 27–38.

Table 1.1. Labor cost indicators

| | Real Labor Cost | | Unit Labor Cost | | Cost of Labor per Unit of Product[a] |
Year	Index 70=1	Yearly variations	Index 70=1	Yearly variation	Index 70=1
1970	100.00		100.00		100.00
1971	104.51	4.51	112.58	12.58	102.64
1972	109.45	4.7338	121.38	7.82	103.17
1973	119.33	9.03	137.74	13.47	105.89
1974	124.56	4.38	164.15	19.18	107.93
1975	131.10	5.2592	206.92	26.050	118.10
1976	135.03	2.99	238.36	15.20	115.82
1977	137.50	1.83	287.42	20.58	116.27
1978	139.39	1.37	327.04	13.79	115.58
1979	140.70	0.94	373.58	14.23	112.33
1980	141.57	0.62	444.03	18.86	109.62
1981	143.02	1.03	537.74	21.10	110.08
1982	145.35	1.63	628.93	16.96	112.21
1983	147.82	1.70	718.24	14.20	113.66
1984	149.27	0.98	779.25	8.49	111.67
1985	152.62	2.24	849.69	9.04	111.89
1986	152.76	0.10	893.08	5.11	109.91
1987	156.25	2.28	942.77	5.56	109.26

Source: OECD, Economic Indicators, 1988.
[a]The Cost of Labor per Unit of Product is defined as Real Labor Cost divided by Productivity.

growth rate of imports was substantially higher than growth of exports. Other major European nations experienced much stronger growth of exports during these years. Even the United Kingdom performed better than Italy, with a roughly balanced growth of exports and imports (see Table 1.3). In short, Italian exporters lost a substantial share of their markets to other European producers. According to Organization for Economic Cooperation and Development (OECD)

Table 1.2. Productivity trends (GDP per employee, average annual percentage changes)

	1951–1979	1951–1958	1958–1963	1963–1969	1969–1973	1973–1979
Total	4.6	4.7	7.1	5.7	4.4	1.5
Agriculture	5.0	6.2	7.3	7.5	4.8	4.1
Industry	4.7	4.6	6.6	6.2	4.5	1.9
Services	2.2	1.4	4.9	3.0	2.6	—

Source: Guido Rey, "Italy," in Andrea Boltho, ed., The European Economy: Growth and Crisis (Oxford: Oxford University Press, 1982). Used by permission of Oxford University Press.

Figure 1.1. Profit shares vs. compensation in Italy, 1950–1979

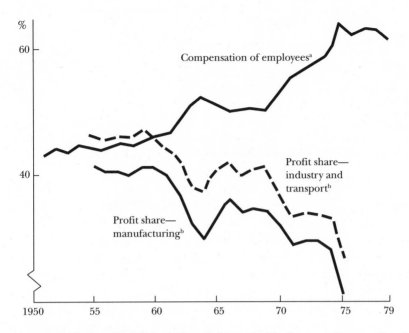

Source: Guido Rey, "Italy," in Andrea Boltho, ed., *The European Economy: Growth and Crisis*, (Oxford: Oxford University Press, 1982). Used by permission of Oxford University Press.
[a]In percent of national income.
[b]Gross operating surplus in percent of gross value added.

estimates, Italy lost 10 market share points in 1973 alone (OECD 1984: 31). This loss in market share was even more remarkable given that the lira had depreciated significantly since the collapse of the Smithsonian Agreements (Templeman 1981: 312).

With firms caught between increased labor costs and the rise of import penetration, industrial investment, particularly in the private sector, stagnated during the early 1970s. Moreover, increased regulation of labor promoted efforts at circumvention among private firms. Instead of increasing productivity by raising the capital labor ratio, managers sought to depress wage bills and avoid restrictive union practices by decentralizing production toward smaller scale establishments or self-employed operators working at home (Salvati 1975; Frey 1975).

The seventies was a decade of high inflation in most European nations. Yet, because of its extremely high dependence on imported

7

Table 1.3. Growth of real exports and imports of goods and service, average annual growth rate

Country	1970–1974	
	Exports	Imports
Italy	6.7	7.9
France	11.4	8.6
West Germany	8.3	7.6
United Kingdom	6.5	6.5
United States	10.5	6.2
Total OECD	10.1	8.5

Source: OECD, Economic Outlook no. 47, 1990, pp. 189–90.

raw materials, especially oil,[12] Italy experienced one of the highest price-level increases among the OECD nations (see Table 1.4. This was exacerbated by the various strategies pursued by labor, management, and the government. Following the first oil shock, unions secured a rigid wage indexation system (tying wages to cost-of-living increases) in the *scala mobile*.[13] Firms contributed to this wage price spiral by defending their market power through cartelization. And the Italian government, unable or unwilling to implement a coherent strategy, enacted a series of stop-go measures that further aggravated the industrial sector's problems. For instance, to offset the negative effects of escalating wage demands on firm productivity, the government provided extensive subsidies to large private and public firms in trouble. The result was an enormous budget deficit (see Table 1.5).

Decisions to devalue the lira fueled inflation further. Although the breakdown of the fixed exchange rate system seemed initially to provide Italy with some additional leeway for accommodating its domestic distributional conflict, increased budget deficits and growing inflation rendered the lira especially vulnerable to speculation (OECD 1988a: 74). The result of this effort to square the circle was a stop-go cycle. Restrictive policies to combat external imbalances were followed by

[12] After Japan, Italy is the second largest importer of petroleum among the major industrial nations. See Samuels 1984. In fact, Italy's deterioration of terms of trade in the wake of the oil shocks was rather more pronounced than that of the other major European economies. See OECD, Economic Surveys 1984: 34.

[13] The *scala mobile* is a cost-of-living adjuster that indexes wages to inflation rates. As discussed in greater detail in Chapter 3, this wage indexation system was modified in 1975 in such a way that it actually fueled (rather than merely protected workers against) high rates of inflation. For more on the historical evolution and particularities of this system, see Lange 1986: 29–46.

Table 1.4. Consumer price indexes: Year to year percentage changes

Country	1972	1973	1974	1975	1976	1977	1978	1979	1980	1981	1982	1983	1984	1985	1986	1987	1988	1989	1990	1991	1992
United States	3.3	6.2	11.0	9.1	5.8	6.5	7.7	11.3	13.5	10.4	6.1	3.2	4.3	3.5	1.9	3.7	4.1	4.8	5.4	4.2	3.0
Japan	4.5	11.7	24.5	11.8	9.3	8.1	3.8	3.6	8.0	4.9	2.7	1.9	2.2	2.0	0.6	0.1	0.7	2.3	3.1	3.3	1.7
West Germany	5.5	6.9	7.0	6.0	4.5	3.7	2.7	4.1	5.5	5.9	5.3	3.3	2.4	2.2	-0.1	0.2	1.3	2.8	2.7	3.5	4.0
France	6.2	7.3	13.7	11.8	9.6	9.4	9.1	10.8	13.6	13.4	11.8	9.6	7.4	5.8	2.7	3.1	2.7	3.6	3.4	3.2	2.4
United Kingdom	7.1	9.2	16.0	24.2	16.5	15.8	8.3	13.4	18.0	11.9	8.6	4.6	5.0	6.1	3.4	4.1	4.9	7.8	9.5	5.9	3.7
Italy	5.7	10.8	19.1	17.0	16.8	18.4	12.1	14.8	21.2	19.5	16.5	14.6	10.8	9.2	5.8	4.7	5.1	6.3	6.5	6.5	5.3
Canada	4.8	7.6	10.9	10.8	7.5	8.0	8.9	9.2	10.2	12.5	10.8	5.8	4.3	4.0	4.2	4.4	4.0	5.0	4.8	5.6	1.5
Total of 7 countries	4.3	7.5	13.3	10.9	8.0	8.1	7.0	9.3	12.2	10.0	7.2	4.7	4.7	4.0	2.1	2.9	3.4	4.5	5.0		

Source: OECD, *Historical Statistics*, 1992.

Table 1.5. Italy's net public debt (percent of GDP)

	1973	1976	1979	1982	1985	1986	1987
Italy	52.1	60.6	63.7	74.3	96.3	99.2	103.9
Big Seven	17.2	21.0	21.2	25.1	30.8	32.3	33.3

Source: OECD Economic Outlook, 1987, reported in Vincent Della Sala, "The Italian Budgetary Process: Political and Institutional Constraints," *West European Politics,* 2 (July 1988): 110–25.

expansionary measures to stimulate growth, which in turn provoked more severe external imbalances.

Many of these problems persisted well into the 1980s and 1990s. Government debt grew throughout the 1980s so that by 1992 it amounted to about 104 percent of the country's GDP. The lira, which briefly regained confidence in the late 1980s and was even able to maintain itself within the narrow band of the European Monetary System (EMS) for a few years, came under growing strain in the 1990s and was radically devalued in the fall of 1992. Other difficulties, however, appeared to be resolved, or at least significantly improved. For example, from its peak of 21.2 percent in 1980, inflation was gradually brought under control so that by 1993 it was well within the European average (see Table 1.4). Likewise, export performance, which had suffered tremendously in the 1970s, rebounded in the following decade so that by the late 1980s Italy outperformed all other European nations. During these same years, rates of GDP growth increased (Table 1.6), unit labor costs decreased (Table 1.1), manufacturing productivity grew (Table 1.7), and even private investment in new equipment and machinery outpaced that of Italy's major European competitors (Table 1.8).

In sum, although still macroeconomically fragile and plagued by a variety of other worrisome problems, the Italian economy has nonetheless generated impressive rates of growth, exports, labor productivity, firm profitability, and private fixed investment. How do we put together these two contradictory images of Italy?

EXPLAINING THE ITALIAN PARADOX

There are two basic explanations for Italy's apparently paradoxical economic performance, each associated with a particular image of

Table 1.6. Growth rates of real GDP, in percent

Country	1980	1981	1982	1983	1984	1985	1986	1987	1988	1989	1990	1991	1992
United States	-0.3%	2.3%	-2.6%	3.9%	7.2%	3.8%	3.2%	3.5%	4.5%	2.8%	0.9%	-1.2%	2.1%
Japan	4.9%	4.0%	3.2%	2.7%	4.3%	5.0%	2.6%	4.1%	6.2%	4.7%	5.2%	4.1%	3.1%
West Germany	1.9%	0.2%	-0.9%	1.6%	2.8%	1.9%	2.2%	1.4%	3.7%	3.2%	4.7%	3.7%	1.4%
France	1.1%	0.2%	2.3%	0.8%	1.5%	1.8%	2.4%	2.2%	3.8%	3.6%	2.6%	3.3%	1.3%
United Kingdom	-2.0%	-2.0%	1.7%	3.7%	2.2%	3.6%	3.9%	4.8%	4.2%	2.3%	0.8%	-2.2%	-0.6%
Italy	3.9%	-0.2%	0.2%	1.0%	2.7%	2.6%	2.9%	3.1%	4.1%	3.0%	2.0%	1.3%	0.9%
Canada	0.5%	3.8%	-3.2%	3.2%	6.4%	4.7%	3.3%	4.1%	4.7%	2.4%	0.4%	-1.7%	0.9%
Total of 7 Countries	1.1%	1.8%	-0.5%	2.9%	5.0%	3.6%	3.0%	3.4%	4.6%	3.2%	2.2%	0.4%	1.4%

Source: OECD, *Historical Statistics*, 1992; OECD, *Main Economic Indicators*, 1993.

Table 1.7. Indexes of manufacturing productivity, output per hours (1982 = 100)

Country	1980	1981	1982	1983	1984	1985	1986	1987	1988	1989	1990	1991
United States	94.4	96.4	100.0	102.9	105.6	108.0	112.6	117.2	122.0	122.5	125.7	128.1
Canada	99.9	104.8	100.0	107.3	116.3	119.8	117.9	119.0	119.5	119.0	120.1	121.7
Japan	92.1	95.5	100.0	101.9	106.1	112.0	110.3	119.5	126.5	135.2	144.2	146.5
France	90.6	93.4	100.0	102.5	104.5	108.8	110.8	113.0	121.0	127.9	129.4	129.1
West Germany	98.4	100.5	100.0	105.3	108.9	112.9	113.4	111.5	115.5	119.0	122.9	125.4
Italy	95.5	97.8	100.0	105.2	115.7	122.3	123.7	127.2	130.5	135.1	140.6	145.2
United Kingdom	89.9	94.5	100.0	108.5	114.0	118.2	122.9	130.4	137.5	143.5	146.0	149.8
					Annual percentage change							
United States	-1.9	2.1	3.8	2.9	2.6	2.3	4.3	4.1	4.0	0.5	2.6	1.9
Canada	-3.8	4.9	-4.5	7.3	8.5	2.9	-1.6	0.9	0.4	-0.4	0.9	1.3
Japan	3.7	3.7	4.7	1.9	4.2	5.5	-1.4	8.4	5.8	6.9	6.7	1.6
France	0.8	3.0	7.1	2.5	1.9	4.1	1.9	2.0	7.1	5.7	1.1	-0.2
West Germany	-1.8	2.1	-0.5	5.3	3.4	3.7	0.5	-1.7	3.6	3.0	3.3	2.0
Italy	4.8	2.4	2.3	5.2	9.9	5.7	1.1	2.8	2.6	3.6	4.1	3.2
United Kingdom	-0.4	5.2	5.8	8.5	5.1	3.7	4.0	6.1	5.5	4.4	1.7	2.6

Source: U.S. Bureau of Labor Statistics, Data Diskette, December 1992.

Table 1.8. Machinery and equipment expenditures as a percent of GDP

Country	1982	1983	1984	1985	1986	1987	1988	1989	1990
United States	7.7	7.6	8.0	8.0	7.7	7.7	7.9	7.8	
Japan	10.2	10.0	10.6	11.0	11.0	11.3	12.0	12.8	13.7
West Germany	7.8	8.1	7.8	8.4	8.4	8.5	8.7	9.2	9.8
France	8.5	8.2	7.8	8.3	8.4	8.8	9.3	9.6	9.7
United Kingdom	7.4	7.4	8.0	8.5	8.1	8.3	8.6	9.1	8.5
Italy	10.2	9.3	9.7	9.6	9.2	9.7	10.2	10.2	10.0
Canada	7.6	6.7	6.5	6.7	7.0	7.2	7.7	7.8	7.2
Total of 7 countries	8.4	8.2	8.5	8.7	8.5	8.6	9.0	9.3	9.3

Source: OECD, *Historical Statistics,* 1992.

Italy. The first explanation draws on the insights and analytic categories of what I refer to as the "national models" school of comparative
political economy. Since the publication of the classic work of Andrew
Shonfield, *Modern Capitalism: The Changing Balance of Public and Private
Power,* if not before, comparative political economy has focused on the
institutional arrangements and/or patterns of state-society relations
of different nation-states to explain divergent patterns of industrial
development, decline, and adjustment.[14] This approach stresses how
individual nations with particular histories and varying positions in
world markets develop specific institutional arrangements to govern
their economies. More than simply describing institutional differences,
this approach often assumes that certain national systems with particular organizational features are more "mature" and/or "efficient" than
others and prescribes the active diffusion or replication of these "best
(institutional) practices" across nations.[15]

During the 1970s and 1980s, scholars and policymakers alike

[14] For examples of this work, see, among others, Albert 1993; Garrett and Lange
1986; Hall 1986; Katzenstein 1978: 295–336; Maurice, Sellier, and Silvestre 1986;
Soskice 1990; and Zysman 1983.

[15] Shonfield, however, was quick to recognize that this process of institutional "borrowing" among nations is often guided by misleading perceptions of how they actually
work in their original context. For example, in discussing the development of planning
in France, Shonfield observes: "It is ironical to reflect that the first generation of French
planners under M. Monnet, groping for a method of inflicting the long-term public
interest on private enterprise, turned naturally to Labour Britain for their model. They
found what they wanted in the industrial Working Parties, the precursors of the abortive
Development Councils, established by Sir Stafford Cripps in the late 1940s. When the
French established the *commission de modernisation* for their key industries and used them
as the basis for constructing a nation-wide plan with a clear order of priorities, they
believed themselves to be taking over an essentially British device, merely adapting it
slightly to their own purposes" (1965: 88).

13

Table 1.9. Big Seven: Personal savings rates as a share of disposable personal income

Country	1970	1980	1985	1986	1987	1988	1989	1990	1991
United States	8.2	8.1	6.6	4.3	4.5	4.5	4.5	5.2	5.4
Canada	5.6	13.6	13.3	10.6	9.2	9.9	10.6	10.4	10.2
France	18.7	17.6	14.0	13.2	10.8	11.0	11.7	12.2	12.7
West Germany	13.8	12.8	11.4	12.2	12.6	12.8	12.5	13.9	13.7
Italy	29.5	21.6	18.0	15.3	15.7	15.4	14.5	16.1	15.6
Japan	17.6	17.9	15.6	16.4	14.7	14.3	14.2	13.6	14.1
United Kingdom	9.2	13.3	9.8	8.2	6.9	5.4	6.8	9.0	9.4

Source: Handbook of International Economic Statistics 1992 (Washington, D.C., September 1992).

pointed to institutional arrangements associated with particular nation-states as the best way to reverse economic decline and promote industrial adjustment. Some suggested etatist France (Cohen 1969; Zysman 1977) and Japan (Johnson 1982) with their highly technocratic state bureaucracies providing various forms of administrative guidance to leading economic sectors; others looked to northern European neocorporatist systems of centralized interest intermediation, peak-level bargaining, and Social Democratic politics (Schmitter 1981; Cameron 1984; Katzenstein 1984); and still others to the United States, with a regulatory framework designed to promote free markets, competition, and individual entrepreneurship (Gilder 1989).

Although the Italian economy possesses elements of etatism, neocorporatism, and liberalism—the Italian state's extensive involvement in the economy rivals that of France (Cassese 1987; Shonfield 1965: 196); historically liberal economic assumptions have guided its macroeconomic policy (Hildebrand 1965); and several industrial sectors and regions achieved various corporatistlike agreements (Perulli 1984; Chiesi and Martinelli 1989)—none of these elements has come to dominate the national political economy as a whole. Instead, recognizing the country's Byzantine institutional arrangements, the standard literature on European political economy often describes Italy as an "anomalous" or "exceptional" case.

Seen through the analytic lenses of the national models approach, Italy's current maladies are not at all surprising. In fact, they are to be expected given the country's dysfunctional institutions and clientelistic sociopolitical arrangements. What cannot so easily be accommodated within this dominant framework are the more dynamic features of the Italian economy. For accounts that emphasize the importance of national institutional arrangements it remains something of a mystery how Italy—once seen as the "sick man" of Europe—managed to outperform its etatist, neocorporatist, and neoliberal neighbors throughout most of the 1980s.

Even when Italy's economic successes are acknowledged, they are often explained away as temporary or conjunctural phenomena: the product of favorable exchange rates, cheap oil prices, and rising unemployment (which in turn reduces the militancy and cost of labor). Once these favorable conditions evaporate, so too will Italy's economic successes. This explains why, after several "fat" years in the 1980s, Italy's economic maladies have resurfaced. In other words, given that there were no major structural reforms of the Italian political economy, Italy remains essentially a "backward" and "inefficient" nation. Its economic successes were temporary anomalies, unlikely to be repeated in the near future.

While the national models approach to comparative political economy is useful in pointing out the important role that national institutions play in regulating the political economy, its explanation for Italy's mixed economic performance may be too simple. Although this view captures Italian failures, the more vibrant aspects of the Italian economy cannot be simply written off as temporary or conjunctural phenomena. Barca and Magnani (1989: 45), for instance, have shown that, because of the Italian economy's extensive system of wage indexation, double-digit rates of inflation, and continued dependence upon foreign sources of oil (purchased in expensive U.S. dollars), the currency devaluations of the 1970s and 1980s did not help Italian industry nearly as much as is often assumed.

Likewise, although all industrial producers experienced a reduction in energy costs due to technological innovations and the Organization of Petroleum Supporting Countries (OPEC's) internal crisis, a 1985 study showed that Italian industry still consumed 25 percent more energy than its French and German counterparts (Silvani 1985). Thus, Italian industry benefited from lower oil costs but no more than its principal competitors did. Finally, although unemployment rose (see Table 1.10)[16] and union power declined throughout the 1980s, labor

---

[16] As in other European nations, unemployment in Italy increased dramatically during the 1980s. But this growth in unemployment was often concentrated in certain segments of the labor force—women, youth, unskilled Southern workers—who have been histori-

costs in Italy actually increased over the course of the decade (Table 1.11). By the 1990s, among the "Big Seven"[17] Italian hourly labor costs were second only to German rates (see Table 1.12). Thus, it appears as if the decline of unit labor costs observed in Italy in the 1980s (Table 1.1) was achieved not through an overall decline in labor costs but rather through increased labor productivity, itself the result of firm restructuring and technological innovation. This process of successful industrial adjustment is precisely what needs to be explained, and accounts that focus on Italy's "anomalous" institutional structures and/or temporary shifts in factor costs appear unable to do this.

The second explanation for Italy's paradoxical economic performance pays little attention to national institutions. Instead it focuses on certain peculiarities of the Italian economy. This second school of thought sees Italy *not* as an "anomalous" case but rather as a paradigmatic illustration of the "new competition" (Piore and Sabel 1984; Goodman 1989; Best 1990; Inzerilli 1990; Pyke, Becattini, and Sengenberger 1990). This second view focuses primarily on Italy's industrial districts of dynamic small- and medium-sized firms. Citing the extremely high rates of growth and innovative firm strategies within these districts, this approach sees Italy's economic vitality as stemming from the ability of these highly specialized and flexible firms to compete successfully in world markets.

With time; so this second view goes, this alternative model of production will diffuse throughout the Italian economy and even to other national systems. Far from merely a passing phenomenon, Italian economic success represents the country's future. To the extent that this view acknowledges Italy's current difficulties, it explains them away as problems of transition inherent in any major shift from one regime of production to another.

In many ways, scholars working from this perspective are correct. Between 1971 and 1981 the shape of Italian industry underwent

---

cally underemployed and who could not necessarily fill the jobs required by firms undergoing adjustment. Thus, how much this growth in unemployment really affected the costs of industrial labor is open to debate. For more on this, see Accornero and Carmignani 1986. For more on the difficulties particular national labor features and modes of measurement pose for comparative studies of unemployment, see Moy 1988: 39–50.

[17]The Big Seven are the seven industrial countries that meet at annual economic summits: Germany, France, United Kingdom, Japan, United States, Canada, and Italy.

Table 1.10. Unemployment as a percentage of total labor force

Country	1972	1973	1974	1975	1976	1977	1978	1979	1980	1981	1982	1983	1984	1985	1986	1987	1988	1989	1990	1991	1992
United States	5.5	4.8	5.5	8.3	7.5	6.9	5.9	5.7	7.0	7.5	9.5	9.5	7.4	7.1	6.9	6.1	5.4	5.2	5.4	6.6	7.3
Japan	1.4	1.3	1.4	1.9	2.0	2.0	2.2	2.1	2.0	2.2	2.4	2.6	2.7	2.6	2.8	2.8	2.5	2.3	2.1	2.1	2.2
West Germany	0.9	1.0	2.1	4.0	4.0	3.9	3.7	3.3	3.3	4.6	6.4	7.9	7.9	8.0	7.6	7.6	7.6	6.8	6.2	4.4	4.8
France	2.7	2.6	2.8	4.4	4.4	4.7	5.2	5.9	6.3	7.3	8.1	8.3	9.7	10.2	10.4	10.5	10.0	9.4	9.0	9.4	10.2
United Kingdom	3.1	2.2	2.1	4.8	4.8	5.2	5.1	4.7	5.7	9.0	10.4	11.2	11.1	11.5	11.6	10.4	8.3	6.1	5.5	8.7	9.9
Italy	6.3	6.2	5.3	6.6	6.6	7.0	7.1	7.5	7.4	8.3	8.4	9.3	9.9	10.1	10.9	11.8	11.8	11.8	10.8	9.9	10.5
Canada	6.2	5.5	5.3	7.1	7.1	8.0	8.3	7.4	7.5	7.5	10.9	11.8	11.2	10.4	9.5	8.8	7.7	7.5	8.1	10.2	11.2
Total of 7 countries	3.7	3.3	3.7	5.4	5.4	5.3	5.0	4.9	5.5	6.3	7.7	8.1	7.4	7.3	7.3	6.9	6.3	5.8	5.6	6.3	6.9

Source: OECD, Historical Statistics, 1992.

Table 1.11. Average hourly labor costs, 1980–1988, in national currencies

	1980	1981	1982	1983	1984	1985	1986	1987	1988
Italy (lire)	8.024	9.477	11.173	12.659	14.014	15.807	17.262	18.642	20.950
Percent change	—	18.1	17.9	13.3	10.7	12.8	9.2	8.0	12.4
Index	100	118.1	139.2	157.8	174.6	197.0	215.1	232.3	261.1
France (franc)	50.34	58.80	66.68	73.35	77.38	81.25	84.91	88.73	92.99
Percent change	—	16.8	13.4	10.0	5.5	5.0	4.5	4.5	4.8
Index	100	116.8	132.5	145.7	153.7	161.4	168.7	176.2	184.7
Germany (deutsche mark)	25.88	27.38	28.58	29.64	30.83	33.17	34.80	36.36	37.71
Percent change	—	5.8	4.4	3.7	4.0	7.6	4.9	4.5	3.7
Index	100	105.8	110.5	114.5	119.1	128.2	134.5	140.5	145.7
United Kingdom (pound)	3.98	4.27	4.73	5.12	5.42	5.77	6.12	6.42	6.81
Percent change	—	7.3	10.9	8.1	5.9	6.5	6.0	5.0	6.0
Index	100	107.3	119.0	128.6	136.2	145.1	153.8	161.5	171.2
Spain (peseta)						1282.5	1397.1	1494.9	1584.6
Percent change						—	8.9	7.0	6.0
Index						100	108.9	116.6	123.6

Source: FIAT, Relazioni Industriali, "Retribuzione-costo del lavoro: Confronti internazionali, competitivita" (Turin: Fiat Internal Company Document, September 1989): 46.

Table 1.12. Indexes of hourly compensation costs for production workers in manufacturing, 1975–1992

Country	1975	1980	1985	1990	1991	1992
United States	100	100	100	100	100	100
Canada	94	88	84	107	110	105
Japan	47	56	49	85	93	100
France	71	91	58	102	98	104
West Germany	100	125	74	147	145	160
Italy	73	83	59	117	117	120
United Kingdom	53	77	48	85	88	91

Source: U.S. Bureau of Labor Statistics, Office of Productivity annd Technology, June 1993.

Note: Foreign compensation costs converted to U.S. dollars at prevailing market exchange rates. Index US = 100.

significant change. The number of small- and medium-sized firms (firms with a maximum of 99 employees) increased by 21 percent. Employment within these firms rose almost 29 percent during these same years (Rey 1989: 71). During the 1970s, these same firms outperformed their larger counterparts in terms of growth of value added, investment, employment, and even average income per employee. Absenteeism and industrial conflict were also lower in small- and medium-sized firms (Bellandi 1989: 49). These trends appear to have continued well into the 1980s (Rey 1989: 79; Barca and Magnani 1989: 171–97).

Although this second view is important in illustrating the very real and significant role small firms and industrial districts played in the resurgence of Italy's economy in the 1980s, it too suffers from several shortcomings. Often these accounts exaggerate the importance of the industrial districts but rarely do they discuss some of the darker sides of small firm production systems (Harrison 1994). Moreover, as subsequent chapters will make clear, not just small firms but also large enterprises contributed to Italy's economic revival in the 1980s. Throughout the 1980s, many large firms that had previously been in trouble restructured themselves (sometimes even imitating certain flexible features associated with the industrial districts) and regained their competitiveness (Regini and Sabel 1989). By the end of the decade it appeared as if these larger firms were outpacing the small-firm sectors in terms of productivity, profitability, and the ability to innovate (Barca and Magnani 1989: 225–85; Consolati and Riva 1989).

Moreover, not all agglomerations of small firms produced economic growth, stable employment, and technical innovation. Some so-called districts failed outright while others degenerated into collections of sweatshops (Amin 1989; Blim 1990). As some of the leading scholars of industrial districts have made clear, this model of economic development did not characterize all of Italy but only specific regions (Bagnasco 1986).[18] The successful districts are concentrated primarily in the Center and Northeast of Italy. In these regions, commonly referred to as the "Third Italy," local entrepreneurs and unions were able to build on preexistent sociopolitical resources to promote high rates of economic growth in the 1970s and 1980s. These same actors were also able to use their well-developed organizational capacities to obtain disproportionately large shares of government assistance (discounted loans, subsidized credits, etc.) which further enhanced industrial development in these regions (Weiss 1988).

Thus, we have two accounts that explain pieces of the Italian puzzle but not the entire picture. Seen through the lenses of the national models approach, Italy's economic difficulties are easy to understand but its successes are less comprehensible. Conversely, accounts that focus on Italy's industrial districts shed light on the economy's dynamic features but tend to obscure many of the country's structural shortcomings.

AN ALTERNATIVE, MICROPOLITICAL APPROACH

The alternative, micropolitical explanation developed in this book paints a more differentiated picture of the Italian political economy. Italy is neither a completely chaotic country nor one composed primarily of dynamic small-firm districts. It is a heterogeneous composite of diverse subnational patterns that coexist within the same national territory. In contrast to accounts that focus on national institutional arrangements to explain differences in economic performance across nations, I look at the microlevel, at the strategic choices of the economic actors themselves, to understand diverse patterns of industrial politics *within* the same nation-state. Moreover, rather than view economic

[18]Nor can this model of development be replicated wholesale in other industrial settings. In fact, some of the strongest proponents of this view are quite clear about its limits. See, for example, Piore 1990: 225–27.

behavior as the product of various structural factors (firm size, production process, etc.), my approach stresses the role of politics in shaping the alternative conceptions and strategies of local economic actors.

Cases of both industrial decline and entrepreneurial vitality are present within the Italian economy, but they are situated in different localities characterized by alternative patterns of associationalism, intergroup relations, political representation, and economic governance. In other words, the divergent patterns manifest within the Italian economy are the product of the very different sociopolitical networks within which firms and unions are embedded.[19] Divergent sociopolitical networks create different mixes of resources and constraints that shape the strategic choices of local economic actors. These sociopolitical networks not only structure relations among local economic actors, but also provide these local actors with very different linkages or channels of communication and representation to the central policymakers in Rome.

Thus, although Italian firms throughout the country faced similar challenges (e.g., increased international competition) and identical or analogous public policies, they nonetheless responded in a variety of ways. Both their understanding of the challenges they faced and their capacity to respond were shaped by the particular features of the context in which they were embedded. This accounts for the variety of economic patterns manifest within contemporary Italy and why so many government programs aimed at either rationalizing the economy or restructuring it produced only mixed results. Analyzing the underlying sociopolitical factors shaping divergent outcomes is a central goal of this book.

THE ARGUMENT IN BRIEF

The standard literature on state building in the West often portrays the process as an evolutionary sequence in which previously independent administrative units are enveloped by a centralizing power that over time imposes a uniform legal code and standardized language

[19] For more on the concept of economic embeddedness, see Polanyi 1944; and Granovetter 1985: 481–510.

and culture throughout the national territory.[20] The actual historical experiences of most modern states, however, were far more complicated than this ideal-typical model suggests. In this regard, Italy is no exception. Italian political development was clearly *not* a progressive and evolutionary process but rather one characterized by a high degree of uncertainty, conflict, and internal differentiation.

Most studies of Italian state-building stress how the existence of strong mercantile capitalist states in the North, a powerful papacy in Rome, and a backward monarchy in the South all prevented Italy from uniting into a full-fledged nation-state until the latter part of the nineteenth century.[21] Moreover, the way Italy eventually achieved unification—essentially the result of political compromises (between northern and southern ruling classes and between the Savoy monarchy and foreign leaders)—led to the incomplete integration of vast areas and numerous groups into the new Italian state. Other reasons for the failed consolidation of the Italian nation-state include the preservation of traditional social structures after unification in 1860 and the fact that the new state did not promote political, agrarian, and other reforms.

Incomplete socioeconomic integration and political unity at the beginning were not rectified but rather exacerbated by Italy's subsequent political history. Following unification in 1860, Italy experienced successive governments in the late nineteenth century which practiced the politics of *trasformismo* (exchanging favors, clientelism, and local autonomy in return for political support of the governing coalition); the collapse of the Liberal regime under fascism; the outbreak of World War II and the ensuing resistance; and the emergence of a highly polarized political system in the postwar era. All of these events reinforced rather than abated local and regional differences within Italy.[22] Thus, notwithstanding the Italian state's highly centralized administrative structure (modeled after the Franco-Napoleonic

---

[20] For more on the standard sequence, see Bendix 1964; various essays in Binder 1971; Poggi 1978; and Tilly 1975.

[21] See, for example, Fried 1963: chap. 2; Anderson 1979; Beales 1981; Gramsci 1971; and Hellman 1987: chap. 16.

[22] For more on how these events hindered the development of a strong and homogeneous Italian nation-state and perpetuated local socioeconomic and political differences, see, among others, Graziano 1978: 290–326; Tarrow 1977a; Ginsborg 1990; Putnam 1993: chap. 2; and Rusconi 1993.

state),[23] Italian politics have in practice accommodated, perhaps even encouraged, local and regional differentiation.

The composite pattern of Italy's economy is the legacy, I argue, of Italy's uneven political and economic development in which different areas were industrialized and enfranchised at different times. The terms, circumstances, and sequencing of these events had long-lasting effects on the socioeconomic resources and political character of Italy's various regions.[24] Region here means not the recently created (1970) administrative structures situated between the national and local (communal) governments (see Nanetti 1988; and Putnam 1993 for more on these) but rather the long-lasting social and political patterns that have historically shaped the Italian economy. Arnaldo Bagnasco (1988) and Carlo Trigilia (1986) describe these "localistic" patterns of economic regulation for the Third Italy, but they exist, in different forms and with varying characteristics, throughout the Italian economy.

Out of these divergent regional histories, distinct patterns of associationalism (Putnam 1993), political representation (Barnes 1977) and economic governance (Bagnasco 1977; Carocci 1975; chap. 7) emerged. It is difficult to quantify precisely the number of distinct political-economic patterns that coexist within the Italian economy. The estimates range from 3 to 955.[25] In this book, I do not even try to count Italy's various local economies. Instead, from the array of distinct subnational arrangements, I identify three ideal-typical patterns. These three patterns, which I label hierarchical, polarized, and policentric, are ideal-types[26] and as such cannot fully capture the rich-

---

[23] For an interesting comparison of the administrative structures, legacies, and attempts to reform these two states, see Gourevitch 1978: 28–63.

[24] For more on the uneven penetration of the periphery by the center and its impact on Italian politics, see Tarrow 1977a: 66–67; and Trigilia 1986: 43–132. See Lipset and Rokkan's "Introduction" in their edited volume, *Party Systems and Voter Alignments* (1967) for a discussion of how the sequencing of various developmental processes had long-lasting effects on the politics of different nation-states.

[25] Bagnasco (1977) identifies three distinct socioeconomic patterns associated with the three major territorial divisions (North, Center, and South) of the country but, according to Paul Ginsborg, "in purely historical terms it would be better to talk not of three Italys but of three hundred" (1990: 3). Saville (1976) identifies seven different patterns whereas Sforzi (1989) divides the Italian economy into 955 distinct "local labor market areas." Political scientists have also wrestled with the problem of dividing Italy into distinct political areas. For an interesting review of this literature, see Cartocci 1987: 481–514.

[26] For more on the use and limits of ideal-types, see Watkins 1978: 82–104.

ness of detail of any one of Italy's many local economies. But they nonetheless help us organize what might initially appear to be an endless variety of local arrangements and illustrate how particular contextual features shape economic behavior in clearly distinct ways.

Although I derived these three ideal-typical patterns from my own field research on industrial adjustment in the Italian automobile, textile, and petrochemical industries, my argument about how local sociopolitical networks shape economic behavior is influenced by and builds on previous research on center-periphery relations in Italy (Tarrow 1977a; Dente 1985), the role of secondary associations and organized interest groups in democratic governance (Berger 1972; Cohen and Rogers 1992; Putnam 1993), the importance of social and political networks in structuring interactions among different individuals and groups (Granovetter 1973, 1982; Knoke 1990; Cohen and Dawson 1993); and the social, political, and institutional foundations of alternative production systems (Piore and Sabel 1984; Bagnasco 1988; and Streeck 1991).

Like Robert Putnam (1993), I find that the "vibrancy of associational life" is important in promoting different patterns of social solidarity and local politics in Italy. But perhaps just as important as the actual number of associations are their qualitative features and patterns of interaction. In her book on French peasant organizations, for instance, Suzanne Berger (1972) illustrated how membership in voluntary associations alone did not always promote greater levels of citizenship since some interest groups actually insulated individuals and hindered their participation in politics. In other words, associations differ in terms of their qualitative features and the way they aggregate interests. These differences have a tremendous impact on both local patterns of political and economic behavior and on the types of connections that link local interests and central policymakers.

Thus, when analyzing local economies in Italy, I have tried to pay attention not just to associational density but also to the qualitative features of the various local actors. Cohen and Rogers (1992) have argued that secondary associations with certain attributes (leadership accountability to group membership, inclusiveness of group membership, cooperative modes of interaction with other groups) are more likely to effectively aggregate and represent interests and thus facilitate democratic governance than are other groups with qualitatively different features (hierarchical intragroup relations, parochial concerns, conflictual politics). Moreover, Granovetter (1973, 1982) has claimed that economic actors linked to one another through many "weak" ties will more easily receive and transmit information than will actors linked by a few "strong" ties.

Building on both bodies of research I argue that local firms and unions are more likely to remain open and responsive organizations when they are tied to other like-minded entities through multiple, horizontal ties. Economic actors embedded in these dense but relatively egalitarian networks will more easily be able to share information, form alliances, build trust,[27] and resolve conflicts through negotiation than will other firms and unions situated in more fragmented or hierarchical networks. As a result, different sociopolitical networks will shape the understandings, resources, and hence the strategic choices of local economic actors in very different ways.

Policentric, polarized, and hierarchical local economies differ along three critical dimensions: the structure of intergroup relations, patterns of associationalism, and linkages to central policymakers.

Policentric systems are characterized by a dense network of encompassing and open associations and interest groups that are linked to one another through many horizontal ties. In these local systems, interests are well organized and communication among different groups is quite frequent. Often different actors within these localities combine to pool resources to purchase collective goods and/or upgrade local infrastructures. Whenever disagreements or conflicts arise between any two local actors, chances are that communication between them will not break down entirely but will continue through indirect, third-party channels. Moreover, other interest groups or associations within the network will most likely attempt to repair ties between the conflicting parties by facilitating negotiations or arbitrating differences. Finally, the horizontal ties linking local actors to one another are stronger and more numerous than any connections linking local interests to central authorities or national representatives in Rome. In fact, vertical linkages are employed *not* as a conduit of communication or control for the central authorities but as a channel through which local groups can express their interests and tap centrally controlled resources to finance local endeavors.

[27] See Sabel 1992 for an interesting discussion on the role of trust in economic adjustment strategies.

Polarized local economies are in many ways the mirror image of po-licentric systems. These subnational orders are characterized by a small number of more parochial and organizationally underdeveloped interest groups and associations usually clustered together into two opposing camps. Although the ties linking organized actors or groups within each camp are quite strong, linkages between the two clusters are often tenuous. Thus whenever conflicts arise between groups asso-ciated with the two opposing camps, they often develop into zero-sum struggles in which gains achieved by one side are seen as equivalent losses by the other. Because local groups and associations are organized into two competing camps, they are unable to repair relations or mediate disputes between conflicting parties. Moreover, vertical ties linking the two opposing local clusters of associations to national-level actors are much stronger than any connections among the various local actors. As a result, local actors often implement strategies developed at the national level and may become dependent on the center for re-sources and information. In certain cases, local struggles reflect or serve as proxies for conflicts between opposing national interests.

Hierarchical local economies are hybrid systems. Like the policentric orders, they, too, may be characterized by numerous organized inter-est groups and associations, but the linkages among the local actors are fragmented and hierarchical. As a result, information does not flow freely among local actors but rather is limited to communications between actors linked by vertical ties. Relations among the various local groups are also segmented into different hierarchically organized clusters. Actors situated at the higher levels of each vertical chain often possess more power and resources than actors at lower levels. To the extent that conflict arises among actors either within or across clusters, they are resolved not through negotiation among peers but through top-down decision-making. (Figure 1.2 depicts these three ideal-typical patterns.)

By structuring relations, information flows, and the distribution of resources among local actors in different ways, these divergent sociopolitical networks create alternative patterns of economic behav-ior. Thus, during the recent wave of industrial restructuring, Italian firms and unions embedded in policentric networks sought to negoti-ate the changes underway whereas local economic actors situated in

Figure 1.2.   Three ideal-typical network structures

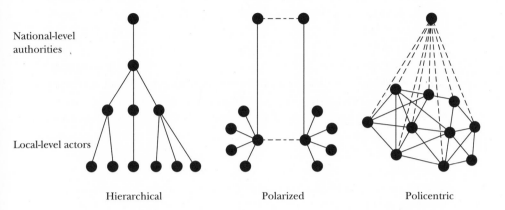

Hierarchical   Polarized   Policentric

polarized settings often engaged in highly conflictual struggles. Industrial change in hierarchically organized areas varied depending upon whether patrons at the upper levels of the chain could either insulate lower-level actors from the changes underway or provide them with new opportunities or resources. When both these strategies failed, lower-level actors were often left to fend for themselves in the new competitive environment.

In sum, notwithstanding the absence of a strong state capable of developing and implementing a coherent economic policy, Italian firms and unions did not simply reinvent themselves de novo. Instead, both their understanding of the challenges they faced and their ability to respond were shaped by the local context in which they were embedded. This accounts for both the diversity of economic patterns currently present in Italy as well as some of the country's current maladies.

Although historical legacies of political and economic development shaped the original attributes of the three subnational orders I describe, economic actors are not simply shackled by local historical legacies. Instead, they actively pursue an array of different strategies and struggle with one another over competing strategic choices. These periodic political struggles among local economic actors may reconfigure and recombine legacies of the past in ways that alter the local economic order. Such struggles may be instigated and heavily influenced by broader shifts in the nature of competition, technological innovation, and/or government regulation. But the basic cleavages, resources, and range of potential strategies are primarily determined by the existing local organizational resources and structure of sociopolitical relations already at hand.

I liken this process to quilt-making, where fragments of old textiles are recombined and sewn together into new arrangements. Except for the thread holding together the patchwork, all the other ingredients are old or, rather, have already been around but in different forms, previously serving different functions.[28] Of course, the pattern is also new but it, too, is constrained by the array of fabrics and colors already available.

THE COMPOSITE ECONOMY: THE ITALIAN CASE RECONSIDERED

Earlier I described how serious political and economic problems plagued the Italian economy in the 1970s and 1980s. To address these problems, Italian political, business, and labor leaders attempted a major structural reform of the country's political economy. Like many American and European social scientists writing at the time, Italy's elite came to perceive their nation's problems as stemming from the lack of a strong and coherent national model. Thus, they sought to build a new Italy through a series of institutional reforms aimed at replicating practices found in other, apparently more stable and efficient nations. This reform process was unplanned, piecemeal, and rife with contradictions but it touched several key political-economic institutions. Reform efforts included the construction of a modern welfare state (Ferrara 1984; Granaglia 1989); the rationalization of public finance and macroeconomic policy (Della Sala 1988; Epstein and Schor 1989); attempts to overhaul Italy's electoral system (Pasquino 1986); a decentralization of political and administrative power (Dente 1985; Nanetti 1988; Putnam 1993); the formulation of a coherent industrial policy (CER-IRS 1986; Ferrera 1989); and a complete reconfiguration of the industrial relations system.

With few exceptions and to differing degrees, these attempts to

---

[28] Both Wolfgang Streeck and James Coleman, in discussing very different problems, have argued that structures or associations developed for one (perhaps noneconomic) purpose can later serve an entirely new and important role in regulating socioeconomic behavior. See Streeck 1991: 21–61; and Coleman 1988: S95–S120.

construct a new national model failed. They failed in part because of the inherent difficulties in exporting or replicating institutional practices developed in one national context to another and/or due to the growing difficulties of these other national models[29]—but especially because they fell victim to political maneuvering and infighting among Italy's key socioeconomic actors. Italian unions, business associations, political parties, and various components of the Italian state all participated in this would-be reform process. Yet each of these actors held a particular vision of the new Italy (and their place in it) and thus interpreted the proposed reforms in slightly different ways. The outcome was familiar: notwithstanding the conclusion of several highly innovative accords among the social partners and the passage of ambitious laws in Parliament, political infighting and bureaucratic sluggishness prevented all but a few of the reforms from being fully implemented.

The political stalemate resulting from this failed reform process reinforced certain idiosyncratic features of the Italian system (decentralized decision-making, local differentiation, etc.) in two distinct but mutually reinforcing ways. First, during these years Italian industry was undergoing a fundamental transformation. This fact was largely obscured by national debates over institutional reform, often ignored by politicians and social scientists alike. Like enterprises in all OECD nations, Italian firms were forced to restructure to survive the new terms of international competition. Without a major structural reform of the Italian economy or a coordinated initiative by the state or peak business and labor associations to protect them from adverse economic conditions, individual firms and even entire industries were forced to fend for themselves. As a result, Italian firms embarked on an ambitious process of adjustment, experimenting with alternative organizational arrangements and strategies and new relations with labor. But, as we saw above, the strategies of economic actors were in many ways shaped by their local context, and, as a result, very distinct, local patterns of economic behavior and industrial adjustment emerged from this ad hoc and uncoordinated process of industrial restructuring.

Second, the political struggles ignited by the process of institutional

---

[29] For more on the difficulties other national institutional arrangements face, see Hall (1986) on France and the United Kingdom; Friedman (1989) on Japan; Martin (1991) on Sweden; and Herrigel (1995 forthcoming) on Germany.

reform mobilized different groups to promote and/or defend their interests and roles in the new order. These political struggles, in turn, both redefined the organizational features of the key socioeconomic actors and reconfigured in subtle and not so subtle ways the institutional framework within which they operated. Many of the proposed reforms entailed the centralization of economic decision-making. Peak business and labor organizations sought to gain the upper hand in collective bargaining and wage determination while the central state attempted to orchestrate industrial policy. Each of these propositions met stiff opposition within the government as well as within the union and business federations. Individual industry federations resisted attempts by Confindustria (Italy's private big business association) to dictate labor or industrial strategies (Chiesi and Martinelli 1989), and various sectoral and local unions countered efforts by the confederal leadership to usurp their recently won power and responsibilities (Golden 1988b; Locke 1990a). Within government, different ministries and regional administrations competed for resources and control over the proposed new programs (Adams 1985; Pennisi and Peterlini 1987; Ferrera 1989).

These political struggles, combined with the growing inability of peak-level actors and central authorities to understand, let alone control, macroeconomic events, led to a shift in the locus of industrial politics *not* to the center but rather to the local level. In ways remarkably similar to the process Peter Katzenstein has described for Germany,[30] Italian institutions evolved to provide greater decision-making autonomy and flexibility to organized actors at the local and regional levels of the economy (Dente 1985; Nanetti 1988). But, as Robert Putnam

[30] Peter Katzenstein describes institutional change in Germany as a subtle process of shifting power and responsibilities *within* the existing framework. Rather than dismantle existing institutions in the face of major shifts in the broader political economy, Germany's institutional framework adapted by: 1) empowering institutions that had been previously less central politically; 2) disempowering others that had played key roles in the previous era; and 3) transforming the actual roles various institutions play in the new economic order. For more on this, see Katzenstein 1989: 329. Although perhaps less smooth and orderly, the process of change Italian institutions underwent in the 1970s and 1980s was very similar. According to Peter Lange and Marino Regini, "Beneath the surface of the relative failure of major state efforts at sweeping reform, there is a reality of constant change in how affairs are regulated. These changes are sometimes through state action, sometimes in response to it and sometimes in spite of it. The Italian system stifles intentional state-directed systematic change but permits the vitalism of society to be transformed into relatively constant incremental changes in regulatory modes and regulatory roles of different institutions" (1989: 255).

illustrated for the case of administrative reform, increased decentral-ization had radically different consequences in the different regions of the country. "The reform freed the more advanced regions from the stultifying grasp of Rome, while allowing the problems of the more backward regions to fester" (Putnam 1993: 68).

In sum, contrary to the dominant interpretation of Italy's current maladies, Italian political and economic leaders *did* in fact attempt to reform the country's institutional arrangements and policy-making processes, but they failed. And because of their failure, differences among Italy's disparate regions increased and the national system as a whole suffered further setbacks to its effectiveness and integrity.

The remainder of this book tells the story in detail but from two different angles. The first two chapters analyze various attempts to reform Italian institutional arrangements and recast them in the image of other, supposedly more efficient nations. Chapter 2 focuses on economic policy and explores three attempts by the Italian govern-ment to streamline and strengthen its governance of the economy. I examine efforts to reform Italy's large state holding companies (ENI and IRI), to relaunch economic planning, and to develop a national industrial policy. Each of these reform efforts failed to achieve its stated goal of rationalizing economic policy in Italy. If anything, the partial and/or distorted implementation of some of these programs actually reinforced preexisting differences within the Italian economy.

Chapter 3 shifts to an analysis of Italian industrial relations and examines several failed attempts by Italy's union, business, and politi-cal elite to construct a new, more stable system of industrial relations. The reform of Italian labor law through the Statuto dei Diritti dei Lavoratori,[31] the attempt by Confindustria to forge a Swedish-like Basic Agreement through wage indexation, and experiments with neocorporatist income policies in the late 1970s and again in 1983–84 were all designed to recast Italian industrial relations in the image of other, more mature national systems. All three initiatives failed. Instead of promoting greater centralization, standardization, and qui-escence these reform efforts unleashed a series of intraorganizational

---

[31] The Statuto was not a complete failure. It represents a significant piece of legislation that continues to have a major impact on Italian labor relations. However, its impact is not exactly what some of its original authors and supporters had in mind. In this way, and as Chapter 3 will show, the Statuto illustrates precisely what I mean by the unintended consequences of reform.

struggles that resulted in the further decentralization of Italian labor relations. Although increased fragmentation and local variation caused serious organizational challenges for the established unions, they also may have created the preconditions for Italian labor's renewal. In short, the first part of this book illustrates how Italy's failed reform process reinforced certain traditional features of the country's political economy (regional differentiation, multiple and competing centers of decision-making, local autonomy, etc.), which, in turn, produced mixed results for Italy's diverse local economic orders.

In Chapters 4 and 5, I retell this story from a local-level perspective. These chapters illustrate the important role local sociopolitical networks played in shaping adjustment patterns in two very different industries. Italy's failed reform process and consequent decentralization of industrial politics did not mean a return to laissez-faire markets. Beneath Italy's facade of institutional chaos lies a dense network of regulation. This regulation does not fit neatly into traditional categories: it does not emanate from a strong, central government, and it takes on a plurality of forms in different localities of the country. To illustrate how different local sociopolitical networks shape economic behavior in distinct ways, Chapters 4 and 5 analyze cases of industrial adjustment in the Italian automobile and textile industries.

Analyzing comparable developments in two industries with varying technologies, industry structures, and work forces permits me to control for certain key variables (hence, alternative explanations) like firm size, capital and labor ratios, type of technology, and skill level of the work force. I also studied matched pairs within each sector in order to control for sectorally specific factors. This research involved archival work, multiple plant visits, and over 150 interviews with academics, company managers, rank-and-file workers, union officials, and local and national political representatives. Often I returned to the same firm or union office to discuss my findings.

Chapter 4 examines the reorganization of the Italian automobile industry. This sectoral case study is interesting for a variety of reasons. First, the industry is composed of two leading firms, Fiat and Alfa Romeo, which have historically played major roles in Italy's economy and have often set the pattern of industrial relations elsewhere in the country. The development of work relations and the balance of power in these firms usually reflects the situation elsewhere in the country. Second, because of the importance of these firms and the unions organizing them, Fiat and Alfa have acted as advanced laboratories for Italian industrial relations. Since the Hot Autumn, they have experimented with various forms of work organization and labor-management relations.

Finally, union experiences with industrial adjustment at these two firms have been radically different. Whereas Fiat reorganized by reasserting managerial control and repressing the unions, Alfa experienced a more negotiated process. Moreover, although both firms emerged more competitive as a result of the reorganization, the outcomes for the two unions differed sharply: Alfa's unions managed to preserve, perhaps even to enhance their strength, while Fiat's unions lost membership and practically all influence on the shop floor. This divergence is especially interesting given that both firms share the same unions, use similar technologies, and operate within the same national setting. This divergence is explained by the very different local sociopolitical networks in which the two companies are embedded and which shaped their alternative managerial and union strategies.

Chapter 5 analyzes the reorganization of the Italian textile industry. If any industry is strongly associated with the resurgence of Italian industry, it is the textile industry. In the 1980s, "Made in Italy" became synonymous with the high quality, stylish products that dominated the fashion industry throughout the world. Closer examination of how this so-called sunset industry, once closely identified with Italian "backwardness" (Frey 1975), became a leading, high value-added exporter in its sector reveals an array of very different adjustment strategies.

The chapter focuses on Biella, Italy's leading woolen textile district, to illustrate that, within certain constraints, firms could construct different solutions to common problems. Notwithstanding similar product markets, technologies, labor unions, and government regulations, textile firms, drawing on resources provided by diverse local sociopolitical patterns, developed alternative strategies of adjustment. The case study on Biella illustrates not only the way local sociopolitical features shape the strategic choices of economic actors but also how through politics these historical legacies can be reconfigured to make very different kinds of resources and choices available to local economic actors.

The sixth and concluding chapter is divided into two sections. The first section reviews the book's key findings. The second considers their implications for other advanced industrial nations and for future research in comparative political economy. Reconceptualizing the Italian economy as a composite of diverse subnational systems helps us understand current trends within that country, but it may help explain recent developments in other advanced industrial nations as well. In Chapter 6, I argue against viewing Italy as an anomalous or exceptional case and seek to extend the lessons of the Italian case to a variety of other countries with very different historical legacies and institutional arrangements.

Paying greater attention to local economies and the variety of experiences that coexist *within* and not simply across different national institutional frameworks does not mean that national institutions no longer matter. Of course they do. But how they matter in today's political economy is an open question that requires further research and perhaps the construction of different theoretical categories. In the concluding chapter I generalize from the Italian case and develop this alternate approach.

CHAPTER TWO

Governing the Economy? Institutional
Reform and Economic Policy

The [Italian] state's activities are more extensive than France['s]—
though as we shall see, they are much less significant as adjuncts of
a coherent national policy.
—Andrew Shonfield, *Modern Capitalism*

In this chapter I examine several efforts by Italy's political and
economic elite in the 1970s and 1980s to rationalize the state's role in
the economy and develop a coherent national policy. Throughout the
postwar period, government intervention in the Italian economy has
been extensive but not especially effective. This unfortunate combination resulted from the uneasy coexistence of two radically different
conceptions of economic regulation held by those in charge of the
Italian economy. Unlike the situation in most other advanced industrial nations, in Italy the new economics of Keynesian demand management did not play a dominant role in postwar economic policy (De
Cecco 1989).[1] Luigi Einaudi and the other neoclassical economists
in control of the Bank of Italy resisted Keynesianism while private
entrepreneurs and the neomercantilist managers in charge of Italy's
large state holding companies (Instituto per la Ricostruzioni Industriale [IRI], Ente Nazionale Idrocarburi [ENI] ignored it. The former
associated greater government intervention in the economy with the
evils of fascism, while the latter believed that countercyclical policies
would do little to resolve Italy's longstanding structural problems.

[1]For more on the spread of Keynesianism in Europe, see Hall 1989. For postwar
Italy, see De Cecco 1989; Prodi 1974: 45–63; and Holland 1972b, especially 5–8.

35

Even when Keynesianism finally did gain ground in the mid-1960s, these two groups interpreted and adapted it to their particular needs and economic visions.

Without a clear orthodoxy steering economic policy, two very different patterns of economic intervention developed. On the one hand, the Bank of Italy sought to shape Italy's postwar development through tight control over monetary policy. Bunking conventional (Keynesian) wisdom at the end of World War II, Italy's monetary authorities promoted a severe austerity and stabilization plan that forced down inflation, restored business confidence, and generated large reserves of foreign currency. These three conditions lay the foundation for Italy's subsequent economic "miracle" (Hildebrand 1965; Salvati 1984). On the other hand, fearing that macroeconomic policy alone would be unable to remedy Italy's longstanding structural problems, managers of Italy's state holding companies actively intervened in the economy. These were the years in which IRI (and later ENI) launched major development programs in the steel, shipbuilding, petrochemical, and transportation industries (Holland 1972b).

These two divergent strategies coexisted (more or less) peacefully and in certain ways reinforced each other throughout most of the postwar era. For instance, the Bank of Italy's restrictive monetary policies undermined trade union efforts to increase wages and permitted Italian firms (private and public) to grow at impressive rates by capturing ever-greater shares of international markets due to the low and stable prices of their products. Likewise, by developing Italy's steel and energy resources and improving its transportation and communications infrastructure, IRI and ENI were, in turn, underwriting the central monetary authority's noninflationary, export-led model of economic development by providing Italian manufacturers with inexpensive inputs and intermediary goods. Together, these two strategies produced impressive rates of economic growth and development in the late 1950s and early 1960s.

The collapse of the international monetary system, growth of inflation, and rise of union power described in Chapter 1 not only eroded the favorable conditions underlying Italy's export-led model of growth, but also increasingly rendered the traditional strategies of both the central bank and the state holding companies ineffective. For instance, attempts by Italy's monetary authorities in 1970 to weaken the unions and end the Hot Autumn struggles by enacting restrictive policies, though it succeeded in provoking an economic slump, had no noticeable effect on union demands or worker militance. Similarly, in the wake of the oil crises, the state holding companies, which had concentrated much of their investment in capital-intensive industries like steel and petrochemicals, found themselves burdened with enormous debt and excess capacity in uncompetitive industries. As a result, they too had to forfeit their propulsive role in the Italian economy and shelve several ambitious industrial development projects.

In an effort to fill the void created by the decreasing ability of both the Bank of Italy and the state enterprises to play their traditional roles in the Italian economy, the Italian Parliament passed a number of makeshift industrial and regional assistance laws. But this action only exacerbated the situation by adding to the government's growing deficits (which the Bank was required to finance) and by forcing the state enterprises to absorb increasing numbers of failing firms and redundant workers. By the end of the decade, the situation had deteriorated so dramatically that it appeared that many IRI- and ENI-affiliated firms, as well as the major Italian banks supporting them, would fail.

The threat of a major industrial and financial crisis generated a chorus of demands for a "return to orthodoxy." Other industrial nations heard similar calls during these same years (Gourevitch 1986). However, although in other countries this demand often resulted in a shift from Keynesianism to monetarism and the retreat of the state from the economy, in Italy "orthodoxy" meant very different things to the different groups in charge of economic policy. Thus, while the economists in control of the Bank of Italy fought to reestablish the bank's autonomy and the primacy of monetary policy, other would-be reformers sought to relaunch economic planning or to develop an etatist industrial policy. Even the public managers in charge of IRI and ENI promoted various reforms aimed at strengthening their presence in the economy. All of these groups looked abroad to economic practices in other nations to support their positions at home. Thus, although Italy's monetary authorities hoped to remake the Bank of Italy in the image of the German Bundesbank, other political and economic interests sought to emulate an array of institutional practices found elsewhere in Europe and the United States.

As a result of this heterogeneous and in many ways internally contra-

37

dictory reform process, none of these efforts entirely succeeded. To give but one example, let's briefly examine the consequences of the loudly announced but quietly celebrated "divorce" of the Bank of Italy and the Italian Treasury. Their 1981 divorce freed the bank from its requirement to purchase unsold state bonds, which had provided the government with unlimited financing.[2] Throughout the 1970s the governor of the Bank of Italy had sought to reassert the central bank's autonomy and regain control over the amount of money injected each year into the economy. This autonomy had been severely curtailed at the end of the 1960s and throughout the 1970s, first informally and then legally, as the bank was forced to buy treasury bills left unsold at public auctions. The divorce freed the bank from this requirement and established a cap of 14 percent on government overdrafts. By limiting its resources in this way, reformers hoped that the Italian government would be constrained to become fiscally responsible.

It is quite apparent today that this reform aimed at disciplining government spending failed. In many ways, the divorce was an Italian-style divorce, or what Italians call "separati in casa," which means that both partners pretend they are divorced but continue to live together. This is an apt comparison because, by the time the Bank of Italy regained its autonomy, the secondary market for treasury bonds (which the bank had helped create) was so well developed that bonds were practically as liquid as money and earned significant interest. In fact, as soon as the bank stopped financing government spending with the creation of money, interest rates on treasury bonds increased in order to guarantee their sale on the market. Given their high interest rates (which the bank maintained) and tax-free status (which the government granted), treasury bonds suddenly became very attractive for individuals and firms alike. As a result of this growing demand, the government easily continued to finance its deficits and was in no way constrained to reform its spending practices.

The consequences for Italian public finances, however, were disastrous. Since the growing stock of short-term treasury bonds expired at very short intervals (between six and twelve months), the government frequently had to refinance its debt through the issuance of even more bonds. Moreover, in order to sustain the market for treasury bonds,

---

[2] For more on the so-called divorce between the Bank of Italy and the Italian Treasury, see Cotula 1984: 219–655; Padoa-Schioppa 1987: 265–86; Epstein and Schor 1989: 147–66; and Goodman 1992: chap. 5.

very high interest rates had to be paid. As a result, the government dug itself into an ever-deeper hole as its basic debt, and the costs of servicing it, continued to grow. In short, the Bank of Italy's regained independence, intended to give it the power to control inflation, impose austerity, and relaunch the Italian economy (see Giavazzi and Spaventa 1989), in practice actually contributed to the creation of a huge cumulated public debt that today threatens Italy's macroeconomic stability and its place within the European Community.

This chapter analyzes three other, quite different efforts by the Italian government to rationalize its role in the economy: attempts to develop a national industrial policy, to relaunch economic planning, and to reform Italy's large public enterprises (IRI, ENI). Each of these efforts failed, not simply by failing to meet its stated goals, but also by unintentionally reinforcing precisely those features of the Italian system (regional differentiation, multiple and competing centers of economic decision-making, etc.) it had been designed to eliminate. In other words, these reform efforts did not fail universally, but had very different effects depending on the extent to which various firms and regions possessed the resources necessary to take advantage of these policies.

The remainder of this chapter is divided into two sections. The first section analyzes two very different approaches to economic reform: the attempt to develop a coherent national industrial policy in the late 1970s and efforts in the mid-1980s to relaunch planning. The second section illustrates the ambitious but internally contradictory nature of the reform process through a case study of Italy's public enterprise system.

Two Approaches to Economic Reform

Several alternative strategies were pursued to revive and restructure the Italian economy in the 1970s and 1980s. Earlier I described the attempt by the central bank to discipline government spending and promote noninflationary growth through institutional autonomy. In this section I discuss two other approaches to economic reform. The first approach was the development of a comprehensive industrial policy. In 1977, the Italian government created a new institution, the Interministerial Committee for the Coordination of Industrial Policy

(CIPI), whose mission was to develop and oversee policy aimed at rationalizing existing industries and launching new, high-technology sectors. During the late 1970s and early 1980s, CIPI sought to centralize control over industrial policy-making by abrogating all previous laws pertaining to industrial development or adjustment and by developing a number of sectoral restructuring plans.

The second approach employed to promote rational economic governance was in the area of planning. Italy's initial experience with economic planning in the mid-1960s was part of a political bargain to bring the Socialist party (PSI) inside the governing coalition. Yet these early plans failed because of the inability of Italy's planning technocrats to mobilize sufficient political support within the civil service, state holding companies, and private sector. In the early 1980s, planning was relaunched through the Fondo Investimenti e Occupazione (FIO). Unlike the plans of the 1960s and 1970s, the Medium-Term Plan of 1981–83 rejected Keynesian demand-management policies and instead emphasized supply-side factors and incomes policies. Moreover, it restricted government intervention to the public sector. In this section I will first describe the initial design and stated objectives of these two efforts and then analyze the distorted implementation and/or unintended consequences of these reforms.

Toward a New Industrial Policy

Industrial policies, or positive adjustment policies as they are sometimes called (OECD 1979), have been part of the economic tool kit of most industrial nations throughout the postwar era.[3] Subsidized loans, tax credits, and the provision of diverse services to industry have all been used by governments to achieve a variety of objectives—greater productivity, increased exports, a presence in certain sectors—for which the market alone appeared inadequate. (See McKay and Grant 1983 for a review of various forms of industrial policy in the OECD nations.) Since World War II, Italy has also employed industrial policies for a variety of purposes: economic development in the South, promoting small- and medium-sized enterprises, and increasing the efficiency of domestic firms prior to entrance into the Common Market.

[3]This section relies heavily on Adams 1985; Ferrera 1989: 111–28; and Fornengo 1986: 33–90.

However, because of its heterodox approach to economic governance, Italy never possessed an industrial policy in the sense of having a single, coherent program or agency responsible for national industrial development. Instead, throughout the postwar period, different ministries and government agencies promoted a series of highly particularistic initiatives. These policies were rarely coordinated and sometimes even contradicted each other. Their objectives ranged from supporting particular sectors (Law 1101 of 1971 for textiles; Law 1329 of 1965 for machine tools) and developing specific regions (Law 853 of 1971 for the South; Law 902 of 1976 for the depressed areas of the Center-North) to the promotion of exports (Law 374 of 1976) and applied research (Law 1089 of 1968).[4]

This piecemeal approach to industrial policy was accentuated by the fragmentary nature of the policy-making process. Ostensibly, the Ministry of Industry and Commerce presided over industrial policy. Yet policies involving the South were controlled by the Ministry for the South; export-promotion by the Ministry of Foreign Trade; shipping by the Ministry of Commercial Shipping; and the public enterprises by the Ministry of State Holding Companies. "If one adds the trio of key economic departments (Treasury, Budget and Economic Planning, and Finance), and keeps in mind that portfolios are distributed according to the needs of coalition and fractional arithmetic" (Kreile 1983: 194), the magnitude of the problem becomes clear. Because of this fragmentation and due to the almost exclusive reliance on subsidized credit as the means to implement these laws, the Italian approach to industrial policy proved quite unsuccessful.

To reverse this situation and rationalize government intervention in the economy, the government of "National Solidarity" (1977–79) passed the Industrial Restructuring and Reconversion Act (Law 675 of 1977). This law sought to change profoundly Italy's rules of industrial policy-making by establishing clear roles and boundaries among the government, civil service, Parliament, and relevant interest groups. A complex machinery involving government ministers and committees of experts in consultation with union representatives, business groups, and local authorities was established to analyze the problems afflicting Italian industry and to develop a comprehensive plan for their resolution.

[4]For an excellent review of various industrial policy laws, see Piattoni 1986.

Law 675 also created a major institutional innovation, the Interministerial Committee for the Coordination of Industrial Policy (CIPI), which brought together the ministers of Budget and Planning, Treasury, Industry, State Holdings, Labor, and the South to work collectively on the formulation and implementation of a national industrial policy. Italy's prime minister formally chaired CIPI (in practice, the committee was chaired by the minister of industry) and its meetings were often attended by the governor of the Bank of Italy, the secretary general of planning, and the minister of European economic affairs.

CIPI was assigned the job of articulating a comprehensive four-year industrial plan that would guide government intervention in the economy. Individual sectoral plans would be used to establish priorities by targeting specific industries deemed particularly promising or in need of reorganization. During these years, plans for the electronics, automobile, chemical, textile-apparel, steel, paper, food and agriculture, leather goods, aeronautics, and machine tool industries were drawn up. These sectoral plans were to be accompanied by a number of intersectoral plans concerning the efficient use of energy, export promotion, and environmental protection. Law 675 also established the Fund for Restructuring and Reconversion (about 5 trillion lire) to provide credit subsidies to firms undergoing restructuring efforts in conformity with CIPI's sectoral plans. A further appropriation of an equal amount was granted in 1983.

The industrial policy apparatus and procedures promoted by the new law blended two very different approaches to industrial policy. On the one hand, CIPI's centralized organization and its use of sectoral plans resembled elements of France's etatist model of industrial policy. On the other hand, its highly participatory process, in which business associations and trade unions participated in the formulation of the sectoral plans and a bicameral parliamentary committee approved them, emulated various Scandinavian practices (Ferrera 1989). With these institutional arrangements in place, it appeared that Italy had finally achieved a coherent and powerful industrial policy.

A New Approach to Planning

Italy first attempted economic planning in the mid-1960s as part of a political bargain involving the entrance of the Socialist party (PSI) in the governing coalition (La Palombara 1966; Pasquino and Pecchini

1975). Planning in Italy was consciously modeled on the French experience (Shonfield 1965: 196). In seeking to replicate French arrangements, the Budget Ministry was transformed into the Ministry of Budget and Economic Planning and a Secretariat of Planning was established. Like France's early plans (see Hall 1986 for more on this), Italy's first plan, the Pieraccini Plan (1966–70)[5] laid out a series of goals or "indicators" it was designed to achieve within its five-year horizon.[6]

Most of these goals were never achieved, however. Following the Bank of Italy–sponsored disinflation of 1963–64, Italian growth rates never fully returned to their previous miraculous levels. Moreover, the other two major issues addressed by the plan—unemployment and structural imbalances between the North and the South—persisted. In fact, just about all of the plan's objectives—support for research and development, the reform of the social security system, infrastructural development, and the promotion of exports—went unfulfilled. The two subsequent planning documents, the Preliminary Report on National Planning (1971–75), the so-called Progetto '80, and the Second National Economic Plan (1973–77) met similar fates in the sense that they were drafted but never implemented by the Italian government. The second plan was not even passed by the legislature, due to its early dissolution in 1972.

Several explanations have been advanced to account for the failure of Italian planning. These include: the fragmentation of policy-making and lack of coordination among the various ministries and agencies involved in the plan (Prodi 1974; Scognamiglio 1979b; Kreile, 1983); the isolation of the planning apparatus within the Italian civil service (Pasquino and Pecchini 1975); and the overly centralized and ambitious nature of the first plans, which rendered them practically impossible to implement (Pennisi and Peterlini 1987).

[5]It took about ten years of debate before Italy's first plan was launched. In 1954, Enzo Vanoni, the Christian Democrat minister of budget, laid out an employment and income development scheme (the so-called Schema Vanoni) which rekindled the debate over planning in Italy. In 1962, the Republican budget minister, Ugo La Malfa, attached another document (the so-called Nota Aggiuntiva) to the budget which also advocated the development of economic planning in Italy. During Moro's first Center-Left government, an actual plan (the Giolitti plan, 1965) was developed, but the government fell before it could be approved. Thus by the time the Pieraccini plan was implemented, thirty-one months had passed since its initial parliamentary debate. For more on the early trajectory of planning in Italy, see La Palombara 1966; Holland 1972b, especially 82–88; and Pasquino and Pecchini 1975: 70–86.

[6]See Bianchi 1990: 607–39 for an interesting review of Italy's planning experience.

All of these explanations appear to be valid in the sense that all of the factors contributed to the demise of Italy's first experience with planning. The early plans elaborated a number of etatist goals (e.g., the maintenance of high growth rates and the elimination of structural inequalities between the North and the South) over which the planning apparatus had little control and/or which were impossible to achieve within five years. Moreover, given that no major overhaul of Italy's bureaucratic apparatus accompanied the planning process, the plan's goals were virtually impossible to implement. The Italian civil service did not even have the means to collect data from private firms, let alone influence their strategies. Reflecting on this failure, Giorgio Ruffolo, the general secretary of planning, who Stuart Holland once referred to as the Jean Monnet of Italy, stated:

> The economic plan for 1966–1970 has been defined as a "book of dreams."[7] If by this, one meant that the plan's proposals had no relation to concrete problems, he would be contradicted by the plain fact that the problems identified by the plan have been crucial to recent political, social, and economic events. If, on the contrary, one meant that the plan was impotent, that is, lacking in operational instruments, he would be perfectly supported by the facts. It is sad but nevertheless true that the Planning Commission has always been in a very weak position vis-à-vis the central administration and the enterprises, public and private. In other words, the political system has prevented the innovative potentialities of planning from becoming a permanent and strong conditioning factor of policy-making.[8]

Following the Hot Autumn and the demise of the Center-Left government, even the tenuous political support promoting global economic planning in Italy was swept away. Not until the early 1980s, did a serious discussion of economic planning resurface in Italy under a radically different guise. We now turn to an examination of this effort.

The Fondo Investimenti e Occupazione

The Medium-Term Plan (1981–83) sought to relaunch economic planning and reinvigorate the Ministry of Budget and Planning.[9] Un-

---

[7] This refers to a comment Amintore Fanfani, a leading Christian Democrat politician, made about the plan.

[8] This quote is taken from Prodi 1974: 48. However, it is worthwhile reading through Ruffolo 1973 for more on the failure of Italian planning.

[9] This section relies heavily on Pennisi and Peterlini 1987.

like Italy's previous planning experience, which was pushed by Socialists and left-wing Christian Democrats, the 1981–83 plan was sponsored by people closely tied to centrist political parties and Confindustria, Italy's large-scale private business association. Moreover, this new effort embraced a completely different approach to planning. Instead of relying on Keynesian demand-management policies and identifying specific indicators or goals to be fulfilled, it emphasized supply-side factors and a restricted role for the government.

In many ways, Italian readings of James Tobin's post-Keynesian synthesis shaped this new approach to planning.[10] Italy's new generation of planners believed that stable monetary policy plus strict incomes policies would stimulate, in the medium term, accumulation and investment and, thus, promote long-term, noninflationary growth. These policies would be formulated and managed respectively by the Bank of Italy and the social partners. The only direct role for government was its use of public spending to direct the new wave of growth.

The plan of 1981–83 embraced this vision by elaborating a series of policies based on the controlled growth of demand, stable monetary policy, and severe incomes policies. Together, these three measures were expected to stimulate a massive wave of productivity and enhance investments in the private sector. The plan also elaborated a new set of procedures guiding economic policy. In order to avoid some of the problems associated with Italy's first planning experience, the new planning apparatus clearly delineated the roles and responsibilities of the different actors.

Through the Interministerial Committee for Economic Policy (CIPE), the government would establish a set of developmental goals and allocate funds to accomplish these goals. Local and regional governments as well as other parastatal agencies (the public enterprises) would then submit proposals for specific projects aimed at realizing these goals. Within the Ministry of Budget and Planning, a committee of technical experts (the Nucleo di Valutazione degli Investimenti Pubblici) would evaluate these proposed projects, ensuring their congruence with the macroeconomic parameters and developmental goals of the plan. The committee would then submit its evaluation of the

[10]See, for example, Grilli, La Malfa, and Savona 1985 for a good example of Italian post-Keynesian analysis. All three of the authors played central roles in the formulation of the Medium-Term Plan of 1981–83.

various projects to CIPE, emphasizing the trade-offs different choices entailed. CIPE would make the final decision on which projects to fund, but the originators of the approved projects were solely responsible for their implementation.

This more decentralized and interactive process was designed to enhance the role of local and regional governments in the planning process, hence making the process more democratic and less taxing on the central bureaucracy. At the same time, the new procedures were believed to increase the transparency and efficiency of economic decision-making in Italy.

The 1982 budget gave birth to the Medium-Term Plan by establishing the funds (Fondo Investimenti e Occupazione) and administrative apparatus (the Nucleo di Valutazione degli Investimenti Pubblici) it required. The next several years witnessed the development of this new planning system as the government established development goals, local and regional governments submitted project proposals to implement these goals, and the technical experts within the Ministry of Budget and Planning evaluated them. By the mid-1980s, it appeared that a new approach to planning had truly taken root in a land of economic anarchy.

The Results of Reform

Both of these reform projects sought to render economic governance in Italy more efficient and organized and both initiatives, to one degree or another, were modeled on institutional arrangements found in other nation-states: the Industrial Restructuring and Reconversion Act on various French and Scandinavian industrial policy arrangements and the Medium-Term Plan on Anglo-American supply-side policies. Yet when recreated in the Italian context, both of these foreign-inspired experiments produced at best only partial results. Certainly they did not radically alter Italy's ad hoc approach to economic policy.

For example, the Industrial Restructuring and Reconversion Act created a completely new institution (CIPI) to develop and implement a coherent national policy. Notwithstanding these institutional innovations (and perhaps because of them), most of Law 675's objectives were never fulfilled. It took three years for the first funding applications to be processed, and only a fraction of the funds allocated for restructuring was disbursed by the time the original law expired (Ranci 1987; Ferrera 1989). What few funds were allocated in these early years were heavily skewed in favor of projects presented by large firms in essentially three sectors: steel, chemicals, and automobiles (see Table 2.1).

Some of these implementation problems had nothing to do with Law 675's design. For instance, much of the delay stemmed from the European Economic Community (EEC) Commission's objection to several sectoral plans that it interpreted as providing government subsidies. The EEC Commission saw these sectoral subsidies as an infringement of Articles 92 and 93 of the Treaty of Rome because they altered the conditions of competition among firms. Subsequent negotiations between the Italian government and the EEC delayed the grant of the first credits until 1983—six years after the passage of Law 675 and ten years after the initial oil shock that had originally provoked a crisis among most Italian firms. By that time, however, individual firms had either gone under or found their own way out of their problems.

At the same time, many of the investment banks (such as Istituti di Credito Speciale) that were supposed to provide subsidized credit to firms undergoing restructuring were themselves in weak financial

Table 2.1. Distribution of funds from Law 675: Industrial Restructuring and Reconversion Act projects and financing approved by CIPI as of December 31, 1984

Sector	Number of projects	Investments (million lire)	Percent of funds
Textiles	36	307,664	2.93
Steel	17	2,994,730	28.52
Chemical	43	2,397,684	22.61
Food-Agriculture	11	107,343	1.02
Paper	7	129,129	1.23
Electronics	6	69,237	0.66
Mechanical Engineering	12	252,188	2.40
Aeronautics	11	646,620	6.16
Automobile	22	3,596,915	34.25
Total	165	10,501,510	100.0
Located in:			
North-Center	132	5,836,326	55.58
South	33	4,665,284	44.42

Source: Graziella Fornengo, "Le politiche dei ristrutturazione e salvataggio," in *Le leggi della politica industriale in Italia,* Franco Momigliano, ed. (Bologna: Il Mulino, 1986), p. 44.

shape and, thus, resisted what they saw as yet another attempt by the government to involve them in unprofitable ventures (CER-IRS 1989: 204).[11] Instead of following the indications laid out by the sectoral plans, these banks provided funding only to those firms that could back up their loans with real guarantees. As a result, many small- and medium-sized enterprises—which had been specifically targeted by the law—were unable to gain access to the funds.

Yet much of the Industrial Restructuring and Reconversion Act's failure was nested in its original design. The last chapter described Italy's uncoordinated and ad hoc institutional reform process. Because different groups with very different visions of the new Italy struggled with one another over proposed changes in Italy's institutional frame-work, most attempts at building a new Italy failed. But they failed for

[11]The evolution of the Italian banking system is an interesting story in and of itself. In many ways, it resembles the French system of state-controlled credit. Through IRI (which owns most major banks) and the Bank of Italy, the government can (theoretically) direct the flow of resources toward its desired projects (see Zysman 1983 for more on the French system; Shonfield 1965; and Posner 1978 for more on the Italian system). At the same time, following the collapse of most major Italian banks (which were modeled directly on the German universal banks), reform legislation in 1936 reorganized the banking system into two distinct and specialized sectors—savings and loans banks and long-term credit/industrial investment institutes. As a result, the structure of the postwar Italian banking system also resembles the American system (and was most likely modeled on analogous banking reforms [1935] in the United States). In the first two decades of the postwar era, the Italian government also established a number of regional credit institutes aimed at financing industrial development throughout the country.

As a result of contradictory government policies in the 1970s, this mixed-model system began to show severe strains. On the one hand, as the government relied increasingly on the long-term credit institutes to finance its own deficits (regardless of interest rates), it began to crowd out industrial firms needing long-term loans for new investments. On the other hand, the government promoted a number of policies aimed at providing subsidized credit through these same long-term credit institutes to firms undergoing adjustment. Yet given that these institutes already felt overly exposed because of their prior support of not very successful, government-inspired investment projects (such as the chemical and steel industries in the South) and that they were doing relatively well simply by servicing the government's debt, they resisted renewed attempts by the government (i.e., Law 675) to induce them to provide cheap credit (not very remunerative for the banks) to industrial firms in need of restructuring. Moreover, given that the Bank of Italy was courting these credit institutes in an attempt to win back its own institutional autonomy (Epstein and Schor 1989), investment banks felt they could successfully resist government pressures to participate in these new schemes. Thus, notwithstanding the excess liquidity in the Italian system during these years, industrial firms had difficulty raising investment funds through traditional, established channels. And given that Italy's capital market was extremely weak and underdeveloped (again, as a result of government and Bank of Italy policies), industrial firms turned to savings and loans banks to borrow. This, in turn, merely recreated the mixed banking practices Italian reforms in the 1930s had sought to prevent. For more on this, see Scognamiglio 1979a: 115–54.

different reasons. Some reforms (i.e., electoral reform) never emerged from parliamentary debate. Others, however, were implemented but in highly compromised ways. Law 675 falls into this latter camp.

The Industrial Restructuring and Reconversion Act was one of several significant reform initiatives promoted by the government of national solidarity (1977–79), an informal coalition between the Christian Democrats (DC) and the Italian Communist Party (PCI). Industrial policy was central to the PCI's program as both a way of rationalizing the state's role in the economy (the elimination of DC-controlled clientalism) and promoting employment, and the Communists demanded this reform in exchange for their support of austerity measures (Regini 1984). Industrial policy, according to the PCI, was to be defined and implemented through various industry plans. Within the DC, however, there was considerable opposition to sectoral planning. Party leaders advocated instead a mixture of macroeconomic policies (incomes policies, monetary reform) and the continuation of highly specialized, piecemeal legislation aimed at supporting individual investment projects (Adams 1985: 77–80).

Law 675 represented a compromise between these two positions. Sectoral planning was accepted as the basis for distributing government assistance, but no specific sectors or criteria were identified. To placate the strong Mezzogiorno lobby in the DC, 40 percent of the Fondo Ristrutturazione e Riconversione was allocated to the South. Likewise, democratic control over the process was guaranteed both through the creation of a bicameral legislative committee to oversee the process and the inclusion of labor unions and business associations in the development of the sectoral plans. Yet, decision-making power rested with CIPI, an interministerial committee consisting mainly of Christian Democrat leaders, many of whom were openly opposed to any form of industrial policy. Thus, the new institutional framework responsible for the implementation of Law 675 consisted of contradictory features based on radically different conceptions of and varying degrees of support for industrial policy. Subsequent events illustrated the disruptive power of these internal contradictions.

For example, the sectoral plans that were to guide the entire process turned out to be little more than detailed accounts of the current state of various industries. These plans were supposed to target specific industries but, instead, eleven sectors—virtually coextensive with Italy's entire industrial structure—were selected for government intervention. Labor and business participation in this process was minimal, and long-term relations between the Ministry of Industry and various industry experts were eschewed. Yet given that the minister of industry responsible for the drafting of the sectoral plans was Carlo Donat-Cattin, a Christian Democrat leader who had actively opposed sectoral planning during the parliamentary debate over the law, none of these deficiencies should come as a surprise. Similarly, the bicameral control commission designed to oversee the entire process was quickly transformed into a debating forum between supporters and opponents of the various sectoral plans. This, in turn, further delayed the implementation of the law.

In short, procedural difficulties and political opposition combined to ensure the law's complete demise. After being denounced repeatedly by various political parties, unions, business groups, and the government itself, Law 675 was finally abrogated in 1988 (CER-IRS 1989: 203–4; Padoa-Schioppa 1990: 149).

Italy's second experiment with economic planning met a similar fate. Notwithstanding the Medium-Term Plan's different policy orientation, constituency, and technical apparatus, this second experiment with economic planning in Italy was no more successful than the first. Interestingly enough, it appears that history merely repeated itself in this case. Although CIPE approved the plan's goals and encouraged the Nucleo di Valutazione to evaluate the various proposals submitted by local and regional governments to realize these goals, allocations from the Fondo Investimenti e Occupazione followed strictly clientalistic criteria. Completely ignoring the planning staff's work, several ministers insisted that their pet projects or electoral constituencies receive the funding instead.

Moreover, the government never provided adequate support for the technical dimensions of the planning process. The Nucleo di Valutazione had to borrow computers, research staff, and even office space from other agencies simply to do its work. When this work was ignored and the plan's objectives were thwarted, most of the planning technocrats resigned their positions and initiated legal action against the government (Pennisi and Peterlini 1987). Once again, insufficient institutional capacity and lack of political support prevented economic planning from being realized in Italy.

Both Law 675 (Industrial Restructuring and Reconversion Act) and the Medium-Term Plan were highly ambitious and innovative attempts to reform economic governance in Italy. Law 675 sought to create new institutional arrangements aimed at building consensus among the social partners and directing industrial adjustment in Italy. The Medium-Term Plan tried both to restrict and rationalize the government's role in the economy by elaborating clear macroeconomic goals and guiding government spending to conform with these objectives. Informed by various French and Scandinavian experiences, Law 675 envisioned a very active role for the state in the economy. The Medium-Term Plan, however, was much more sympathetic to recent American and British experiences and thus sought to severely restrict government intervention. Notwithstanding their different approaches to economic reform, both Law 675 and the Medium-Term Plan failed to achieve their goals.

Initially it may appear that these two reform efforts failed for different reasons. The final design of Law 675 was so thoroughly compromised by the time it passed Parliament that it is hard to imagine that it could have ever achieved its goals. The Medium-Term Plan was more thoughtfully and coherently designed, but its implementation was sabotaged by recalcitrant government bureaucrats and ministers. Closer examination, however, reveals that both experiments fell victim to the same political conflicts among competing groups with alternative visions of the new Italy. All key political-economic actors agreed that Italian institutions were in need of reform, but no single plan or approach could satisfy most, let alone all, of these actors. As a result, many of the proposed reforms simply failed to emerge from debate, and those few which did manage to pass through Parliament were so altered and compromised (either in their design or during their implementation) that they stood little chance of achieving their goals. In short, both Italian efforts to develop a comprehensive industrial policy and relaunch economic planning were undermined by the political struggles unleashed by Italy's institutional reform process.

The following section of this chapter further illustrates the innovative, ambitious, but internally contradictory and conflictual nature of Italy's reform process through a case study of Italy's large state holding companies (IRI, ENI). In the 1960s, Italian public enterprises performed so well that other advanced industrial nations admired and sought to emulate them (Holland 1972a). By the 1980s, these same companies were seen as the Achilles' heel of the Italian economy (Bognetti 1981). To restore them to their prior strength, three very different reorganization projects were promoted. The Gestione e Partecipazione Industriale (GEPI), an industrial rescue and reprivatization agency modeled after the British Industrial Reconversion Corporation, was created as a defensive measure to protect the state holding companies from being saddled with growing numbers of ailing private firms. At the same time, IRI-affiliated firms also sought to restructure themselves through the Protocollo IRI, a neocorporatist reorganization scheme informed by German and other northern European experiences. Finally, efforts at privatizing numerous, nonstrategic public firms were also attempted throughout the 1980s. Thus within the same public enterprises, three very different reform strategies coexisted and competed with one another. The following case study analyzes this pluralistic approach to institutional reform and considers its implications for the current state of public enterprise in Italy.

REVITALIZING ITALIAN STATE ENTERPRISE: A CASE STUDY OF FAILED REFORM

Italy's state enterprise system was launched in 1933, with the creation of the Istituto per la Ricostruzione Industriale (IRI). "IRI was born through the combination of virtually accidental factors when three of the most important private Italian banks in Italy were nationalized in 1933. But its inspired extension in the postwar period has provided governments with a concrete example of what otherwise appeared difficult or impossible to achieve—state enterprise as efficient and dynamic as leading private enterprise groups, yet still directly serving the end of government policy and the interests of society as a whole" (Holland 1972b:1). IRI was established initially as a temporary agency to manage the industrial securities of three recently rescued banks: Banca Commerciale Italiana, Credito Italiano, and Banca di Roma. By 1937, in what Shonfield has described as "perhaps the most absent-minded act of nationalization in history" (Shonfield 1965: 179), IRI became a permanent agency.[12] Immediately following the war, a debate over the future of IRI ensued. The Liberal party (PLI), the Republican party (PRI), parts of the Democrazia Cristiana (DC), and the

---

[12] For more on the early history of IRI, see Holland 1972a: especially 56–62; Martinelli 1981: 85–98; Bianchi 1987: 269–90; and Maraffi 1990.

traditionalist wing of Confindustria (Marzotto) advocated the disman-
tling of IRI; the Communist party (PCI), the Socialist party (PSI), and
the left wing of the DC, along with the unions and the modernization
wing of Confindustria (Valletta of Fiat) advocated its continuation. The
former saw IRI as tainted by its fascist origins and as a potential threat to
the free market, while the latter viewed public enterprise as an essential
instrument in the postwar reconstruction of the Italian economy.

A compromise was eventually reached in which the state holding
companies would continue to operate but only in certain strategic
sectors (steel, energy, infrastructure) aimed at supporting private economic development. With this same goal in mind Ente Nazionale
Idrocarburi (ENI) was established in 1953 to develop Italy's energy
industry. Six years later, ENI entered the chemical industry as well. By
fostering direct links with oil-producing nations and creating import-
substitutes for foreign plastics and fertilizers, ENI claimed to reduce
input costs and stimulate private industrial growth. IRI, too, expanded
into transportation and telephones in order to facilitate the extension
of Italian markets.

Throughout the 1960s this strategy was highly successful—so successful that Italian state enterprise came to be seen by a number of
foreign observers as a model in its own right (Shonfield 1965; Posner
and Woolf 1967; Holland 1972b, 1974). Not only had these parastatal
corporations played critical roles in developing Italian industry, but
they had done so within the framework of a liberal market economy.
IRI and ENI are not nationalized corporations. The so-called IRI
formula entails only partial government ownership of company stock,
enough to control managerial strategy. In the 1950s and 1960s, IRI-
and ENI-affiliated firms were managed as private companies—competing with private and other state-controlled firms, selling stock to
raise investment funds, and paying dividends on their earnings.

In the 1970s, however, this system began to unravel. While employment in the state holding companies expanded, investment and economic performance plummeted. Because of these poor results and
due to increasing government intervention in managerial decisions,
private investors defected. This, in turn, forced IRI and ENI to rely
increasingly on government grants to finance their investments and
cover their operating losses, which only further encouraged the government to intervene in their affairs. Table 2.2 illustrates this down-
ward trend. From 1970 on, with the sole exception of 1973, the entire

53

state holding system operated at a loss. These losses grew over the course of the decade. Similarly, after 1973, investment levels declined as well.

Several explanations have been advanced for this reversal in economic performance. They include: the increasing politicization and declining competence of public enterprise managers (Grassini 1981); weak and poorly coordinated government control over IRI and ENI business activities (Prodi 1981; Cassese 1981; Martinelli 1981); the "improper burdens" imposed on the state holding companies by the government such as absorbing redundant workers and failing firms, investing in high-risk, and low-return projects in the South (Grassini 1979; Bognetti 1981); and the concentration of IRI and ENI firms in crisis-ridden industrial sectors like steel, shipbuilding, and petrochemicals (Bognetti 1981).

But it is difficult to disaggregate the precise weight of the various factors and assess these different explanations, since they are in many ways interrelated. For example, over the course of the 1960s and 1970s, Italian legislation required that the state holding companies locate growing percentages of their new and total investment in the South. This, in turn, encouraged IRI and ENI to overinvest in large-scale, capital-intensive projects in the South simply in order to maintain or up-grade their plants in the North. Because of poor government control and the growing links between public sector managers and certain factions of the ruling Christian Democrat and Socialist parties, not all of these projects were economically sound. Often they were pursued for purely political, clientalistic reasons. And since private investors refused to go along, IRI and ENI were forced to raise investment funds from bank loans and government grants.

Thus, by the time the economic crisis of the 1970s hit, IRI and ENI were already burdened with overcapacity in no longer competitive industries (see Table 2.3) and rising interest payments on loans taken out to pay for these projects.[13] Moreover, neither holding company possessed the managerial skills necessary to emerge from this situation. In short, the public corporations that had once constituted the most dynamic sector of the Italian economy and had appeared as models for other industrialized nations were, by the end of the 1970s, suffer-

---

[13] By the end of the decade, IRI could not even meet its interest payments, which the government had to cover directly. See Bianchi 1987 for more on this.

Table 2.2. Selected performance indicators of Italy's public enterprise system

	1970	1971	1972	1973	1974	1975	1976	1977	1978
Investments (billion lire)	4344.2	5551.1	6375.7	6365.8	5200.5	5075.1	5043.7	4577.3	4283.0
Employment (thousands)	462.4	531.6	584.8	617.9	687.3	706.7	715.0	710.7	706.8
Economic results (billion lire)	−33.8	−75.1	−85.4	62.0	−100.0	−744.2	−664.2	−1316.0	−1407.0

Source: Giuseppe Bognetti, "Il sistema delle partecipazioni statali negli anni '70," in *La crisi delle partecipazioni statali: Motivi e prospettive,* Emilio Gerelli and Giuseppe Bognetti, eds. (Milan: Franco Angeli, 1981), pp. 18–20.

ing from financial insolvency, managerial involution, and political corruption.

As early as 1975, with the Chiarelli Commission of the Chamber of Deputies, but continuing throughout the 1980s, several attempts were made to restructure Italy's public enterprises.[14] We now turn to an analysis of three of these efforts: GEPI, Protocollo IRI, and privatization. Although the first effort, GEPI, was conceived prior to the crisis of Italy's public enterprise system and was initially a defensive initiative, in the sense that it sought to restructure private firms so that the state holding companies would not have to absorb them, the other two initiatives were aimed directly at IRI- and ENI-affiliated firms.

Table 2.3. Selected economic results of various industrial companies, 1978

IRI	Gain or loss, in billion lire	ENI	Gain or loss, in billion lire
Finsider (steel)	−581.1	Agip (oil and gas energy)	207.0
Finmeccanica (autos)	−238.6	Snam (engineering services)	26.1
Fincantieri (shipbuilding)	−83.9	Agip Nucleare (nuclear energy)	1.1
Stet (telecommunications)	+40.0	Anic (chemicals)	−247.2
Finmare (shipping)	−42.1	Nuovo Pignone (motors, machine tools)	4.0
Alitalia	+14.0	Lanerossi (textiles)	−103.0

Source: Giuseppe Bognetti, "Il sistema delle partecipazioni statali negli anni '70," in *La crisi delle partecipazioni statali: Motivi e prospettive,* Emilio Gerelli and Giuseppe Bognetti, eds. (Milan: Franco Angeli, 1981), p. 22.

[14]See Gallo 1986; Pennacchi 1981a; and Gerelli and Bognetti 1981 for various analyses and proposals concerning the reorganization of the state holding companies.

All three reform projects were modeled after seemingly successful reorganization arrangements in other European countries.

Gestione e Partecipazione Industriale (GEPI)

Inspired by the British Industrial Reorganization Corporation,[15] GEPI was established in 1971 as a private joint-stock company with the specific purpose of restoring ailing private firms to financial self-sufficiency. IRI, ENI, and Ente partecipazioni e Finanziamenti Industrie Manufatturiere (EFIM)—the three main state holding companies—held 50 percent of GEPI's shares. GEPI was seen as a preventive measure against the further indiscriminate use of the public sector to rescue failing private firms. To implement this mission, GEPI would link up with one or more private partners when taking on a rescue operation. According to Franco Grassini, GEPI's first general director, this strategy "reflected the insight that the state possessed unlimited funds but insufficient entrepreneurial capacities. Thus, it turned to the private sector for this entrepreneurial talent" (Grassini 1979: 102).

Theoretically, one of these interested private partners would eventually purchase the firm. To help private firms with temporary and surmountable managerial problems, GEPI employed several strategies. Sometimes, it would directly purchase shares in individual companies and then reorganize them. Other times, it would set up or participate in setting up financial holding companies to manage firms in

---

[15] GEPI's inception in many ways illustrates the extensive (but not very efficient) borrowing of institutional practices among countries. According to Romano Prodi (1974: 50), GEPI was modeled after the British Industrial Reorganization Corporation (IRC). Interestingly, however, Stuart Holland, one of the main architects of the IRC, was highly taken with IRI and claims that the IRC was, itself, modeled after IRI. Holland was the economic assistant to the special economic advisor to the British Cabinet in 1966–67 and personal assistant to the British prime minister in 1967–68—precisely when the IRC was being established. "In other words, if the ends which the IRC was supposed to pursue were recognizably similar to IRI's, it differed initially in the means which it was supposed to employ to fulfil them, and employed resources which were a fraction of those available to IRI. On the other hand, there were considerable qualitative similarities in the way in which IRC operated and IRI's operation. For instance, both agencies were seen as means for state promotion of entrepreneurship in a market environment by entrepreneurs rather than government departments. Its chairmen and board included men whose main experience had been in finance or industry rather than administration. ... None of these parallels need to be forced, since it is well appreciated that the Prime Minister's Special Economic Advisor both knew the IRI model in detail and recommended the establishment of the IRC as an instrument of state intervention in industry which would back up the sectoral planning target of the Department of Economic Affairs" (Holland 1972b: 244–45).

crisis. GEPI also provided subsidized credit to finance firm restructuring efforts. When rescuing a private firm, GEPI would insist that it go through bankruptcy procedures as a way of holding the companies' owners, managers, and creditors responsible for the current state of the firm.

Initially, GEPI implemented its mission with tremendous success. Between 1971 and 1978, GEPI oversaw the restructuring of 176 firms with about 57,000 employees. Ninety of these firms, with 39,483 employees, were located in the North, twenty-seven (5,265 employees) were in the Center, and fifty-nine (12,434 employees) were in the South. In eighty-two of these companies, GEPI had significant private partners and, out of these, about half had been sold back to private entrepreneurs (Kreile 1983: 208). GEPI also played a significant role in the reorganization of the now highly successful cotton spinning and weaving industry located between Bergamo and Brescia.[16]

Yet stemming the tide of failing private firms was, at best, only a partial solution to IRI's and ENI's problems. They still had to reorganize their own operations, and their apparent inability to do so was being publicly denounced by the early 1980s. The 1981 annual report of the Ministry of State Holding Companies lamented that "the crisis of the largest Italian firms shows its deepest intensity in the public-owned firms: in the last five years they lost more than 9,500 billion lire with an alarming rate that shows no signs of decreasing. . . . The system of public shareholdings, that is, the main instrument of industrial policy organization in our country, has become terribly costly in terms of collective resources absorbed, while the results are worsening day by day (Bianchi 1987: 281). To remedy the crisis, the minister in charge of state holdings initiated a series of measures aimed at rationalizing and reinvigorating IRI and ENI. Among these, he named new directors to both these state holding companies. Both new directors refused to take on new rescue operations and, instead, began radical reorganization processes of their core businesses. These re-

---

[16] Based on extensive interviews with several textile company managers in this region, including Sergio Gambarelli, general manager of Leglertext, S.p.A., Ponte San Pietro (Bergamo), May 25, 1987; and Alberto Archetti, president of Gruppo Tessile Niggeler and Kupfer, Capriolo (Brescia), June 11, 1987. Managerial views on this issue were echoed by labor representatives as well in several interviews, including Bruno Ravazio, regional secretary of Filtea-CGIL Lombardia, Milan, July 6, 1987; and Mario Agostinelli, regional secretary of CGIL Lombardia, Sesto San Giovanni, June 11, 1987. For more on the restructuring of the Italian cotton textile industry, see Canziani 1989.

structuring efforts included highly diverse, somewhat contradictory strategies borrowed from other nations. For example, on the one hand, IRI and ENI sought to emulate the more participatory and apparently more efficient labor-management arrangements of Germany through the Protocollo IRI.[17] On the other hand, however, the directors of these two state enterprises were intrigued by Britain's radical privatization drive and hoped to employ this rationalization strategy as well. We now turn to an examination of these two very different approaches to public enterprise reform.

The Protocollo IRI

Agreed to initially in December 1984 as a two-year experiment but renewed and extended in February 1986, the Protocollo IRI between Italy's largest state holding company and the three major union confederations sought to promote neocorporatistlike arrangements within IRI-affiliated firms. Building on IRI's early legacy as an innovative employer and pacesetter in industrial relations[18] but highly influenced by central European experiences with comanagement as well (Treu 1986b), the Protocollo established new institutions aimed at enhancing union participation in firm restructuring efforts. The agreement served the needs of both sides. On the one hand, IRI's new director, Romano Prodi, knew that IRI's situation was critical and thus, desperately needed labor's cooperation in rescuing it. On the other hand, the unions were reeling from their own political and economic troubles[19] and welcomed this opportunity to (re)legitimate themselves as essential participants in firm governance and economic restructuring.

Essentially, the accord between these two groups established a number of bilateral committees of experts at various levels (firm, territory, corporate) of the holding company. These bilateral committees were composed of equal numbers of union and management representatives and were empowered to discuss all issues concerning the investment, restructuring, and employment policies of IRI-affiliated firms.

---

[17]ENI did not promote a group-level accord, but rather encouraged its various operating companies to do so.

[18]For more on these experiences, see Walter Kendall, "Labor Relations," in Holland 1972b: 219–33; and Martinelli 1981: 94.

[19]Including an attempt by certain segments of private business to circumvent unions entirely. For more on this, see Federmeccanica 1985.

In this way, unions would be able to influence strategic decisions in the early stages of their formulation. As differences in opinion were expected from both sides, the agreement also set up procedures to promote consensus or a convergence of views. Arbitration and conciliation processes were created and a cooling-off period was required before either side took action. A number of manpower programs aimed at shedding redundancies, retraining workers, and enhancing internal mobility were also included in this agreement.

Early assessments of the Protocollo IRI by both union and management representatives were very positive (see Treu 1986b; Ricci and Veneziani 1988). Bilateral committees were established within several sectors (steel, shipbuilding, electronics, autos, and telecommunications) and in several regions (Liguria, Lombardia, and Campania). Conciliation and arbitration mechanisms were also created. Given the poor institutionalization of Italian industrial relations (Cella 1989) and the antilabor climate of the early 1980s, these developments appeared as radical innovations in the Italian context.

Privatization—Italian Style

Equally radical was the initiation of privatization efforts among the state holding companies. While simultaneously promoting concertative labor relations to help reorganize its industrial activities, the new directors of IRI and ENI also turned to the market to resolve their financial problems. In other words, they began to privatize firms that they had acquired during previous bailouts and now were perceived as secondary to their strategic mission.

Denationalization efforts had taken place throughout the postwar period, but they usually had involved only minor firms. Beginning in 1983, ENI and IRI privatized between four and five major firms per year, including well-known giants like Alfa Romeo and Lanerossi.[20] Between 1980 and 1986, IRI alone sold off twenty-five companies with about 50,968 employees. From sales realized between 1983 and 1986 5,389 billion lire flowed into IRI coffers. Tables 2.4 and 2.5 illustrate this trend for IRI, but similar developments took place in the other state holding companies as well (Table 2.6).

---

[20] These and the following figures were taken from Bianchi, Cassese, and della Sala 1988: 87–100. For more on this process of privatization, see Bianchi 1988: 109–25; and Stefani 1988: 935–50.

Table 2.4. Privatization of IRI-affiliated firms, 1950–1985

	1951–1960	1961–1970	1971–1980	1981–1982	1983–1985
Purchase of enterprises	15	23	55	9	1
Sales of enterprises	9	17	18	7	20
Balance	6	6	37	2	−19
Employees acquired	22,503	21,114	71,162	9,520	740
Employees lost	5,362	9,601	13,323	4,259	7,113
Balance	17,141	11,513	57,839	5,261	−6,373

Source: Patrizio Bianchi, Sabino Cassese, Vincent della Sala, "Privatization in Italy: Aims and Constraints," *West European Politics* 11 1 (January 1988): 92. Used by permission of Frank Cass Publishers.

Privatization not only helped the state holding companies emerge from their financial difficulties but also served an important political function. As we saw earlier, the companies had placed themselves in a vicious cycle in which their growing dependence on government funding had forced them to give up much of their operational autonomy. In order to regain their independence and return to their original institutional mission, IRI and ENI sold off major components of their holdings. According to several well-placed analysts, "The only way for the agencies to break out of this vicious circle, which condemned them to being slaves of the government, was to regain the financial autonomy which for 30 years represented the shield behind which they could freely go about their business. Privatization offered them a means of breaking out of this circle."[21]

Thus, over the course of the 1970s and 1980s, three very different and in certain ways contradictory strategies—privatization, neocorporatist bargaining, and direct intervention in the restructuring of ailing private firms—were all pursued to revitalize Italy's state holding companies. Backers of each of these strategies conceived of the problems afflicting the public enterprises in slightly different ways and thus pursued alternative approaches to reform.

For the supporters of GEPI, the key source of IRI's and ENI's troubles was the growing number of ailing private firms they were called on to take over and rescue. Many of these firms were in industries completely unrelated to the core business activities and competencies of either ENI or IRI and thus could not be efficiently managed

[21] This quote is taken from Bianchi, Cassese, and della Sala 1988: 98. Patrizio Bianchi, who directs the Bologna-based research institute Nomisma, is a very close collaborator of Prodi.

Table 2.5. IRI sales between 1983 and 1986

Firm	Year	Sector	Employees
Maccarese (Liquidat.)[a]	1982	Agriculture	546
FAG	1983	Mechanical industry	666
Umbra Cuscinetti	1983	Mechanical industry	185
CBF	1983	Mechanical industry	76
Italsnack	1983	Food industry	124
Sweet Mark	1983	Food industry	131
Elettr. S. Giorgio	1984	Mechanical industry	768
Safog	1984	Mechanical industry	224
Idrisag	1984	Mechanical industry	20
Star	1984	Food industry	2,770
Ducati Mecc.	1985	Mechanical industry	411
Ansaldo Motori	1985	Mechanical industry	784
Cirio[b]	1985	SME group	1,087
Alivar[b]	1985	SME group	3,230
Italgel[b]	1985	SME group	1,318
Sidalm[b]	1985	SME group	4,143
Autogrill[b]	1985	SME group	512
Sico[b]	1985	SME group	4,761
Supermaercato G.S.[b]	1985	SME group	1,130
Other S.M.E. Comps.[b]	1985	SME group	—
Rivoire	1985	Chemical industry	673
Rivoire Sud[c]	1985	Chemical industry	23
Pantox[c]	1985	Chemical industry	32
Italdata	1986	Electronics industry	382
Continentalmare	1985	Maritime transport	11
Sovitalmare	1985	Maritime transport	6
Sartelec	1986	Telephone trenching	—
Sidalm Peru	1986	Food industry	—
OMG	1985	Mechanical industry	189
Fimit Sud	1985	Car accessories	95
Gallino Sud	1985	Car accessories	309
Isai international	1985	Finance	10
Intrigas	1985	Gas production	50
Italso	1985	Food industry	105
Circum Vesuviana	1986	Transport	2,658
Alfa Romeo (group)	1986	Motor vehicles	36,000

Source: Patrizio Bianchi, Sabino Cassese, and Vincent della Sala, "Privatization in Italy: Aims and Constraints," *West European Politics* 11 1 (January 1988): 97.Used by permission of Frank Cass Publishers.

[a]Opposed sales.
[b]Uncompleted sales.
[c]Sold to other public enterprises.

even after their takeover. As a result of this understanding of IRI's and ENI's problems, a group of reformers within the public enterprise system pushed for GEPI as a way of stemming the tide of these lame ducks and keeping IRI and ENI out of the business of bailing out failed private firms.

Table 2.6. Takeovers and sales of public enterprises in Italy, 1983–1986

	IRI	ENI	EFIN
Takeovers	5	15	8
Sales	9	7	8
Balance	−4	+8	0

Source: Patrizio Bianchi, Sabino Cassese, and Vincent della Sala, "Privatization in Italy: Aims and Constraints," *West European Politics* 11 1 (January 1988): 96. Used by permission of Frank Cass Publishers.

Proponents of privatization had a distinctly different view of the problems afflicting the public enterprises. For this second group of would-be reformers, IRI and ENI's growing dependence on government resources, and hence their decreasing autonomy from the government, was the principal cause of their downfall. The so-called IRI-formula had worked because public enterprises were run essentially as private firms: they raised investment funds on the market, paid dividends to their private investors, and competed aggressively with other public and private firms. As government influence in the management of these public enterprises increased, many of the companies lost their managerial autonomy. Rather than concentrate their efforts on increasing market share or returns on investment, these firms became increasingly attentive to the direction of government policies or, even worse, the whims of their political patrons in the Christian Democrat or Socialist parties. By privatizing affiliated firms, IRI and ENI were simultaneously rationalizing their businesses, improving their finances, and reasserting their managerial autonomy.

Finally, supporters of the Protocollo saw IRI's problems as arising essentially from the inefficiency of its own operations. Only if IRI-affiliated firms restructured themselves would they return to their past glory and only if they worked out an agreement with their powerful unions would IRI firms be able to successfully restructure their businesses, shed redundant workers, and enhance the efficiency of their operations.

However, like Italy's experiences with economic planning and industrial policy, these three very different strategies failed—both individually and collectively—to achieve their goal of revitalizing Italian public enterprise. Nearly a decade after the first efforts to reform IRI and ENI were initiated, both state companies continue to face serious economic difficulties and are once again the focus of political controversy. In short, over the course of the 1980s, many resources were expended and several reform projects pursued, but not one of these efforts was able to produce significant change.

For instance, although GEPI in its early years remained true to its institutional mandate of rescuing and reprivatizing industrial firms temporarily in trouble, it eventually succumbed to political pressures and began rescuing firms alone, simply to maintain employment levels (Prodi 1974: 50; Grassini 1979: 103). After 1977, GEPI's activities were restricted to the South, and in the 1980s, special laws were passed that required GEPI to serve as a retraining center/employment agency for growing numbers of redundant workers parked within its juridical boundaries. Thus, what began as an attempt to keep failing firms and their work forces off the public sector's rolls evolved into what some called "the fourth state holding company" specializing in industrial bail-outs. As of June 1987, GEPI was still involved in 202 firms with 30,837 employees. Out of 202 firms, only 43 had significant partners. Twenty-four of these firms, with 6649 employees, were located in the North. The remaining 178 companies (of which only 19 had private partners) were all centered in the South (CER-IRS 1989: 209–13). GEPI's role in restructuring private firms appeared so ineffective by the latter half of the 1980s that a highly influential report on Italian industry recommended that it be either returned to its original mandate or shut down completely (CER-IRS 1986: 17).

The other two approaches to reforming Italian state enterprise— the Protocollo IRI and privatization—met similar fates. As we saw already, privatization efforts among the state enterprises accelerated after 1983. The income earned from these sales allowed both ENI and IRI to resolve their financial problems and reassert their autonomy from the government. However, when compared with other national privatization efforts, the Italian experience appears quite modest. For example, between 1980 and 1986, IRI privatized 25 companies with 50,968 employees. During roughly the same time period, British firms employing 400,000 people were denationalized. Similarly, funds realized from the sale of state enterprises in Italy during the first half of the 1980s amounted to only a fifth of the income nine French privatizations generated in one year (1986–87).[22] Moreover, because privatization efforts in Italy followed no set legislative or

---

[22]These figures are taken from Bianchi, Cassese, and della Sala 1988: 88.

administrative guidelines, the state holding companies could not be assured that their intentions to sell off individual firms would be realized. Thus, although IRI successfully privatized Alfa Romeo, it was blocked in its efforts to sell off SME, a much smaller food business (See Bianchi 1988 for a comparison of these two cases).

The implementation of the Protocollo IRI was equally uneven. In two follow-up studies (Ronchi 1986; Ricci and Veneziani 1988), researchers found highly differentiated patterns of implementation in different sectors and regions of the economy. Essentially, in firms and regions with a tradition of bargaining and the open exchange of information between labor and management, the Protocollo was implemented, sometimes even expanded, by the local bilateral committees. However, in other firms and regions lacking these attributes, the bilateral labor-management committees either did not meet or met but could not agree on how to proceed with a common approach to industrial restructuring.

In many ways, developments within the public enterprise system mirror the larger debates and political struggles endemic to Italy's institutional reform process. Different groups with alternative agendas and visions of the new Italy—but all coexisting within the same state enterprises—pushed for divergent programs and adjustment strategies. Sometimes, as in the case of IRI's management, the same actors simultaneously pursued two apparently contradictory strategies. As a result of this highly politicized and incoherent process, none of the reform initiatives succeeded in fulfilling their goals. Often efforts pursued in one direction (privatization) merely undermined other strategies (Protocollo IRI) undertaken in another. As is quite obvious by looking at the sorry state of Italian public enterprise today, the consequences of this ad hoc, poorly coordinated, and internally contradictory process have been disastrous for what was once seen (by Italian and foreign observers alike) as a model of efficiency and technological know-how.

In this chapter I reviewed a variety of different attempts to rationalize economic governance in Italy. To one degree or another, all of these reform efforts failed in that they were unable to achieve their stated objectives. New institutions were created and new policies launched, but their impact on reordering political-economic relations was minimal. As in the cases of GEPI and the Medium-Term Plan, for example, sometimes these reform initiatives actually reinforced traditional, clientalistic practices. Yet a closer look at several of these failed reform processes reveals that they were not all universal failures. In fact, in certain regions and sectors of the Italian economy, they were actually quite successful.

For example, following legislation (once again, Law 675 of 1977) that restricted GEPI's activities to the South, its demise was assured. Yet even before 1977, GEPI had already developed a mixed record, with most of its successful interventions in the North and, even then, not always with private partners. For GEPI to effectively fulfill its mandate, it relied on a set of external resources (the availability of talented and well-funded entrepreneurs, a cooperative or at least non-obstructionist work force, a sound industrial base on which to rebuild the company). These supporting conditions, however, were available only in certain Italian localities, not all. As a result, GEPI was able to achieve tremendous success reorganizing textile companies in highly developed areas like Bergamo and Brescia, but its opportunities (and rate of success) were far more limited in the South (Grassini 1979: 105; CER-IRS 1989: 207–13).

The same was true for the other reform strategies as well. For example, the Protocollo IRI depended upon the good will and favorable disposition of various union and management groups for its implementation. As we saw earlier, the Protocollo was implemented only in firms and regions with a strong tradition of labor-management bargaining and the open exchange of information. Where these underlying conditions did not exist, the Protocollo was either ignored or sabotaged. Likewise, the Nucleo di Valutazione required that local and regional governments submit proposals with precise information and particular (cost-benefit) analyses illustrating how their proposed projects were congruent with the overall objectives of the Medium-Term Plan. Yet since only certain regional and local governments possessed these technical capacities,[23] access to the Fondo Investimenti e Occupazione (FIO) was heavily skewed in their favor. This was the principal justification government ministers employed when completely circumventing the planning process.

Ironically, these reforms, which were originally designed to be im-

[23]For more on the differential capacities of Italian regions, see Putnam, Leonardi, Nanetti, and Pavoncello 1983: 55–74.

plemented uniformly throughout the national territory and which sought to eliminate structural inequalities between regions, actually contributed to reinforcing prior differences. In other words, because GEPI, the Protocollo IRI, and the FIO were implemented primarily in firms or areas with particular organizational attributes and embedded in localities with distinct underlying sociopolitical features, these same firms and regions were the ones to benefit most from these reforms. The same was true for Law 675. As we saw earlier, most of the Fondo Ristrutturazione e Riconversione was allocated to large firms operating in three industries: chemicals, steel, and automobiles. This was due not only to political pressures (IRI and ENI were deeply involved in all three sectors) but also to the fact that only these large firms possessed the internal capacities necessary to negotiate the labyrinth of bureaucratic procedures required to access these funds and the assets to back up their loans from the special credit institutes.

This was not the first time government funds were allocated disproportionately in favor of stronger firms and more dynamic regions. In fact, many previous government-subsidized credit initiatives available either to all firms within a particular industrial sector or to only those companies with particular characteristics (i.e., small- to medium-sized firms) often resulted in favoring industrial districts located in particular regions of Italy (Weiss 1988) and/or large firms (Piattoni 1986), since they both possessed the organizational capacities and resources necessary to tap these government funds. As a result, government initiatives often reinforced rather than abated preexisting differences and usually subsidized rather than directed local-level developments already under way.

In an odd way, both of Italy's traditional approaches to economic regulation—the macroeconomic-monetarist approach pursued by the Bank of Italy and the microinterventionist strategy sponsored by the state enterprises and their allies in government—converged to reinforce various traditional features of the Italian political economy. The Bank of Italy's attempt to remedy Italy's economic problems by tightening government spending and imposing tough austerity measures—policies it could once again pursue because of its regained autonomy—were eventually undermined by the growth of the secondary market for treasury bills which the bank itself had promoted. No longer able to induce the bank to print new money, the government turned to individuals and firms and sold short-term, high interest-yielding bonds. As a result, government spending continued unabated and the public debt exploded.

Neomercantilist public enterprise managers promoted a completely different approach to economic regulation, one aimed at intervening directly in the economy to "correct" structural imbalances and guide development. Yet as we just saw, in the 1970s and 1980s these more microinterventionist strategies not only failed to achieve their stated goals but often ended up supporting the more dynamic firms and regions. Thus, they actually reinforced prior structural inequalities between strong and weak firms, industries, and economic regions.

The failure of these various efforts to rationalize Italian economic policy in the 1970s and 1980s did not, however, translate into a reaffirmation of laissez-faire marketism. In the absence of a coherent national policy, Italian firms and industries were nonetheless guided and regulated in their strategies by the underlying sociopolitical character of different local economic orders. These local sociopolitical orders shaped the way the various economic actors understood the changes underway and the range of strategic options these actors could viably pursue.

Firms and industries located in localities with particular features (dense networks of associations, well-developed interest groups) were better able to adjust to changing economic conditions *and* take advantage of the various incentives and resources made available to them through the different reform projects than were other firms situated in local economies with very different attributes. This explains why the same policy (whether planning or restructuring or even privatization) produced such different results in different areas of the country. The important role local sociopolitical networks play in shaping economic behavior will be more fully illustrated in the latter chapters of this book. But before moving to that level of analysis, we now examine another set of reform measures aimed at remaking Italy. Chapter 3 focuses on a completely different policy arena—industrial relations— once considered critical to the health (or lack thereof) of the Italian economy.

CHAPTER THREE

Building a "Mature" System
of Industrial Relations

Uncoordinated economic policies were not the only problems plaguing Italy in the 1970s. Italian industrial relations, often characterized
as highly conflictual (Shalev 1983), politicized (Lange and Vannicelli
1982), and poorly institutionalized (Cella 1989), were also seen as a
major source of Italy's political and economic woes. In fact, many
Italian business, government, and even labor leaders came to believe
that before Italy could ever hope of joining the ranks of the other
advanced nations, it would need to reform its system of labor relations.

This chapter analyzes various efforts during the 1970s and 1980s
to construct a new, more "mature" system of industrial relations in
Italy. Most of these reform projects failed. In many ways their failure
exacerbated the organizational fragmentation and political divisions
already plaguing Italian labor relations. At the same time, however,
these failed institutional reforms led to a reconfiguration of various
industrial relations rules, practices, and organizational boundaries
which may contain the seeds of labor's renewal.

This chapter is divided into five sections. The first section briefly
describes the postwar evolution of Italian industrial relations. The
second section reviews several failed attempts at reforming this system
which sought to replicate certain key practices and/or institutions characteristic of other, supposedly more mature, national systems of industrial relations. The reform of Italian labor law through the Statuto
dei Diritti dei Lavoratori (1970), the revision of the wage indexation
system, scala mobile (1975), and attempts at promoting neocorporatist
policies and relations during the period of national solidarity in 1976–
79 and again in 1983–84 will all be analyzed. The third section then

examines the unanticipated consequences of these reforms. Contrary to the intentions of Italy's would-be reformers, all of these experiments with institutional reform inevitably encouraged the further decentralization and fragmentation of Italian industrial relations practices. Section four further illustrates the unintended consequences of this reform process through a case study of the Confederazione Italiana dei Sindacati Lavoratori (CISL).

Established during the height of the Cold War, initially as a breakaway from and later rival organization to the Communist-dominated Confederazione Generale Italiana del Lavoro (CGIL), the CISL sought to develop its own distinct organizational culture around two fundamental principles: 1) the importance of firm-level union activity and 2) the professionalization of union activists. As a result of these features, the CISL emerged during the 1960s as a highly innovative labor union. Many of the key changes in Italian industrial relations during this period, for instance, the establishment of firm-level union organizations and the introduction of "articulated" (firm-level) collective bargaining were promoted by the CISL. Moreover, most of the innovative strategies developed during the Hot Autumn—the *inquadramento unico* (unification of blue and white collar job classification schemes), egalitarian wage policy, and the strategic unity of Italy's three major labor confederations—were, in fact, initiated by various CISL-affiliated industrial unions, especially the Metalworkers Federation, (Federazione Italiana Metallurgici or FIM.

By the end of the 1980s, however, the situation appeared completely reversed. No longer a source of strategic innovation in Italian labor relations, the CISL appeared to be a much more bureaucratic and politicized organization (closely tied to particular factions of the Christian Democratic party). The fourth section illustrates how this turnaround came about. Essentially, like many other Italian political and economic elite in the 1970s and 1980s, the leadership of the CISL became increasingly convinced that Italy's problems stemmed from its archaic and inefficient institutional arrangements. As a result, the union abandoned its original focus on shop floor bargaining and promoted a series of strategic and organizational changes aimed at launching neocorporatist incomes policies in Italy. When these efforts failed and the Italian economy underwent a massive wave of restructuring, the CISL found itself lacking the organizational capacities necessary to respond adequately to the new challenges it faced. As a result, like other labor confederations in Italy and throughout the West, the CISL—which once seemed perfectly positioned to negotiate industrial change—now found itself plagued by strategic uncertainty and organizational weakness. These internal difficulties, in turn, rendered the union vulnerable to political pressures from key Christian Democratic politicians to support government policy and act as a "transmission belt" for the party.

Although this process of failed reform provoked a number of organizational challenges for the established unions, it also appears to have created the preconditions for labor's renewal. The concluding section of this chapter analyzes both the current challenges and potential benefits accompanying industrial relations reform in Italy.

A Brief Synopsis of Italian Industrial Relations

The Italian labor movement emerged from the destruction of twenty years of fascism and the Second World War as a highly politicized, centralized, and unified organization called the Confederazione Generale Italiana del Lavoro (CGIL). The union movement, like Italy's first postwar governments, consisted of a broad coalition of antifascist resistance forces: Communist, Socialist, Republican,[1] and Catholic currents coexisted within the trade union confederation.

The union movement was fostered by these political parties. Because the postwar labor movement had to rebuild more or less from scratch, union structures at all levels were creations of the central confederations in Rome. Rank-and-file workers and prefascist trade unionists had little to do with the reconstruction of the Italian union movement. Indeed, many of the CGIL's initial union leaders were recruited directly from political parties and had little previous union experience.[2]

With the advent of the Cold War, both government and labor coalitions dissolved. The Catholic current broke away from the CGIL and established itself as the Confederazione Italiana dei Sindacati Lavoratori (CISL), while the Republican and Social-Democrat trade union leaders set up the Unione Italiana dei Lavoratori (UIL).

[1]The Italian Republican party (PRI) was a small, centrist party with significant influence in Italian politics, especially economic affairs. For more on this and other Italian parties, see Farnetti 1985.
[2]See also Turone 1976; La Palombara 1957; and Raffaele 1962.

70

Throughout the 1950s and 1960s, the politics and strategies of the three union confederations were shaped by their political affiliations and rivalries.[3]

Union divisiveness and weakness were exacerbated by business and government policy. The 1950s were years in which the conservative wing of the ruling Christian Democratic party predominated. As a result, very few of the industrial relations reforms stipulated by the Constitution were enacted. For example, Italian labor had no formal legal protection. Because the Christian Democratic government delayed establishing the Constitutional Court until the late 1950s, what labor laws existed (e.g., the "urbanization law," which required workers to demonstrate proof of employment before they could change residence) were all inherited from the fascist regime (Contini 1985). Moreover, because many of the judges, prefects, and magistrates dealing with labor issues were trained during the fascist era, they often interpreted legal doctrine to the disadvantage of workers.

Business took advantage of this situation to circumvent labor market legislation (Reyneri 1989) and to purge their factories of union activists (Accornero 1976; Pugno and Garavini 1974). These years are considered the "golden age" of Confindustria, Italy's main business association (Becchi Collida 1989), since business was all-powerful and was able to use its power to pursue a low-wage, export-oriented strategy. This strategy not only generated enormous profits for individual firms, but also created the conditions for Italy's postwar economic "miracle" of the late 1950s and early 1960s (Salvati 1984). For instance, during these years Confindustria insisted on highly centralized collective bargaining since this worked to the advantage of business. Confindustria would set wages and other working conditions to the most backward and unproductive sectors of the economy (such as agriculture) and then generalize these terms to all of industry. Because unions were themselves highly centralized and also because they were weak in both the labor market and the political arena, they were unable to resist this low-cost, labor-sweating strategy.

All this changed with the Hot Autumn, the period of intense social and labor mobilization that began with the student demonstrations and mass rallies over pension reform in 1968 and lasted until the end of the 1970 contractual round (Brandini 1975; Pizzorno, Reyneri,

---

[3]See Neufeld 1960 for an interesting analysis of this period.

Regini, and Regalia 1978; Sabel 1982). This wave of strikes and protests overturned almost all of the social, political, and economic patterns established in the postwar period. For example, increased collaboration among the three confederations led to a form of reunification in 1972 with the signing of the federative pact. Within the Federazione Unitaria CGIL-CISL-UIL, each confederation retained its autonomy at all levels of the union hierarchy, but new joint structures aimed at coordinating decisions among the existing organizations were also created (Lange and Vannicelli 1982). The federation dissolved in 1984, due to disagreements between the Communists in the CGIL and the rest of the labor movement over a referendum sponsored by the Italian Communist party (PCI) abrogating a government decree revising the scala mobile (system of wage indexation). Since then, the three confederations have continued to cooperate in contract negotiations, notwithstanding periodic antagonism over issues like flexible work hours, internal mobility, and contingent compensation schemes.

Each confederation has both vertical and horizontal structures. The vertical structures are based on industries and branches of industry. Thus, each confederation has a national chemical workers, textile workers, and metalworkers federation. The three confederations are also organized geographically, in what are called horizontal structures (e.g., the Camere del Lavoro of Turin and Milan). During the 1950s, when the union movement was fragmented, weak, and politically isolated, these horizontal structures, especially the confederations, were predominant. With the increase in collective bargaining at the industry and firm levels during the 1960s, however, the national industrial unions became ascendant (Santi 1983).

Following the Hot Autumn struggles and the federative pact in 1972, factory councils—elected by and composed of union and non-union workers alike—were established at the shop floor. These are the official workplace organs of the three confederations, replacing the earlier Commissione Interne[4] (factory grievance committees). Figure 3.1 depicts the organization of the Italian union movement.

The organizational structure of the Italian union movement reflects its tumultuous and uncoordinated development. It also maps the key sources of dissent and tension that existed within the labor movement

---

[4]For an interesting historical reconstruction of the Commisioni Interne, see Baglioni 1968–69: 35–64.

Figure 3.1. Organizational structure of the Italian union movement

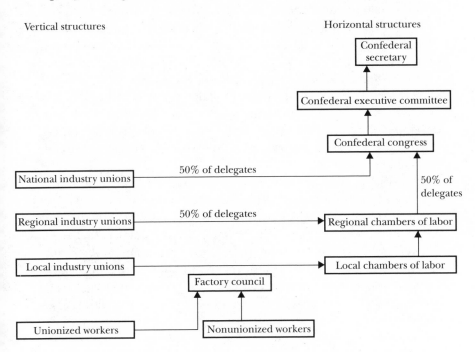

Source: Adapted from Guido Romagnoli and Giuseppe Della Rocca, "Il sindacato," in Gianprimo Cella and Tiziano Treu, eds., *Relazioni industriali: Manuale per l'analisi dell' esperienza italiana,* 2d ed. (Bologna: Il Mulino, 1989): 91.

over how best to respond to the economic crisis of the 1970s. For example, over the course of the decade, different levels of the union hierarchy competed for control over collective bargaining. While the central confederations attempted to negotiate peak-level agreements over social reforms and incomes policies, industry unions resisted these agreements. The industry unions saw them as a challenge to the power and autonomy they had accumulated over the years through negotiating the contratti collettivi nazionali di lavoro (CCNLs), triennial industry-wide collective bargaining agreements over minimum wages, work hours, and job classification schemes. Likewise, the factory councils insisted on revising or renegotiating a variety of clauses already covered in these same national industry agreements in order to enhance their own organizational standing.

Since the roles and responsibilities of the different union structures in collective bargaining were never fully demarcated or completely institutionalized, the various levels of the union hierarchy proved unable to develop a clear, mutually agreeable division of labor. As each level of the union fought to protect its own autonomy and power, the situation stagnated and the union became paralyzed by internal power struggles. Agreements concluded between labor and management at one level were subsequently challenged and renegotiated at another (Deallessandri and Magnabosco 1987). Moreover, wage drift developed as different parts of the union movement competed over who could deliver the best bargain for the workers (Flanagan, Soskice, and Ulman 1983).

Inconsistent business and government policies further aggravated this already precarious situation. At first, Confindustria reacted to the Hot Autumn through traditional repressive means (lockouts and disciplining union activists). Yet, when it became obvious that these measures would no longer work in the altered conditions of the 1970s, internal struggles within the business organization erupted over how best to respond to the new balance of power between labor and management. While one group of entrepreneurs associated with the so-called Pirelli Commission encouraged negotiations with labor and the construction of a new, more stable system of industrial relations, other more traditional business advocates resisted negotiations and used their influence within the association to block proposed reforms (Becchi Collida 1989). The government also was divided. Some advocated a harsh deflation that they believed would discipline the work force as it had in the early 1960s. Others sought to create new institutions and arrangements capable of reconciling labor's demands with continued economic growth and perhaps even greater political stability.

These debates took on greater significance when it became apparent that Italy's crisis of industrial relations was contributing to its economic woes. As we saw in Chapter 1, Italy experienced among the highest inflation and unemployment rates of all OECD nations during the 1970s. According to David Cameron (1984), Italy had the worst "misery index" (the combination of inflation and unemployment) of all advanced industrial nations. Turbulent industrial relations accentuated these problems. Italy witnessed more strikes and strike days during these same years than just about all other industrialized democracies. Moreover, wage militancy was especially pronounced in Italy. Between 1973 and 1980, real hourly wage rates in manufacturing rose 22 percent in Italy, 7 percent in West Germany, 9 percent in the United States, and 11 percent in Japan. As a result, labor costs per unit of output rose more in Italy than for its foreign competitors. In the mid-1970s, labor costs rose an average of 19.4 percent in Italy, as compared to 11.9 percent in France and 5.5 percent in West Germany.[5] In sum, Italy's political-economic troubles were compounded by (some would later argue, were caused by)[6] the country's highly volatile industrial relations system.

Due to this potentially explosive situation, a number of Italian political, business, and union leaders began working on rebuilding the Italian industrial relations system. No single unitary reform effort was promoted by these actors and certainly no clear consensus existed over what the new Italian arrangements should look like. Nonetheless, over the course of the 1970s and early 1980s, a number of initiatives aimed at recasting Italian industrial relations were launched. Many of these reform efforts were inspired by other national models, or at least by what the Italian reformers believed these models to be. Yet, because of the ad hoc and internally incoherent nature of this reform movement, each of these attempts at institutional reform produced mixed or incomplete results at best. Often the results contradicted the initial intentions of those who designed the reforms.

In other words, all of these efforts aimed at making the Italian industrial relations system more centralized, quiescent, and predictable—more like that of other nations—turned out to make the Italian system more decentralized, fragmented, and competitive. Initiatives aimed at abating the peculiarities of the Italian system instead accentuated them.

The next section of this chapter examines some of these reform efforts in greater detail. Three separate institutional reforms will be analyzed: 1) the Statuto dei Diritti dei Lavoratori of 1970, a workers' charter inspired by both American and French labor law principles; 2) the attempt by Confindustria to forge a Swedish-like "Basic Agreement" through the scala mobile accord of 1975; and 3) experiments with neocorporatist incomes policies in the late 1970s and again in

---

[5]Strike rates are reported in Paldman and Pedersen 1982: 519; real hourly wage increases are reported in Garonna and Pisani 1986: 123; per unit labor increases are reported in Salvati 1985: 510. All of these statistics were reported in Miriam Golden 1988b: 16.

[6]Federmeccanica 1985.

1983–84. All three initiatives were designed to recast the Italian industrial relations system in the image of some other, supposedly more stable and mature system. All three failed in their initial intentions, but in a way that may ultimately reconfigure the Italian industrial relations system along more democratic and innovative lines.

RECASTING ITALIAN LABOR RELATIONS IN THE 1970S AND 1980S

The Statuto dei Diritti dei Lavoratori

As stated previously, labor law in the Italian republic virtually did not exist until the late 1950s and early 1960s.[7] The old fascist legal codes remained in force and prefects, judges, and magistrates interpreted them to the disadvantage of workers. Moreover, until the establishment of the Constitutional Court at the end of the 1950s, it was impossible to revise these fascist codes since no body was empowered to judge them unconstitutional. In this context, factories became a legal no-man's-land with management free to persecute union activists, strikers subject to severe sanctions, and collective agreements no longer enforceable.

With the establishment of the first Center-Left government in the early 1960s, things began to change. Legislation enforcing collective agreements, abolishing fascist legal codes, and requiring "just cause" for dismissals was enacted in these years. At the same time, leading jurists began working on a comprehensive labor code, the Statuto dei Diritti dei Lavoratori, which combined elements of French and American labor law. This law, enacted in 1970 on the crest of the strike waves of the Hot Autumn, had two major components. Like the American Wagner Act, the first part consisted of a series of articles guaranteeing the freedom of workers as citizens: freedom of thought and expression were protected, job security was ensured, the roles of security guards and supervisors were strictly limited, and various surveillance techniques were curtailed. The second part provided institutional guarantees for unions: black lists were prohibited, the right

---

[7] For more on the evolution of Italian labor law, see Contini 1985: 192–218; and Napoli 1989: 47–57.

to join a union was affirmed, and unions were authorized to constitute their own structures on the shop floor.

However, the American concept of "bargaining unit" could not be applied easily to the Italian context because, typically, Italian workplaces are not organized by single unions. Unions within Italian companies are not chosen directly by workers through free elections, nor do they possess exclusive representation and contractual rights. As a result, Article 19 of the Statuto embraced the French solution of automatically recognizing what were called the "most representative" unions as the legitimate bargaining agents for employees within large and medium-sized firms. In other words, unions were given the authority to represent workers within a given workplace *not* through any direct vote by the workers, but rather by having already signed either a national or a provincial-level contract in the relevant industry. As a result of the way the Statuto defined representativeness, it essentially provided the three major union confederations (CGIL, CISL, and UIL) with a representational monopoly within most large and medium-sized Italian firms. This, in turn, supported the confederal unions in their attempt to channel worker protest and demands away from the militant factory councils and toward traditional union structures.

Although some radical critics accused the Statuto of straitjacketing worker protest during the Hot Autumn, almost everyone agreed that it was instrumental in supporting the unions at a time when they were facing severe dissent from the rank-and-file and continued intransigence from management. The aim of this legislation was clear. By granting almost exclusive recognition and support to the most representative unions, reformers hoped to contain conflict by institutionalizing relations among the various actors within the labor movement and between the unions and management.

The Scala Mobile Accord of 1975

When it became apparent in the early 1970s that traditional repressive measures on the shop floor and a government-sponsored deflation of the economy were no longer viable strategies for reducing union power, especially since labor had legal protection through the Statuto and a passive if not sympathetic government in office, Confindustria began searching for new ways of moderating labor conflict.[8] In 1972,

[8]This section draws heavily on Flanagan, Soskice, and Ulman 1983: 496–566.

a series of meetings between Confindustria and the three union confederations were held in which organized business proposed to swap employment guarantees for new regulations of collective bargaining, greater formalization of union structures in the factories, and a system of wage coordination. Although the industrial unions, fearing that they would lose power under the new arrangements, blocked these initial negotiations, these early meetings nonetheless set the stage for a subsequent round of negotiations which culminated in the 1975 accord over wage indexation.

The main aspects of this accord were a 100 percent indexation[9] of the scala mobile and a secondary agreement guaranteeing 80 percent of workers' wages in the event of layoffs (Patriarca 1986). Together, these would provide Italian workers with significant wage guarantees against both high inflation and radical restructuring. Confindustria believed these proposals would be so attractive that the industrial unions would be unable to block this renewed attempt by organized business to move the center of gravity of bargaining, and hence union power, closer to the more moderate confederations.

The accord provided benefits for both sides. For the unions, it not only protected workers in their already established bastions (primarily large, well-organized plants in the North) but also extended this bargain to workers in smaller, less organized plants. Together with the *inquadramento unico* (unification of blue and white collar job classifications), the scala mobile agreement defined Italian union strategy for over a decade. Major Italian firms gained as well. Since compensation for price increases would be paid by large firms in any event (because of strong unions within their plants), little was lost by imposing automatic compensation on smaller, potential competitors. Moreover, by removing disputes over price increases, this accord would eliminate a primary source of conflict within large plants, therefore reducing the power of the factory councils as well.

But there was also an ideological component to the 1975 accord. For the unions, the scala mobile accord, like the inquadramento unico,

---

[9]Indexation consisted in automatic wage increases related to changes in a union-controlled price index. Increases, however, were not related to existing wage levels but rather consisted of equal sums for all employees (the *punto unico di contingenza*). As Italy experienced two-digit inflation rates in the late 1970s and early 1980s, these "egalitarian" adjustments provided full protection of wages for workers in the lower job classifications but eroded the real wages of higher skilled workers. As a result, wage differentials were drastically reduced.

allowed them to satisfy the egalitarian demands of their more militant industrial federations. Yet for Giovanni Agnelli, the head of Fiat and president of Confindustria who had negotiated the accord, the aim was to create a privileged class of industrial workers with job and wage security. Not only would these "guaranteed" workers see the long-term benefits of moderation in terms of increased real wages and better working conditions, but together big business and organized labor would be able to fight the inefficient and bloated public sector. According to Robert Flanagan, David Soskice, and Lloyd Ulman; "The objective of Agnelli's exercise appears to have been the transfer of resources to the industrial sector and away from the public sector, which would be accomplished under conditions of rapid inflation as long as inflation was offset by depreciation of exchange rates and as long as 100 percent indexation was confined to the industrial sector. While the real wages of industrial workers in relation to consumer prices were safeguarded, consumer prices, reflecting smaller economywide wage increases, would fall in relation to industrial prices, and the real cost of industrial labor, in relation to industrial prices, would fall." (Flanagan, Soskice, and Ulman 1983: 543–44).

In short, Confindustria hoped to accomplish several things with this one sweeping agreement. First, it hoped that this agreement, like its Swedish counterpart in the 1930s, would simultaneously bring about the centralization and domestication of the Italian union movement.[10] By shifting the center of gravity of bargaining to the more moderate confederations, and by taking price increases and job security out of the bargaining arena, it hoped to restructure Italian industrial relations along more predictable and stable lines. Second, this centralization of wages would also, in the long run, enhance the competitiveness of Italian exports by tying wages in the export-oriented industrial sector to moderate price increases in the Italian economy as a whole. Finally, by enlisting the industrial working class into a "producers alliance" against the public sector, Confindustria was sending clear signals to the state that it was prepared to do battle if the government continued to encroach on the private sector.[11]

---

[10]For more on this Swedish model, see Martin 1984: 192–218; and Swenson 1989: 42–60.

[11]During these years, parts of the dominant Christian Democratic party sought to use their hold on government to take over (either through direct nationalization or by purchasing a controlling share of company stocks) a number of large, private firms. The takeover of Montedison through the secret purchase of the company's shares had

Two Attempts at Concertation

As the economic crisis worsened, partially as a result of the inflationary consequences of the scala mobile agreement (Flanagan, Soskice, Ulman 1983: 545), and the unions' Reform Strategy[12] floundered, organized labor engaged in two separate experiments in concertation.[13] The first, commonly referred to as the Federazione Unitaria's EUR policy, involved a trade-off between wage moderation and greater labor mobility in return for influence over industrial and labor-market policies aimed at restoring economic growth and sustaining employment. The second took place in 1983 when the unions entered into a tripartite agreement aimed principally at reforming the system of wage indexation. Both experiences were clearly inspired by, perhaps even modeled after, seemingly successful neocorporatist arrangements in other nations.

Prodded by the collapse of its prior strategies and by the Italian Communist party's support of austerity, the Italian union movement began moderating its wage demands in return for the right to bargain over private investment decisions in 1976.[14] In 1977 the confederations signed an agreement with Confindustria which revised seniority bonuses and severance pay, eliminated seven paid holidays, gave management greater control over absenteeism, and increased labor mobility within plants and firms. By 1978 the Federazione CGIL-CISL-UIL officially adopted an austerity policy in the form of the EUR document.

This document proclaimed that the unions would exercise self-restraint in both plant- and industrywide bargaining. Demands for investment and information about future company plans would replace claims for higher wages and better working conditions. In return for this moderation, the unions demanded substantial changes in the government's tax, energy, and agricultural policies; a reform of state finance; and a legislative package concerning industrial restructuring

alarmed many private business leaders. For more on this episode, see Galli and Nannei 1976.
[12] For more on the Reform Strategy, see Lange and Vannicelli 1982: 125–42.
[13] This section draws heavily on Golden 1988b; Lange and Vannicelli 1982; and Regini 1984: 124–42.
[14] Almost as a prelude to the Protocollo IRI, these rights were aimed at reducing information asymmetries regarding the introduction of new technologies and the reorganization of work. These demands were included in certain 1976 national contracts (e.g., metalworkers) but were for the most part never implemented. For more on this experiment, see Treu and Negrelli 1983.

and reconversion (Law 675) which included youth employment guarantees, vocational training initiatives, and pension reform (Lange and Vannicelli 1982: 166–67). In setting the stage for this change in union strategy, Luciano Lama, general secretary of the CGIL, gave a well-publicized interview in which he claimed:

> We have become aware that an economic system cannot sustain independent variables. The capitalists maintain that profit is an independent variable. The workers and their union, almost as a reflex, have in recent years sustained that wages are an independent variable and the size of the employed work force another . . . ; one established a certain wage level and a certain level of employment and then one asked that all other economic quantities be fixed in such a way as to make possible those levels of salary and employment. . . . It was an absurdity, because in an open economy the variables are all dependent on one another. . . . The imposition of excessive workers on firms is a suicidal policy. We retain that the firms, when it is determined that they are in a state of crisis, have the right to fire.[15]

The right to fire, increased labor mobility, and wages tied to productivity—all of these changes were seen as major concessions by the Italian union movement since they were considered among the key victories achieved by labor during the Hot Autumn. Initially, this turnaround in union strategy produced beneficial results: industrial conflict declined significantly in 1977–78, wage costs decreased, investments grew, and inflation was severely curtailed (Barca and Magnani 1989; OECD 1979: 21). Yet following the second oil shock and the demise of the government of national solidarity, industrial conflict and inflation resurfaced.

The second attempt at concertation took place in 1983 in the form of a tripartite cost-of-labor agreement aimed at revising the scala mobile. Due to Italy's high inflation rates, the 1975 agreement over wage indexation had gained massive weight in the determination of wages. By the early 1980s, it was estimated that the scala mobile accounted for over 60 percent of annual wage increases. This not only caused problems for management, which had to pay for these increases, but also for the unions whose control over wage determination had been severely reduced by indexation. The government, too,

---

[15] Luciano Lama, interview in *La repubblica,* January 24, 1978, reported in Lange and Vannicelli 1982: 169.

wanted a reform of this system since it ostensibly blocked all government measures aimed at fighting inflation.

Although bargaining over this agreement took place at separate tables, with labor leaders in one room, business representatives in another and government officials racing back and forth between them, all three actors signed the January 22, 1983, agreement. The agreement eliminated bracket creep, improved family allowances, established the Fondo di Solidarieta (Solidarity Fund) to raise money for investment, reduced coverage provided by wage indexation by 15 percent, and banned plant-level bargaining for eighteen months.[16] Disagreements over certain clauses of the agreement subsequently broke out between labor and management, and the agreement was not automatically renewed the following year. Yet the anticipated economic results appear to have been fulfilled: inflation was reduced, wage demands were moderated, and economic growth was restored.

THE UNINTENDED CONSEQUENCES OF REFORM

All of these initiatives were designed to make the Italian industrial relations system more stable and productive. And all of them, to one degree or another, were inspired by other national systems: the Statuto by the American Wagner Act, the 1975 accord over the scala mobile by the Swedish Basic Agreement, and the two attempts at concertation by analogous arrangements in central and northern Europe. Yet all of them failed to recast Italian labor relations along the lines of these seemingly more mature foreign systems. Instead, they accentuated the fragmentation and decentralization characteristic of the Italian system.

The Statuto dei Diritti dei Lavoratori, for instance, sought to establish a universal labor code throughout the national territory, thus institutionalizing standard labor practices in all workplaces with more than fifteen employees, and to recast Italian labor relations along more procedural (and, it was hoped, less conflictual) lines. Both goals were frustrated in the Italian context.

A series of studies on the implementation of the Statuto five, ten, and twenty years after it was established found tremendous variation

---

[16]For more details of the agreement, see Golden 1988b: 82–84.

in both its use by unions and its interpretation by magistrates (Melucci 1976; Treu 1984, 1991). These studies examined every case invoking the Statuto in eight very different regions of Italy and found that in areas where the union was politically powerful, economically secure, and embedded in a sociopolitical network that accepted it as a major player (Bologna, Monza), the union rarely invoked the statuto to resolve its problems. When it did seek legal recourse, it did so only in support of individual workers not as an organization. In short, the Statuto was used as a compliment, not as a supplement, to already existing union strategies. On the other hand, in areas where the union was less established as an organization (Porto Marghera-Mestre, Treviso) or where its power was being challenged by industrial restructuring (Prato, Novara), the union used the Statuto more often either to further or to protect its rights as an organization. Likewise, in areas where the union was strong, judges were more inclined to decide in favor of labor, whereas in areas where labor was weak (Sicily) they more often than not upheld traditional managerial practices. In sum, a law that was designed to standardize labor practices throughout Italy, in practice, actually reinforced a variety of diverse, well-established local arrangements.

Moreover, although the Statuto was initially designed to strengthen the more moderate union confederations vis-à-vis radical rank-and-file movements and thus contain industrial conflict, these same features of the law subsequently encouraged labor militancy and various organizational challenges to the established unions. For example, because of the way it limited workplace representation to the most representative unions and defined "most representative" as the ability of the union to negotiate a national or provincial-level industry contract, the Statuto actually created a very strong incentive for nonconfederal worker organizations to provoke strikes and contest previously negotiated contracts simply as a way of gaining access to collective bargaining negotiations.

In other words, given that the only way a nonconfederal union could establish itself *within* the workplace was through its legitimation *outside* the workplace, as a signatory of at least a provincial-level contract, various autonomous unions and anticonfederal worker groups (e.g., COBAS), especially in the public education and transportation sectors, increasingly engaged in a series of highly disruptive wildcat strikes. Only in this way could they demonstrate that they (and not the confederal unions) were the most representative unions and thus force the CGIL, CISL, and UIL, as well as the business associations, to include them in subsequent contract bargaining rounds.

Finally, aside from limiting workplace representation to a clearly defined number of organizations, the Statuto did not specify in any detail how exactly firm-level representation should be established, how elections to these bodies would be regulated, and, once constituted, what precise functions these workplace councils would perform. As a result, over the course of the 1970s and 1980s, provincial and national industrial unions slowly but systematically stripped the factory councils of most of their functions. As relations among the three confederations deteriorated and challenges by nonconfederal unions (autonomous unions and the COBAS) increased, elections to these workplace councils in many firms were held either sporadically or not at all (Regalia 1984). In sum, although workplace democracy and labor quiescence were to be institutionalized through the Statuto, various weaknesses in the design and implementation of the law actually contributed to producing the opposite results instead.

Similar developments characterized the other two reform efforts as well. As we saw earlier, part of the aim of the scala mobile accord of 1975 was the recentralization of collective bargaining toward the more moderate confederations and the containment of prices by privileging industrial workers at the expense of public sector employees. Yet this effort at controlling price increases and moderating labor relations through indexation backfired in several ways. First, public sector workers mobilized to protect their wages. Where established unions failed to articulate these demands, new, competitive organizations (Sindacati Autonomi, COBAS) emerged to fill this representational void. As a result, not only did indexation spread to all sectors of the economy, mitigating Confindustria's plan to contain consumer prices, but also industrial conflict increased dramatically—this time in the public and service sectors (Bordogna 1989).

Autonomous unions and the COBAS were not the only ones challenging the established unions. Because of the particular formula used in calculating wage increases and, given that indexation during the high inflation years of the 1970s accounted for over 60 percent of all wage gains, wage differentials based on different skill levels were significantly reduced (see Table 3.1). As a result, the unions found

Table 3.1. Wage differential indexes related to metalworkers' job classifications in selected years

	1978	1980	1981	1982	1983	1984	1985	1986
Blue-collar skill levels								
1	100	100	100	100	100	100	100	—
2	128	106	108	109	105	107	106	100
3	115	113	116	114	111	113	112	106
4	122	117	121	122	119	119	118	112
5	132	126	131	132	127	127	126	119
White-collar skill levels								
2	104	105	107	108	106	109	—	—
3	117	117	118	118	114	116	114	114
4	127	124	127	127	123	125	120	120
5	148	138	139	140	135	139	132	132
5 Super	161	151	151	157	149	152	145	145
6	195	174	172	183	172	174	164	164
7	248	227	227	224	215	220	209	209

Source: Elaboration on CESOS (1982, 1983, 1985, 1987) data.

themselves increasingly attacked, if not simply abandoned, by their more skilled members who felt underprotected and insufficiently appreciated by the unions' leadership. Many of these workers defected from the unions and established their own associations, such as the Sindacato dei Quadri at Porto Marghera (Gavagnin, Grillo, and Mulas 1988), while others mobilized against the unions in certain key industrial strikes (like the one held at Fiat in 1980. See Baldissera 1984).

In short, what was considered to be a mutually beneficial agreement for both labor and big business in the mid-1970s generated a series of organizational and economic disasters for both parties. Contrary to the initial intentions of Confindustria, the scala mobile did not contain prices but rather acted as an automatic inflationary mechanism. This was borne out by the fact that it became the single most important issue in Italian industrial relations throughout the next two decades. In fact, following the 1984 government decree, six different accords aimed at reforming or modifying the scala mobile were negotiated by the confederal unions, Confindustria, and the government. A final agreement was reached on July 31, 1992, that abolished the scala mobile.[17]

The unions, as well, which had originally interpreted the scala mo-

---

[17] For more on these more recent events, see Locke 1994.

bile accord as a major political and economic victory, subsequently came to see it as a source of internal dissent and weakness within their own ranks. Far from strengthening the central confederations, the 1975 accord delegitimated them in the eyes of their highly skilled industrial workers and their public sector members. Many of the latter subsequently defected to rival organizations like the COBAS which became increasingly aggressive in the late 1980s, often disrupting services in several key sectors (schools, transportation, health care). This further embarrassed the confederations, which were unable to force these workers to abide by agreements they had already negotiated.[18]

Finally, attempts at constructing an Italian variant of neocorporatism not only failed, but also renewed and increased divisions within the union movement, including the demise of the newly united Federazione Unitaria. Both the EUR policy and the 1983 tripartite agreement met stiff opposition within the unions (Golden 1988b). Essentially, industrial unions like the metalworkers correctly saw these two efforts as threats to their own organizational autonomy and power. As a result, they mobilized actively to revise, if not actually resist, these confederal-sponsored initiatives. Interestingly enough, even within the metalworkers union (FLM), clearly the most active opponent of the Federazione Unitaria's austerity measures, provincial unions differed in their degree of support for (or opposition to) austerity. In other words, not only did these efforts at concertation fail to recentralize industrial relations in favor of the confederations, but they also eroded the power of the national industry unions by further fragmenting internal union relations along more historic, local patterns of industrial politics (see Golden 1988b: chaps. 5, 7).

Moreover, attempts at furthering the capacity of the confederations to engage in neocorporatist bargains through an organizational reform in 1979 (the so-called Riforma di Monte Silvano) merely accentuated the unions' problems (Regalia 1986). Although this organizational reform was initially conceived as a way of decentralizing the unions'

---

[18]Another interesting side effect of the scala mobile is that it actually encouraged rather than abated decentralized bargaining in Italy. In order to correct the distortions provoked by this centralized agreement, a number of sectoral, regional, and firm-level accords were negotiated. For more on the unintended consequences of the scala mobile, see Commissione Carniti 1988.

structures in order to match changes in the administrative structure of the Italian state,[19] by the time it was implemented the central confederations sought to use this organizational reform to strengthen their own structures while also weakening the sources of opposition to their policies (certain large national industry unions like the metalworkers and various provincial unions in the North). New zonal, departmental, and regional union structures replaced the old provincial unions, and several smaller national industry unions, especially in the public sector, merged to form larger, more powerful federations.[20] The confederations hoped to use these more centralized and moderate federations to check the disproportionate influence of the metalworkers union.

Again, the anticipated results did not materialize. Since various organizations within the union movement fought hard to protect their autonomy, this organizational reform—ostensibly aimed at rationalizing the unions' structures—resulted in diluting them instead. For instance, at a time of shrinking resources, the Federazione CGIL-CISL-UIL added 453 new structures and about 20 percent additional staff to its ranks (Regalia 1986: 210). Within the public sector, characterized before the reform by an array of smaller, more professionally oriented unions with only loose ties to the three major confederations, the impact of this reform was even more damaging. In these sectors, workers felt that the central confederations were imposing on them an inappropriate, industrial union model of organization—one that failed to recognize their particular needs and interests. Not coincidentally, these same settings later provided fertile ground for the alternative organizing strategies of the COBAS and Autonomous Unions, which emphasized the differences of workers in these sectors. All in all, this effort to promote a "new confederality" appears to have provoked increased fragmentation and particularism as various sectoral and provincial union structures mobilized to resist efforts to centralize the union movement.

Certainly the most glaring failure at reforming Italian industrial relations came in 1984 when the unions split over the renewal of the 1983 tripartite agreement. As we saw earlier, the 1983 accord over wage indexation provoked a series of debates both between the unions

[19]For more on these changes, see Putnam 1993.
[20]CISL, for example, reduced the number of its industry federations from 37 to 17, while the CGIL also consolidated its 39 industry federations into 18.

and Confindustria as well as within the unions' own ranks. However, when the government presented its proposal to fix wage indexation for 1984, regardless of the actual rate of inflation, the Communist component of the CGIL used its majority on the CGIL Executive Committee to reject the agreement's renewal. The government implemented this policy through an executive order and the unions once again split along partisan lines. The Socialists in the CGIL and the CISL and UIL all supported the government's position. The rest of the CGIL staunchly opposed it.

Supported by the PCI, the Communists within the CGIL then promoted an electoral referendum aimed at abrogating the government decree. The campaign was very bitter and pitted various factions of the union movement against each other. The results of the referendum, held on June 9, 1985, were favorable to the government and the moderate union forces that supported the 1984 accord (Lange 1986). Thus, only twelve years after the reunification of the union movement, labor unity once again dissolved in Italy. This not only eliminated the functional equivalent structures necessary for concertation in Italy (Regini 1984) but also dashed many of the dreams associated with the Hot Autumn.

Renewed divisions among the confederations signaled their increasing weakness. Unable to translate the power they had gained during the Hot Autumn into long-lasting social and political change, the confederations embarked on a series of reform efforts aimed at recasting not just labor relations but the entire Italian model of political and economic development. Yet these repeated attempts at constructing a new Italian model failed. Thus, the confederations had not only consumed most of their hard-won political capital (with few results to show for it) but also unwittingly enforced certain long-standing features of the Italian industrial relations system which they had hoped to eliminate.

The next section will examine these developments in greater detail through a case study of the Confederazione Italiana dei Sindacati Lavoratori (CISL). Because historically the CISL has played a prominent role in several of the key developments described above, a closer look at the union's organizational and strategic evolution should provide additional insight into the rationale behind and consequences of recent reform efforts in Italian industrial relations.

THE STRATEGIC AND ORGANIZATIONAL EVOLUTION
OF THE CISL

Established in the early 1950s, the CISL was linked by the affiliations, affinities, and origins of its leaders and its rank and file to the Catholic church and the ruling Christian Democratic party.[21] In many ways, the founding of the CISL reflected the polarization of Italian society into Marxist and Catholic subcultures. As the labor confederation most closely identified with the Christian Democrats, the CISL vigorously opposed Communism and sought to organize workers in Italy who identified politically as Catholics.[22]

In the 1950s, the ideology of the CISL reflected its historical origins. The union espoused a philosophy of "nondemagogic" and "responsible" trade unionism, indicating a willingness to subordinate the short-term interests of its membership to national goals of economic stability and growth. To back up this pledge, the CISL rejected the use of militant trade union action such as strikes and cooperated with the government on a number of programs.

Notwithstanding its origins, the CISL sought to develop a new model of trade unionism—one that rejected both prefascist Catholic corporatist unionism (see Treu 1973) and the Leninist model of unions as "transmission belts" for revolutionary working class parties (Baglioni 1975). Instead, the CISL sought to emulate the practices of labor unions in the United States which were seen as more autonomous organizations, interested not in broader political questions but rather in securing wage increases and other benefits for their membership through collective bargaining (Sciarra 1980: 283–307).

The CISL's early analysis of Italy's socioeconomic problems focused on the country's economic "backwardness." As a result, the union's strategies in the 1950s sought to stimulate economic growth, industrialization, and technological innovation. For example, informed by marginalist economic theory, the CISL's initial wage policy explicitly linked wage gains to productivity improvements. This concern with produc-

---

[21] The close ties between the CISL, the Catholic church, and the Christian Democratic party are described in La Palombara 1964: 310–12.

[22] La Palombara describes the CISL as "manifestly a Christian Democratic organ." See La Palombara 1955: 75. For more on the historical evolution of the CISL, see Greco 1976.

tivity growth reinforced not only the CISL's preference for collective bargaining (over politics) but also its image as a positive and modernizing force in Italian society. Essentially, the CISL believed that through "articulated" (firm-level) bargaining, the union could drive up the cost curves of less efficient firms and thus force them to invest in new, more efficient technology.[23] In this way, the CISL hoped to spark a virtuous cycle in which wage increases would lead to new investments, which, in turn, would enhance productivity and thus lead to subsequent wage gains.

In short, through the union's wage policy the CISL hoped simultaneously to promote (noninflationary) growth and provide distributive gains for its membership. Moreover, to ensure that wage gains would in fact translate into new investment and not simply price increases passed on to consumers by Italy's oligopolistic firms, the CISL also encouraged government intervention in the economy (through the state holding companies and economic planning) aimed at correcting structural imbalances and promoting domestic competition.

Notwithstanding these aspirations to develop a new model of unionism, the CISL of the 1950s acted more or less like a collateral organization of the Christian Democratic party (DC). Many of its innovative proposals (organizational autonomy from political parties, firm-level collective bargaining, and productivity-enhancing wage policy) remained on paper and were not immediately translated into concrete actions. With members of Catholic Action (ACLI), CISL unionists formed the Forze Nuove faction of the party.[24] Moreover, the CISL often colluded with management to marginalize the Communist-dominated CGIL.[25]

During the 1960s, however, the situation began to change as the CISL developed its own organizational structures, trained a new leadership group, and began to implement many of its innovative proposals. Through its internal training school, the Centro Studi CISL outside of Florence, the union developed a new cadre of highly trained union activists. These activists were later instrumental in developing the CISL's capacities to negotiate contracts at the industry and firm

[23] For more on the economic views of the CISL, see Baglioni and Tarantelli 1980; and Marconi and Vicarelli 1980.

[24] For more on this, see Zuckerman 1979; and Weitz 1975: 226–42.

[25] See Carbognin 1980; and Pugno and Garavini 1974 for more on the collusion between the CISL and management against the CGIL.

levels and to ensure the union's autonomy from the DC party.[26] Throughout the decade, the CISL organized local union structures within Italian firms and, beginning with the 1962–63 bargaining round, negotiated firm-level contracts as well. Moreover, the composition of the CISL's membership also changed during these years. Growing beyond its original base among farm workers and civil servants, the CISL became increasingly successful at organizing semiskilled industrial workers in the North. Between 1960 and 1970, the CISL's total membership increased by 36 percent while its membership among industrial workers increased 117 percent (Romagnoli 1980: 55).

However, as the CISL became increasingly active within the factories, it began to shed its initial optimism regarding cross-class collaboration, enlightened economic development, and the automatic benefits of technical progress.[27] Company owners and managers strongly resisted the introduction of firm-level bargaining and thwarted various efforts by the CISL to organize their factories. Consequently, the CISL became increasingly involved in industrial conflict and thus abandoned its earlier position (highly influenced by American industrial relations theory) that strikes were an indicator of "backwardness."

The CISL's wage policy also changed during this period. Whereas the CISL's early policy was based on an understanding of economic growth which privileged firm profitability and capital accumulation and thus encouraged wage moderation, the union's subsequent analysis of the actual behavior of Italian business following the recession of 1962–63 completely altered its views. Notwithstanding an increase in firm profitability between 1964 and 1968, industrial investment continued to stagnate and capital flight increased. As a result, the union shifted its economic views toward Keynesianism and began to stress the importance of aggregate demand for the country's development. This, in turn, led the union to pursue an aggressive wage policy, even during periods of recession.[28]

These years witnessed a radicalization of the CISL, especially as a result of the union's increased contact with neo-Marxist theorists like Andre Gorz and Serge Mallet who stressed the growing alienation of

[26]For more on the innovative role the Centro Studi CISL played in the union's organizational and strategic development, see La Palombara 1956: 29–42; De Cesaris 1971: 80–94; Santi 1977: 95–127; and Costantini 1980.

[27]For more on this, see Romagnoli 1980.

[28]See Carniti 1977: 277–83 for more on the shift in the CISL's wage policy.

industrial workers.[29] These themes resonated especially within the CISL's metalworkers union, the FIM, which became increasingly critical of Taylorist managerial practices within Italy's largest firms. Whereas the CISL had initially understood an increase in the division of labor as an inevitable consequence of industrial modernization, during the Hot Autumn CISL's industrial unions began to contest the extremely hierarchical and "dehumanizing" organization of work within Italian factories. Because CISL unionists had significant knowledge of and experience with bargaining over piece rates, shift arrangements, and the pace, quantity, and organization of work, they were especially effective in challenging these workplace practices.[30] In fact, most of the more innovative union demands of the Hot Autumn— the inquadramento unico, egalitarian wage policy, abolition of piece rates, and substitution of "hardship compensation" for workers employed in especially pernicious positions (paint shops, foundries) with the reorganization of these shops instead—were initiated by FIM activists. The FIM also pushed for the reunification of the Italian labor movement "from below" by collaborating with CGIL- and UIL-affiliated unions.

The CISL experienced tremendous success with its new, more aggressive shop floor strategies, and this success encouraged it to broaden its demands and push for reforms in the political arena. As a result, the CISL, along with the two other major union confederations (CGIL and UIL) began to bypass the political parties in Parliament and negotiate directly with the government over pension, school, housing, health care, and fiscal reform. At the same time, the unions also sought to bargain with management over future corporate strategies and investment decisions.

As we saw earlier, the unions' "Reform Strategy" produced few results and, by the mid-1970s, the unions began once again to rethink their strategy. As Italy's economic crisis worsened after the first oil shock in 1973, the CISL began to see that its dualistic strategy of demanding wage increases and changes in work organization at the firm level and demanding major institutional reforms at the national level had exacerbated the country's political and economic problems.

---

[29] For more on this, see Greco 1976; and Baglioni 1975.

[30] As three CISL activists themselves admitted, "Nobody can better contest the piece-rate system, from either a technical or political perspective, than one who for years negotiated these practices" (Manghi, Cella, and Piva 1972: 40).

Moreover, the union also realized that its egalitarian wage policy had provoked major dissent and even defections by the union's more skilled and professional membership.

In many ways, the CISL's analysis of the role its strategy played in exacerbating Italy's economic crisis of the 1970s signaled a return to its prior positions. Similar to its original interpretation of Italy's economic problems in the 1950s, the CISL in the late 1970s once again stressed the importance of private investment and capital accumulation. According to the union, economic growth would resume only when inflation was brought under control and managerial authority on the shop floor was restored.

As a result of this self-criticism, the CISL embarked on a major reform of its strategies and structures. Earlier I described various attempts in the late 1970s and early 1980s to construct neocorporatist arrangements in Italy. The CISL took the lead in promoting these tripartite arrangements. Yet for the CISL, the arrangements were intended to produce more than antiinflationary income policies. Instead, the union hoped that through tripartite negotiations over macroeconomic policy and increased (and institutionalized) union participation in company decision-making, it could construct a new, more concerted approach to economic governance (Carniti 1985: especially 175–202). Given that the political parties had proven incapable of promoting reform, the CISL believed that only a "social contract" between the unions and organized business could restimulate growth and pull Italy out of its recession. In order to hold up its own end of these deals and implement the new strategy, the CISL (along with CGIL and UIL) embarked on an organizational reform in 1979 (the so-called Riforma di Monte Silvano) aimed at centralizing collective bargaining arrangements and consolidating the unions' structures.

This more responsible and concertative approach to union politics, however, produced at best only mixed results. Italy's experience with tripartite bargaining was extremely short-lived and ended with the breakup of the Federazione Unitaria in 1984. The "proceduralization" of industrial relations at the firm level through the institutionalization of union participation in company decision-making was implemented only within the state holding companies through the Protocollo IRI. And as Chapter 2 illustrated, the implementation of the Protocollo was itself quite uneven and incomplete.

Numerous explanations have been advanced to account for the

failure of these neocorporatist experiments. Some scholars have stressed the institutional weaknesses of the Italian industrial relations system as a whole (Cella 1989); others, the lack of resources necessary to support this political exchange (Giugni 1985); and still others, the strong opposition to these policies within the unions themselves (see, for example, Kemeny 1990). Regardless of the particular reason, the failure of these arrangements also spelled the demise of the CISL's new strategy.

In the late 1970s and early 1980s, the CISL had gambled on a new strategy—one that shifted the union away from its traditional strength in shop-floor bargaining over wages, working conditions, and the organization of production and toward participation in peak-level tripartite negotiations over income policies and institutional reforms. The CISL lost this gamble. As a result, the union found itself internally divided and strategically confused just as the Italian economy began a process of major industrial adjustment. Because it had eschewed shop-floor concerns in recent years, the CISL no longer possessed the organizational resources and internal expertise necessary to negotiate industrial change. As a result, like many other unions with none of the CISL's organizational resources and technical expertise, in the 1980s the CISL suffered a loss in membership and a decline in influence on the shop floor and in the political arena. As a number of CISL unionists and collaborators have lamented, throughout this period the union appeared incapable of coordinating strategy among its various local and national unions, let alone launching new, innovative proposals and bargaining platforms.[31]

In many ways, the evolution of the CISL mirrors (at an organizational level) the broader experiments with and struggles over industrial relations reform in Italy. Having failed to construct a new system of industrial relations, first through various reformist strategies in the 1960s and later by mobilizing rank-and-file workers around more radical positions, by the mid-1970s the CISL became convinced that the only solution to Italy's economic and labor relations crises entailed the construction of completely new institutional arrangements. As a result, the CISL completely altered its own strategies and recast its structures in order to promote neocorporatist arrangements in Italy.

---

[31] See various articles by Gianprimo Cella and Pietro Kemeny and others in a special issue of *Prospettiva Sindacale* 77 21 (September 1990) dedicated to the "reality of the CISL today."

Resources that were once dedicated to training local union militants about the organization of work and new technologies were transferred to fund outside consultants and experts on various macroeconomic and legal-institutional issues.[32] Thus, when the efforts at recasting Italian industrial relations in the 1980s failed, the CISL found itself not simply defeated strategically but also weakened organizationally and once again at odds with the CGIL and the UIL.

ENTROPY RUN WILD OR THE SEEDS OF RENEWAL?

As the case of the CISL illustrates, the failure of various reform efforts to build a new national model of industrial relations did more than just dash the hopes of Italy's would-be institutional reformers. In fact, it left the union movement so internally divided and strategically confused that even the preexisting model of Italian industrial relations—those few arrangements that Italian unions relied on for organizational strength and strategic guidance (vibrant factory councils, national industry bargaining, and the supremacy of the CGIL, CISL, and UIL)—has begun to unravel as well. A quick look at two of these traditional features—national industry bargaining and the predominance of the confederal unions—reveals the extent of the transformations currently underway.

The Decline of National Bargaining

We have already seen how Italian labor law in the form of the Statuto dei Lavoratori was both utilized and interpreted in ways that reinforced local differences among various Italian regions (Melucci 1976; Treu 1984, 1991). A similar localization of practices can also be observed in collective bargaining arrangements. Historically, master agreements negotiated by the national industry unions (such as contratti collettivi nazionali di lavoro [CCNL]) were predominant and structured the contracts of most, if not all, firms in the industry. Like in the United States, leading firms were targeted by the unions for a particular year's bargaining round, and the national contract was usually little more than the diffusion of that company's agreement to the

---

[32]For more on this, see Locke 1990b.

rest of the industry. These contracts were negotiated every three years and renewals were essentially automatic.[33] Negotiations by union locals at individual firms were mere addenda to these more standardized national contracts and usually took place within one year of the signing of the national agreements.

During the 1980s this pattern broke down. Essentially, the national industry agreements became squeezed between confederal-level tripartite agreements and local- or firm-level bargaining (Baglioni and Milani 1990: 37–56). Attempts by the peak-level confederations to engage in macroconcertative deals over the cost of labor, the scala mobile, fiscal reform, and the annual budget increasingly constrained national industry unions as they sought to negotiate their own contracts covering many of these same issues. At the same time, unwilling to be limited by overly broad industry contracts (which lump together within a single "category" extremely diverse economic realities—firms of different sizes and degrees of technological sophistication, engaged in different lines of business, and employing alternative strategies),[34] firm- and territorial-level unions became more active in negotiating their own contracts. These more microlevel contracts usually concern firm restructuring efforts, the introduction of new technology, and shifts in the organization and timing of work.

National unions, as a result, experienced substantial difficulties in developing, let alone implementing, master agreements in a number of industries. Moreover, even when national contracts were negotiated, they appeared progressively emptied of contents. Tables 3.2 and 3.3 list all national contracts signed between the textile workers and metalworkers unions and the relevant employers' associations during the last two decades. Increased vacancy periods (periods without a valid contract) signal the difficulties both these national unions faced in maintaining patterned bargaining within their sectors.

The content of collective bargaining also began to shift away from the national contracts. A 1986 study on collective bargaining in Italy revealed that contrary to past practice, local union contracts were the most innovative and important agreements covering workers in industry. Although national union agreements appeared to be quite

---

[33] Often, new contracts were approved and signed before the expiration of the previous ones.

[34] In the metalworkers category, for example, firms as different as Fiat (autos), Olivetti (computers), Ansaldo (engineering), and Ilva (steel) are lumped together.

Table 3.2. Metalworkers' national contract renewal dates, 1973–1987

Date of signature	Date of contract initiation	Date of contract expiration	Vacancy period, in months[a]
01.08.70	—	—	—
04.19.73	01.01.73	12.31.75	—
05.01.76	05.01.76	01.01.79	5
07.16.79	07.16.79	12.31.81	7
09.01.83	09.01.83	12.31.85	21
01.18.87	01.01.87	12.31.89	13
12.14.90	01.01.91	06.30.94	12

Source: Based on a reading of national and firm-level contracts made available by Fiat Auto and the CGIL.

[a]Vacancy period refers to number of months that elapsed between expiration of the prior contract and the subsequent contract.

generic, at most setting broad parameters on wages and working conditions, local unions were actually negotiating the most significant elements of the contract (Nacamulli Costa and Manzolini 1986). This trend was confirmed in a subsequent study (Baglioni and Milani 1990) that documented how negotiations over the pace and timing of work, bonuses and profit sharing, new technologies, and redundancies were increasingly negotiated at the firm and/or local levels.

In the Italian textile industry, for example, the national contract established a 36-hour workweek, but local unions decided exactly how to implement and regulate this agreement. Thus, in certain localities, the workweek was concentrated in three or four long days, whereas elsewhere it was spread out across the week in the form of six shorter days. This variation in arrangements reflected the needs and desires

Table 3.3. Textile workers' national contract renewal dates, 1973–1990

Date of signature	Date of contract initiation	Date of contract expiration	Vacancy period, in months[a]
07.20.73	01.01.73	06.30.76	
09.23.76	01.01.76	06.30.79	3
12.17.79	07.01.79	05.31.82	6
01.12.83	07.01.83	05.31.86	8
02.22.87	04.01.87	12.31.90	9
05.20.91	07.01.91	06.30.95	5

Sources: Based on a reading of national and firm-level contracts made available by CGIL.

[a]Vacancy period refers to number of months that elapsed between expiration of the prior contract and the subsequent contract.

of the local work force. In more agricultural areas, having shorter workdays permitted textile workers to also tend their fields. In more urban areas, fewer but longer days gave workers longer weekends or larger blocks of time to dedicate to a second job.

Even the sequencing of contract negotiations appears to be shifting in favor of local unions. Whereas before, national agreements were negotiated first and local contracts later, often with a prescribed lag period, more recently many local unions negotiate their own contracts first with the national agreement emerging later as an aggregation and ratification of these prior local deals (Guidotti 1986). Similar trends can be seen in the implementation of laws regulating hiring and firing (Reyneri 1989), the use of redundancy funds or cassa integrazione (Reyneri and Semenza 1990), and union relations with local governments (Regalia 1985, 1986; Nanetti 1988) and business associations (Chiesi and Martinelli 1989; Baglioni 1989).

The End of the Confederal Unions' Hegemony

The organizational and strategic problems stemming from the demise of industrywide bargaining have been further exacerbated by declining membership and growing challenges to the confederal unions by alternative labor organizations. As in other countries, Italian unions have suffered membership losses in recent years. Although this decline is somewhat obscured by the growing number of retirees within the unions' ranks (pensioners and unemployed workers make up 45.6 percent of CGIL and 36 percent of CISL membership), the truth is that the proportion of active employees within the three major confederations declined from 49 percent in 1981 to 41.7 percent in 1990 (*Nuovo rassegna sindacale*, September 30, 1991: 52).

Moreover, a more careful analysis of the membership of these three confederations reveals that its composition is quite varied among the various confederations. The CGIL's membership, for example, is based primarily among semiskilled industrial workers employed in the North, especially in the Lombardia and Piemonte regions, while the CISL is made up primarily of public sector workers from the South (CESOS 1990, 1991). Thus, even to speak of these two confederations (and they are the largest and most powerful) as "national" is already stretching the meaning of the term. Even within these so-called national union confederations, new factions (Essere Sindacati within the CGIL, Fimilano within the CISL, and the "autoconvocati" movement within many large firms) have emerged to contest the dominant political and strategic positions of the confederal unions.

Organizational difficulties within the three traditional union confederations have been aggravated by increased competition by other, "autonomous" unions and new, alternative employee organizations. The so-called autonomous unions (sindacati autonomi) emerged during the 1970s in various sectors like transportation, banking, insurance, health care, and education in response to the perceived inability or unwillingness of the confederal unions to adequately represent white-collar, technical, and professional workers. For instance, both Confederquadri (the confederation of white-collar and clerical workers) and SNALS (secondary school teachers' association) were founded in 1977 in order to oppose various policies then being promoted by the CGIL, CISL, and UIL. Both of these new unions argued that the traditional union confederations were overly political and ideological and thus insufficiently attentive to "economic" (bread-and-butter) issues. Moreover, they called for increased wage differentials between skilled and unskilled workers, greater appreciation of white-collar work, and enhanced "union democracy" (local decision-making)—all issues that ran counter to the dominant strategy of the traditional union confederations in these same years.

Over the course of the 1980s, these autonomous unions grew in number and began to organize their own rival confederations. CISAL (Confederazione Italiana Sinadacti Autonomi Lavoratori), for example, embraces sixty-three federations that organize railway, marine, and health care workers. In 1988, it claimed to have 1.9 million members. CISAS (Confederazione Italiana Sinadacti Addetti ai Servizi) includes thirty-nine different federations in various private and public services and reports eight hundred thousand members. CONFAIL and CONFSAL, two other autonomous union confederations, each claim to have about 1 million members. Given that the three traditional union confederations report only slightly higher membership figures—the UIL reported about 1 million members, CISL a little more than 2 million, and the CGIL about 2.7 million (Squarzon 1990: 151)—the challenge these new unions pose to the traditional union confederations should not be underestimated.

The confederal unions were further challenged in the 1980s by the so-called COBAS (Comitati di Base), which arose in various service sectors (for more on this, see Bordogna 1989; and Bignami 1992). The COBAS are organized along professional lines (engine drivers in the railways, secondary school teachers in the public schools, air traffic controllers, etc.) and are extremely militant. In order to push their demands, they often block critical national services like hospitals, railways, airports, and schools. Like the autonomous unions, they reject the "egalitarianism" of the traditional unions and instead seek to enhance wage and status differentials that benefit their membership. Because of their ability to disrupt critical services, a new law, Legge 144/1990, governing strikes in the service sectors was passed in 1990. Aside from establishing a set of procedures governing the scope and timing of service sector strikes, this law also created a national arbitration board aimed at resolving labor-management conflicts and thus preventing strikes. As a result, the law de facto recognized these new unions as legitimate actors and has given them a place at the bargaining table.

In sum, the attempts to construct a new, more mature system of industrial relations in the 1970s and 1980s not only failed but also unleashed a series of inter- and intraorganizational struggles which resulted in the increased fragmentation of Italian labor relations. The breakdown of national industry bargaining, the balkanization of labor law and labor market regulation, the defection of skilled workers and public sector employees to rival organizations, and centrifugal tendencies within the traditional unions themselves have all characterized Italian industrial relations in recent years.

Yet as the 1990 law governing service sector strikes suggests, out of this apparent morass, the preconditions for a new, more flexible and democratic industrial relations system may be emerging. Increased competition from rival organizations like the COBAS and the autonomous unions, and growing dissent from within, have forced the traditional unions to reexamine several of their organizational strategies and become more responsive to the needs and interests of their membership. For example, the CGIL has recently supported a law aimed at revising Article 19 of the Statuto dei Lavoratori in a way that would transform the factory councils into more democratic and vibrant organizations. Any worker group that can collect signatures from at least 5 percent of the employees can stand for election to the new enterprise councils. This change not only ends the monopoly over firm-level representation the CGIL, CISL, and UIL have enjoyed for over twenty years but also ensures that elections to these worker councils take place regularly. These changes in workplace representation should not only render the factory councils more democratic but also, by including the COBAS and the autonomous unions within the new councils, eliminate a primary source of labor conflict in Italy.

Likewise, the breakdown of national industry bargaining has led to both a series of innovative local-level agreements and to a more general reevaluation of the structure of collective bargaining within the major union confederations. For example, in the textile district of Biella, the local union and business association have negotiated a series of agreements on industrial restructuring, redundancies, retraining and skill development, and flexible work hours. At Zanussi, one of Italy's largest consumer durables producers (15,000 employees), the local union and firm management established several comanagement committees to work out arrangements concerning wages, working conditions, and working time; the introduction of new technologies; and various environmental issues. In Lombardia, the regional business association Assolombarda and the confederal unions negotiated a series of accords promoting labor mobility, equal employment opportunities, employment security, and the reduction of labor costs.

In sum, although recent developments have dashed the hopes of Italy's would-be institutional reformers and accentuated the longstanding, anarchic features of the Italian industrial relations system, they also appear to have planted the seeds for a reconfiguration of Italian labor relations along more innovative and democratic lines. It is still too early to say exactly how this process will unfold. For every fragment of evidence or anecdote supporting the rebirth of Italian labor, a mass of depressing counterfactuals documenting labor setbacks also exist. Much of this, of course, depends upon whether the seeds of labor's renewal actually take root and this, in turn, depends on where they are planted.

Many of the interesting experiments and proposals for reform mentioned above have originated from or are concentrated in particular localities in which organizationally well-developed unions are embedded in and supported by a dense network of other social, economic, and political associations. Conversely, several of labor's most notorious setbacks and/or failed efforts at renewal have taken place in other localities that lack these sociopolitical resources. The following chapters of this book will analyze in greater detail the way in which divergent local patterns of economic governance shaped industrial adjustment and industrial relations in Italy.

CHAPTER FOUR

Industrial Adjustment and Industrial Relations in the Automobile Industry

This chapter analyzes the reorganization of the Italian automobile industry in the 1980s. Like car manufacturers in other West European nations and the United States, Italian automobile producers experienced very serious organizational and financial problems in the late 1970s. A variety of factors, including increased international competition, the rise of fuel costs, changing consumer tastes, more stringent government health, safety, and environmental protection regulation, and increased labor costs all contributed to the crisis of the automobile industry in the West (Altshuler et al. 1984). Yet because of insufficient investment, especially in new product development, and extremely conflictual and rigid industrial relations practices throughout the 1970s, Italian automobile companies were especially hard hit by the crisis. Productivity, profitability, and plant utilization rates of Italian automobile manufacturers were all lower than those of their major competitors abroad (Comito 1982; Amin 1985).

To emerge from this crisis, Italian producers, like their competitors throughout the West, underwent a major restructuring effort that entailed the shedding of redundant workers, an overhaul of the supplier and distribution networks, unprecedented levels of investment in new process and product technologies, and a radical reorganization of work within their plants. Although Italian car companies (like major automobile producers throughout the West) continue to face stiff competitive challenges, both Fiat and Alfa Romeo emerged more efficient and profitable as a result of their restructuring efforts in the 1980s.

This chapter analyzes the reorganization of Italy's two leading automobile producers—Fiat Auto and Alfa Romeo. These two firms are interesting for a variety of reasons. First, both firms have historically played major roles in Italy's economy and have often set the pattern for industrial relations in the country. The development of work relations and the balance of power between management and labor in these firms reveals, often in extreme form (Accorrero 1988: 14–16) the situation elsewhere in the country. Second, in many ways Fiat and Alfa have acted as advanced laboratories for Italian industrial relations. Since the late 1960s, these firms have witnessed several experiments in both the organization of production and the strategy of the union movement. Finally, patterns of industrial adjustment at these two firms have been radically different.

Whereas Fiat reorganized by asserting managerial control and repressing the unions, Alfa experienced a more negotiated process. Moreover, whereas both firms emerged more competitive as a result of their reorganization efforts, the outcomes for the two local union movements[1] differed sharply: Alfa's unions managed to preserve—if not enhance—their strength, whereas Fiat's unions lost membership and practically all influence on the shop floor. This divergence is especially interesting given that both firms share the same ownership, their work forces are organized by the same unions, their plants possess similar technologies, and they operate within the same national setting. This chapter explains these divergent outcomes by analyzing the alternative strategic choices pursued by the key actors at the two companies. These alternative strategies were, in turn, shaped by the very different local contexts in which Fiat and Alfa Romeo are embedded.

The remainder of this chapter is divided into two sections. The next section provides a very brief historical sketch of each of the companies and describes in greater detail the alternative adjustment strategies they pursued in the 1980s. The second section examines

---

[1] A note of clarification. In the early 1970s, the metalworkers federations of the three major union confederations, FIOM-CGIL, FIM-CISL, and UILM-UIL, united as the Federazione Lavoratori Metalmeccanici (FLM). Workers could belong to either the united organization (FLM) or to one of its parent organizations. For most of the 1970s and early 1980s, the FLM acted as a single union, both at the national and local levels. But following the demise of the Federazione Unitaria in 1984, old divisions among the three metalworkers unions resurfaced, even though they continued to negotiate as a single entity. Because of this complicated organizational history, I sometimes refer to the unions at Fiat and Alfa as single local unions (especially when discussing the 1970s), but at other times (particularly when discussing events in the mid to late 1980s), I refer to the various local unions that coexisted at both companies.

various alternative explanations for the divergent outcomes observed before illustrating the role local sociopolitical networks played in shaping the adjustment strategies at both Fiat and Alfa Romeo.

A Tale of Two Companies: Fiat Auto and Alfa Romeo

Chronic Conflictualism: The Case of Fiat Auto

Fiat was founded in 1899. Within a few years, Fiat's founder and chairman, Giovanni Agnelli, began to pursue a strategy aimed at the transformation of automobile production into a large-scale industry. This change in strategy was the result of Agnelli's visit to the United States and his decision to "produce like Henry Ford."[2] This plan by Agnelli to develop large-scale industry in Turin made Fiat not only a major actor in the local economy but also the main architect of fordism in Italy. Fiat, like Ford, began to pay higher wages as a way of attracting skilled workers away from other firms. After the recession of 1907, Fiat took over several of its suppliers as well as its competitors. As a result, Fiat managed to increase its productive integration and reduce local competition simultaneously.

Factory work also began to change. Production was organized by sequence, and American semiautomatic single-purpose machine tools were introduced. Interestingly enough, the metalworkers union, FIOM, not only agreed to these changes (in return for increased piece rates) but also reorganized its structures to match the emergent fordist order (Berta 1978).

By the 1920s, Fiat had acquired 80 percent of the domestic market and had taken major steps towards developing mass production techniques. With the 1921 opening of the Lingotto factory and the 1939 inauguration of the Mirafiori plant, Fiat began to manufacture large volumes of cars with thousands of workers. Production increased from 35,120 cars in 1930 to 55,701 in 1939 (Bigazzi 1986: 77), and employment grew from 20,905 in 1930 to 48,395 in 1939. The Mirafiori plant alone employed 22,000 workers (Volpato 1993: 38).

Two world wars and the autarkic economic policies of the Fascist regime delayed the realization of Agnelli's plans for about thirty years, but by the late 1950s Fiat succeeded in creating and servicing a mass

[2] This section draws heavily on Bigazzi 1986; Castronovo 1977; and Michelsons 1986.

market for automobiles. In 1955 Fiat introduced its first truly popular economic subcompact, the "600" model, and in 1957 the well-known "Cinquacento." With the introduction of these new models, production grew from 100,000 units in 1950 to 500,000 in 1960, and to over 1 million cars in 1966 (Volpato 1993: 47). These large production volumes permitted the company to introduce a number of technical and organizational changes that further reinforced mass production techniques. The Mirafiori plant, for example, was completely restructured along more taylorist lines in the 1950s, and productivity (as measured by number of cars produced per employee) jumped from 2 in 1950 to 7.5 in 1960. By the late 1960s Fiat ran one of the largest automobile production facilities in Western Europe, dominated the Italian market, and exported abroad. Its production grew prodigiously—from 108,700 cars in 1950 to 1,307,800 in 1979. Employment grew as well: from 56,321 in 1949 to 138,949 in 1979 (Michelsons 1986: 301, 307). In fact, over the course of the postwar period, Fiat became Italy's leading automobile producer and largest private enterprise.

Fiat's low-cost/high-volume strategy rested on a highly specialized and hierarchical organization of work and strict control of workers. As a result, Fiat management sought to control workers through a combination of paternalism and repression. Communist unionists were persecuted within Fiat's plants or transferred to special shops where these "destructive" activists (the term Fiat management used at the time) could not cause trouble among the majority of "loyal" and "constructive" workers (Accornero and Rieser 1981; Pugno and Garavini 1974). The company also created its own training school, summer camps, sports clubs, cultural associations, and even a company union in order to maintain order within its plants. Although these practices were successful at weakening organized labor throughout the 1950s and 1960s, over time they generated tensions within the company which subsequently exploded during the Hot Autumn.

The 1970s were difficult years for almost all automobile producers in Western Europe and the United States. Yet Fiat's troubles were exacerbated by three additional and more particular factors: the company's highly centralized and integrated organizational structure, its lack of investment in new process and product technologies, and the highly disruptive consequences of the Hot Autumn for the company's productivity and profitability.

Because of the company's tayloristic work practices and past repression of union activists, the Hot Autumn struggles were especially explosive within Fiat plants. In 1969 alone, 19 million work hours (the equivalent of 277,000 cars) were lost to strikes. High strike levels continued well into the 1970s: over 4 million hours in 1970; over 3 million in 1971, and about 4.5 million hours in 1972 (Volpato 1993: 68). Absenteeism also was rife among Fiat workers in these years. For example, out of a total of 186,501 people employed in the company's automobile operations in 1971, an average of 16,800 were absent on any given day. The numbers climbed even higher in 1973, when it was estimated that almost 19 percent of the company's work force was missing daily from work (Volpato 1993: 69).

Strikes, absenteeism, and a contractually negotiated reduction of work hours (7.5 percent less per week after 1971) all significantly reduced the company's output and productivity. This loss in productivity was not compensated by a reduction in costs but rather the opposite. Wages at Fiat exceeded cost-of-living increases every year between 1969 and 1977. As a result, while the cost of living increased by 102.7 percent in these eight years, Fiat's wage bill grew by 141.3 percent (Volpato 1993: 92).

The company's production problems were further exacerbated by a sharp decline in demand for Fiat cars. Because of the economic recession and a sharp increase in fuel costs, demand for automobiles contracted everywhere. Yet because Fiat had not invested sufficiently in developing new models, its market situation completely reversed in the 1970s. Whereas in the 1950s and 1960s, Fiat could not produce enough cars to satisfy the demand for its products (customers often had to wait months for their new cars to arrive), following the first oil crisis, the company could not sell all of its output. In 1973 alone, Fiat's stock of unsold cars climbed to 300,000 units (Volpato 1993: 94). The costs of financing and later reservicing this enormous stock of unsold cars further deteriorated the company's financial situation.

Since Fiat had been organized for much of its history as a highly centralized conglomeration of various industries, throughout the 1970s the company's organizational and financial problems were obscured. Losses incurred in the automobile sector were offset by profits from other, more lucrative sectors. But following the divisionalization of Fiat in the late 1970s and the creation of an autonomous automobile division[3] with a separate balance sheet in 1979, Fiat's crisis became completely visible. Suddenly, Italy's largest privately owned firm appeared to be on the verge of bankruptcy.

To recover from this crisis, Fiat, like other automobile manufacturers (Katz and Sabel 1985; Streeck 1985), adjusted its production cycle in order to increase product differentiation while promoting greater economies of scale. Moreover, to confront its problems, the firm initiated a deep reorganization process aimed at improving its short-term profitability and its long-term survival in the industry. The main features of this process were:

1) a new product policy that led the company to introduce many new models with frequent restyling and increased commonality of components;

2) a massive investment in new process technologies and the reorganization of work in many areas of the factory;

3) a rationalization of the company's supplier network in order to enhance the quality and standardization of components; and

4) a radical break with the industrial relations climate of the 1970s through massive layoffs and a reassertion of managerial control on the shop floor.

A central feature of Fiat's reorganization process was management's effort to regain control over the shop floor and shed redundant workers. During the 1970s, several experiments with labor-management cooperation had failed (Dealessandri and Magnabosco 1987), and high levels of industrial conflict and absenteeism had disrupted Fiat's operations. Union delegates enjoyed considerable power on the shop floor: regulating work rhythms, determining breaks, and controlling internal labor mobility. As part of the company's restructuring effort, Fiat encouraged its shop floor supervisors and line managers to reassert their traditional roles and authority and to discipline individual workers who failed to obey their orders. The company also proposed plac-

---

[3] Fiat Auto is one of fourteen divisions of Fiat S.p.A. The others include various related and unrelated industries like industrial equipment, tractors, automobile components, machine tools, telecommunications, aviation, publishing. In 1988, the automobile division employed approximately 45 percent of Fiat S.p.A.'s total employees, generated over 60 percent of its profits, and consumed about half of its investment. For more detail, see Fiat 1989.

ing 24,000 (out of about 139,000) workers in cassa integrazione,[4] a state-financed unemployment insurance fund, during the fall of 1980. The local union rejected these proposed changes and broke off relations with the firm. Claiming it was suffering from economic duress (which permits Italian firms to dismiss workers permanently and not merely lay them off temporarily), Fiat, in turn, declared its intention to dismiss 15,000 workers, beginning on October 6. Things heated up as the union blockaded the firm and Fiat sent out letters of dismissal. The ensuing strike lasted thirty-five days, but rank-and-file participation was low.

Finally, on October 14, Fiat foremen and supervisors organized a successful demonstration calling for a return to work. Forty thousand people marched against the union, among them many blue-collar workers (Baldissera 1984). That very night, an agreement completely embracing management's position was signed. The agreement met with resistance from the more militant factions of the local union, but was signed and pushed through for approval by the national industry federations. Despite initial attempts by the local union and the local branch of the Communist party to claim victory in this strike, it marked a major defeat from which the union never recovered.

With the union out of the way, Fiat proceeded with its reorganization efforts. The company completely revamped its product strategy and introduced many new models with greater differentiation in appearance but consisting, in fact, of increasingly common and interchangeable components. This reconceptualization of the automobile as a modular system, each macrocomponent system in itself a finished product, not only enhanced model variation but also permitted Fiat to achieve greater economies of scale. Previously the company's breakeven point was calculated on the basis of the annual volume of automobiles produced. In the 1970s it was estimated that Fiat needed to manufacture at least 2 million cars a year in order to be profitable (a

---

[4]The Cassa Integrazione Guadagni is an unemployment fund originally established by the state in 1947 to provide partial income to laid-off blue-collar workers during downturns in the business cycle. Over the years, the scope and the duration of this unemployment insurance scheme have grown. Now, the fund protects most unemployed white-collar and blue-collar workers alike by providing almost 95 percent of their income for nine months—or, in the case of employees in firms undergoing restructuring, for an unlimited period. Employers apply to both local and national tripartite commissions regulating the fund during restructuring. The labor contract of employees supported by the fund remains valid. The employer must rehire all workers remaining in the cassa once the firm is restructured. For more on this fund, see Treu 1986a.

volume it was never able to achieve in these years). Through the mass production of common and interchangeable components that were shared among Fiat's different models, modular production allowed Fiat to fully achieve economies of scale.

Fiat also invested heavily in new technologies like computer assisted design (CAD) and industrial robots. Over the course of the 1980s, Fiat installed over 2,000 robots in its various operations. Sixty-two percent of these robots were installed in what were previously labor-intensive assembly shops (Volpato and Camuffo 1992). The impact of these new technologies on employment, the organization of work, and the composition of the work force were dramatic. Perhaps the best way to illustrate these changes is by focusing on one particular shop. With the introduction of Robotgate, an electronically controlled, multiheaded welding system in Fiat–Mirafiori's welding shop, employ-ment decreased by about 50 percent (from 247 to 137 workers), while the composition of the work force also shifted significantly. Whereas direct manual workers previously made up over 70 percent of the welding shop's work force, following the introduction of Robotgate, these semiskilled workers decreased to only 15 percent of the work force. Conversely, highly skilled maintenance workers grew from 16 percent of the shop's work force to over 64 percent after Robotgate (Volpato 1993: table 50).

Aside from reducing and reskilling Fiat's labor force, these new process technologies enhanced the ability of the company to retool its operations. Unlike in the past, when a change in model entailed an almost complete overhaul of the plant, with the introduction of Ro-botgate, Fiat was able to change models with greater ease, since 80 percent of the hardware could be adapted to new models. As a result, Fiat was able to launch twelve new models between 1978 and 1986, as opposed to only five in 1970–77 (Volpato 1993: table 48).

Finally, Fiat rationalized and upgraded its network of component suppliers. The company reduced its supplier base from 1,300 firms in 1979 to about 800 suppliers in 1986. Suppliers were chosen on the basis of their prices, technical capacities, and quality records. They were also classified into three major groups: pilot firms that produce macrocomponent systems for Fiat and collaborate with Fiat in product design and development; second-tier suppliers that manufacture less complex components and supply the pilot firms; and companies that produce standard, multipurpose components and parts for both Fiat and other automobile manufacturers.[5] This increased collaboration between Fiat and its suppliers both enhanced the quality of its components and further stimulated product innovation.

The consequences of these various reorganization efforts were positive for the firm. Profits rose from 324 billion lire in 1981 to 1,764 billion in 1988. Productivity, as measured by the average number of cars produced by a single worker, more than doubled, from 14.0 in 1979 to 31.2 in 1989 (Fiat 1989: 69). As a result of these and other improvements, by the late 1980s Fiat reemerged as a significant competitor in the European market.

If the results of Fiat's restructuring were positive for the auto firm, the consequences for the union were not. Immediately following the rupture in relations with the union in 1980, the firm asserted a hard line with the labor movement. Within the factories this translated into a recreation of traditional hierarchies and control on the shop floor, the discriminate use of layoffs to rid the factories of union activists (see Collida and Negrelli 1986: 167), and the halving of the work force (see Table 4.1).

Continuing antagonism between the local union and Fiat management foreclosed all possibility of labor participation in the adjustment processes underway. In many shops, traditional union rules and practices were rendered obsolete by the introduction of new technologies and the reorganization of production. Three examples concerning accords over piece rates and breaks, job classification schemes, and sourcing decisions illustrate this point.

During the 1970s, factory delegates and the Job Analysis offices of Fiat's plants engaged in extremely meticulous, time-consuming negotiations over individual and group work effort levels, piece rates and new piecework times, and working conditions (Contini 1986). As a result, numerous accords were reached regulating piece rates and breaks in different parts of the assembly line, and hazardous work sites (paint shops) were restructured. After 1980, however, with the introduction of new technologies in chassis wielding, engine construction, and the paint shops, work was reorganized in a variety of different shops, and the previous accords became virtually irrelevant.

These new technologies also transcended traditional job classifica-

---

[5]For more on this process, see Enrietti and Follis 1983: 37–45; and Follis 1979: 141–51.

Table 4.1. Employment and production at Fiat Auto, 1979–1986

	1979	1980	1981	1982	1983	1984	1985	1986
Blue-collar workers	113,568	110,049	97,046	88,812	78,993	71,345	64,123	60,283
White-collar workers & management	25,381	24,572	22,156	20,350	19,176	18,312	17,736	17,627
Total employees	138,949	134,621	119,202	108,662	98,169	89,657	81,859	77,910
Personnel in cassa integrazione	0	20,505	18,598	19,109	14,569	10,380	6,501	1,915
Total active laborers	138,949	114,116	100,604	89,553	83,600	79,277	75,358	75,995
Fiat autos produced (in thousands)	1,160.9	1,087.8	963.2	985.3	1,037.9	1,076.2	1,037.3	1,295.0
Lancia and Autobianchi autos produced (in thousands)	146.9	187.7	155.3	146.2	185.0	191.1	227.2	227.6

Source: Figures on employment at cassa integrazione were provided through interviews with managers at Fiat Auto. Production figures from Fiat Auto, *Bilancio Consolidato 1988* (Turin: Fiat Auto, 1989): 13.

Note: Fiat Auto acquired both Lancia and Autobianchi in the late 1960s. Automobiles sold under these names are manufactured in Fiat factories, often alongside Fiat models.

tion schemes as they rendered certain traditional jobs redundant while creating new positions for people capable of both operating and servicing the new process technologies. As more and more workers occupied these jobs, which had skill requirements and responsibilities that did not fit neatly into traditional job classification schemes, the unions found themselves with an anachronistic classification system. The question of what to do with these workers presented a dilemma. On the one hand, a failure to acknowledge their skills would antagonize the new workers. On the other hand, the unions would anger their traditional constituency of semiskilled workers if they appeared to favor the new workers by awarding them the extra bonuses and privileges associated with higher classification levels.

Finally, the reconceptualization of the automobile as a composite of modular macrocomponent systems overhauled prior production and sourcing arrangements. Engines, brake systems, dashboards, and seats could be produced by specialized suppliers working in collaboration with Fiat. Since these "make-or-buy" decisions seemed to be continuously renegotiated by the firm and its suppliers, and since many of the suppliers were also organized by the metalworkers union, it became increasingly difficult for the union to develop a viable position on sourcing issues.

Perhaps more damaging for union practices than the actual changes in production was the way these changes were implemented by the firm. For the first half of the decade, Fiat management circumvented the unions, negotiating directly with workers over issues concerning retraining, flexible work hours, and modifications of their jobs. Although these modifications were significant enough to match the changes underway in the organization of production, they were not so dramatic as to necessitate formal renegotiation of job classification schemes, which would have legally required union participation. This blurring or bending *but not* breaking of already established contractual rules was very characteristic of Fiat industrial relations policies over the course of the 1980s.[6]

A 1986 study of Fiat workers' perception of the technological changes then underway suggests that those workers most vulnerable to being replaced by automation were extremely anxious about their

[6]Based on interviews with both Fiat managers and local union officials in Turin. See the Appendix for a complete list of interviewees.

positions and diffident toward the union. The union was shunned not only because of its failure to protect these workers from replacement by automation, but also because of fears that union contacts would result in company reprisals in the form of dismissals or layoffs (Rieser 1986). Union membership rates reflect these feelings. At Fiat's various Turinese plants, membership in the local metalworkers union, the FLM, fell from 32,898 (32.5 percent of the work force) in 1980 to 11,589 (20.5 percent) in 1986. In certain Fiat plants (Mirafiori) the union reported even lower unionization rates (see Table 4.2).

If the situation was precarious for workers within the firm, it was even more dismal for laid-off workers. The most evident sign of the severe dislocation resulting from Fiat's restructuring and the defeat of the union was the fate of the so-called *cassintegrati*. Of the more than 60,000 workers who exited the firm between 1979 and 1987, a total of 30,590 were supported by cassa integrazione. Of these, only 11,000 returned to their jobs at Fiat. The rest were paid bonuses to retire early or simply resign (Bonazzi 1990: 30–31).[7]

The majority of redundant workers were middle-aged, unskilled, poorly educated workers of southern origin. Many of the disabled and female workers hired during the latter half of the 1970s (because of union enforcement of national hiring policies) were also laid off.

---

[7]To reconcile these figures with those previously presented in Table 4.1, keep in mind that employees were both placed into and removed from cassa integrazione during each of these years:

Fiat Auto: Entry into and exit from cassa
integrazione, 1980–1986, in number of employees

Year	Entry	Exit	Sum
1980	20,505	—	20,505
1981	3,766	5,683	18,598
1982	5,886	5,375	19,109
1983	—	4,540	14,569
1984	370	4,595	10,380
1985	—	3,843	6,501
1986	63	4,586	1,915

Source: Giuseppe Bonassi, "Lasciare la fabbrica," in *La citta dopo Ford*, Arnalso Bagnasco, ed. (Turin: Bollati Boringhiere, 1990): 31.
Note: The figures in the third column match those presented in Table 4.1.

Table 4.2. Unionization at Gruppo Fiat in Turin

Year	Total workers	Members FIM-FIOM-UILM	Union density, in percent
1980	101,311	32,898	32.5
1981	98,461	27,380	27.8
1982	76,541	20,803	27.2
1983	70,156	17,131	24.4
1984	60,817	14,527	23.9
1985	57,338	12,940	22.6
1986	56,619	11,589	20.5

Source: Figures were obtained from internal union documents of the FIOM TORINO.
Note: These are aggregate data and hence do not reveal the even lower unionization rates at particular plants, such as Mirafiori, which supposedly have fallen below 20 percent.

Some unemployed workers used this period to finish their studies or acquire new skills (see Bonazzi 1990), but others experienced tremendous difficulties adjusting to their new lives outside the factory. Rates of suicide, divorce, substance abuse, and psychological illness, especially among workers who had recently immigrated to Turin, reached alarming proportions by 1985 (Cardacci 1985).

Needless to say, the local union lost considerable support among the rank and file, who held it responsible for this debacle. Loss of membership was compounded by other problems, including factional infighting, purges, and persistent paralysis vis-à-vis firm initiatives. Even now, as Fiat begins a new phase of restructuring, the union's bargaining position continues to be extremely weak at Fiat as evidenced by the union's persistent inability to shape managerial decisions concerning sourcing, retraining, and the reorganization of work on the shop floor.

A more careful examination of why company managers and local militants pursued this confrontational strategy raises serious questions about labor-management relations in today's climate of sweeping economic change. But before turning to that task, let us look at a second, very different case of industrial restructuring. Examination of the developments at Alfa Romeo not only provided a comparative perspective through which to better understand the case of Fiat but also highlights how local sociopolitical networks shaped adjustment patterns at these two firms.

Negotiated Restructuring: A Brief Comparison with Alfa Romeo

Founded in 1906, Alfa Romeo did not concentrate its production on automobiles until after World War II (Bigazzi 1988). Instead, automobiles were one among a number of more or less profitable manufactured items which included munitions, railroad stock, and aircraft engines. Following World War I, market limits, financial problems, and management errors constrained Alfa Romeo's car output. In the same period during which Fiat began to reorganize its production along the lines of mass production, Alfa's management, drawing on the firm's experience in manufacturing racing cars, concentrated on high-quality automobiles. In the field of industrial relations, the firm stressed workers' skills, cooperation, and loyalty to the firm. Even after the company's takeover by the state during the Depression, Alfa continued to be characterized by this model of industrial development.

This triad of high-quality production, skilled workers, and cooperative industrial relations continued to underpin the firm's industrial strategy in the postwar period. In fact, Alfa did not really embark on the mass production of autos until the early 1960s, when it opened its Arese plant outside Milan and doubled its production capacity. Even then, the company continued its tradition of high-quality production through technical innovation—winning fame for its technically advanced product development and design—and labor-management cooperation. The results were impressive: Alfa increased production from 27,438 cars in 1958 to 101,570 automobiles in 1969 (Volpato 1983: 222), and over the course of the 1960s doubled its workforce from 11,149 employees in 1961 to 23,969 in 1971 (Frey 1988: 55). By the end of the decade, Alfa Romeo was an internationally recognized leader in luxury sedans and sportscars.

The success of this corporate strategy, however, was not fully appreciated until after it was abandoned for fordism. In 1972, with the opening of its Pomigliano plant outside of Naples,[8] Alfa Romeo sought to break from the past, departing from its traditional product differentiation-based strategy to manufacture the Alfasud, a small, economy car. The firm had little experience either with the mass-marketing strategy that was needed to sell this new product or with the unskilled workers and highly automated and special-purpose equipment that

[8]As we saw in the last chapter, this was part of IRI's and the Italian government's policy to industrialize the South.

were employed to manufacture it (Geroldi and Nizzoli 1986). Those disadvantages, together with the timing of this strategy exactly at the moment when the European automobile industry began to suffer from overcapacity, higher fuel and labor costs, and greater international competition, may explain the disastrous results this change in strategy had for the firm. That the Pomigliano-based division was operated more or less independently from Alfa's older plants, with separate management and autonomous design, purchasing, and marketing offices, may also account for the poor results experienced by Alfa during the 1970s. Following the opening of its Pomigliano plant, Alfa Romeo, once seen as the pride and joy of Italian state enterprise, languished for over a decade before it was finally restructured (Bianchi 1988; Geroldi and Nizzoli 1987: chap. 3).

To further exacerbate the firm's troubles, labor relations at Alfa (both in the North and in the South) became antagonistic in the 1970s. Like Fiat, Alfa Romeo experienced an especially militant wave of strikes and worker mobilization during the Hot Autumn of 1969–72. In fact, the local union at Alfa became so powerful that it was often able to achieve its goals with no more than the threat of strikes (Reyneri 1976). Although absenteeism (about 200 hours per worker per year through most of the decade) and hours lost to work stoppages (from 27 hours per worker in 1975 to 50 hours per worker in 1979) increased dramatically, productivity and product quality plummeted (Costa and Gradara 1984: 98, 105, 122). The climate of industrial relations at the Pomigliano plant became so horrible that industrial sociologists dedicated volumes to studying it as an "anomaly" (see, for example, Salerni 1980).

Alfa's response to these troubles was radically different from Fiat's. For example, in the early 1980s, the local unions and Alfa's management negotiated a series of accords aimed at both increasing the firm's productivity and enriching workers' skills. In accordance with these agreements, which resembled workplace redesign efforts in the United States and Scandinavia,[9] the assembly line was divided into various segments, with a team of ten to twenty workers assigned to each segment. Within these so-called homogeneous production groups, workers rotated various jobs as a way of eliminating monotony and

[9]For more on efforts to redesign work and enhance productivity and quality through small group activity, see Cole 1989.

increasing their skills. Quality control and maintenance work were also relegated to teams.

As a result of these changes, productivity increased, product quality improved, and a number of indirect and supervisory jobs were eliminated from the factory. For example, following the creation of the homogeneous production groups in 1982, the same number of workers (9,595) at the Arese plant assembled almost 100 cars (of the same product mix) more per year than they had in previous years (Frey 1988: 62). The success of this experiment appeared so great that one of Alfa's personnel managers wrote a book arguing that one could "forget about Turin" (that is, Fiat's experience) in this new phase of "negotiated restructuring" (Medusa 1983). Both absenteeism and strikes decreased significantly following the negotiation of these accords in 1982 (see Tables 4.3 and 4.4 for employment, production, and strike rate figures at Alfa during these years).

A variety of factors, including the increased militancy of the local FIM and the subsequent dissolution of union unity at Alfa, the breakdown of the firm's supplier network (which made it nearly impossible to maintain production schedules, let alone product quality), a series of management turnovers, and persistent underinvestment—especially in new product and process technologies—all combined to undermine the effectiveness of the production groups. Cooperative labor-management relations nevertheless continued at Alfa, even after it was sold to Fiat in November 1986.[10]

Illustrative of this continuity was the May 3, 1987, agreement between Fiat and the unions over the restructuring of Alfa Romeo. In this accord, Fiat agreed to invest 55 billion lire in new process technologies, restyle a number of existing Alfa models, and transfer production of various Lancia models (Y-10 and Thema) to Alfa's plants. In return for these investments, the unions abandoned what remained of the production groups, agreed to a number of early retirements and layoffs during the firm's reorganization, and relaxed its contract rules regulating internal labor mobility.

The restructuring plan did meet with some resistance. The radical

---

[10] As in other Western nations in the 1980s, the Italian state began privatizing various assets. As part of that process, the Italian state holding company, IRI, decided to sell off Alfa Romeo, which it had taken over during the Depression in the 1930s. Both Ford Motor Company and Fiat Auto bid for Alfa. Fiat won the bid and took control of the firm in 1987. For more on this experience, see Bianchi 1988.

Table 4.3. Employment and production at Alfa Romeo, 1979–1986

	1979	1980	1981	1982	1983	1984	1985	1986
Employees in Alfa Romeo S.p.A.	41,384	35,051	34,137	33,703	31,956	30,264	28,832	27,968
Employees in cassa integrazione	—	—	—	3,398	2,269	5,313	6,444	7,697
Autos produced at Arese	111,100	117,819	97,415	103,776	98,713	72,830	74,027	86,453
Autos produced at Pomigliano	96,400	101,752	99,872	84,997	108,213	127,273	85,598	81,621

Source: Marco Frey, "Ristrutturazione ritardata e conseguenze occupazionali: Il caso Alfa Romeo," *Economica e Politica Industriale*, no. 59 (1988): 66 for employment figures; 81 for production figures.

Note: Until 1980, Alfa Romeo consisted of two divisions; Alfa Romeo S.p.A., which included the Arese plant in the Milan area, and Alfasud, which consisted of the Pomigliano operations. The two divisions were conglomerated in a complete reorganization that centralized operations under Alfa Romeo S.p.A.

Table 4.4. Work hours lost due to union actions and absenteeism at Alfa Romeo, 1980–1986

	1980	1981	1982	1983	1984	1985	1986
Hours lost due to union actions	785	669	1,071	778	565	152	365
Hours lost due to absenteeism	9,152	6,423	3,927	3,147	2,664	1,936	2,585

Source: Marco Frey, "Ristrutturazione ritardata e conseguenze occupazionali: Il caso Alfa Romeo," Economia e politica industriale, no. 59 (1988): 67.

faction of the local FIM rejected the plan and tried to mobilize the local work force against it. A referendum held in the late spring of 1987, however, resulted in the ratification of the plan. With the union involved, the costs of the reorganization in terms of layoffs were lower than anticipated. For instance, at the time of the May 3, 1987, accord 6,000 Alfa employees were already in cassa integrazione. Following the agreement, another 1,500 workers were laid off. Although the original plan envisioned layoffs lasting until the end of 1990, by the end of 1988 virtually all Alfa employees were back at work. Moreover, in 1989 Alfa began to hire new workers. Almost 2,000 new blue- and white-collar employees were hired at both the Arese and Pomigliano plants. Consistent with these results was the continual decline of strike and absentee rates to almost negligible levels in 1988 and 1989 (Fiat 1990: 14).

In short, negotiated restructuring at Alfa seems to have resulted in gains for both sides. Alfa increased its sales by 29 percent and productivity by 50 percent between 1986 and 1988 (Fiat 1990: 14) and once again became profitable. Whereas Alfa was still losing 286,534 million lire during the first year of the firm's reorganization in 1987, in 1988 net profits amounted to 138,195 million lire and 343,743 million lire in 1989.[11] Moreover, as of 1991 all laid-off workers had returned to their jobs. Union membership figures reflect this outcome. Not only were union membership rates significantly higher at Alfa following the restructuring of both firms (in 1988, 44 percent at Arese and 52 percent at Pomigliano) than at Fiat (in 1986, 20.5 percent), but also the more cooperative forces at Alfa (FIOM, FLM, UILM) appear to have fared better than the militant FIM during the firm's reorganization (see Table 4.5).

Thus, we have two cases, one of chronic conflictualism resulting in the defeat of the union and the other of a more negotiated solution

[11] These figures were taken from Ricerche e Studi: 1988, 1989, 1990.

Table 4.5. Unionization rate at Alfa Romeo Arese plant

	May 1987		April 1988	
FIOM-CGIL	4,462	(30.5)	3,300	(26.6)
FIM-CISL	2,211	(15.0)	1,200	(9.7)
UILM-UIL	655	(4.5)	513	(4.1)
FLM	708	(5.0)	450	(3.6)
Total	8,036	(55.0)	5,463	(44.0)

Source: Marco Frey, "Ristrutturazione ritardata e conseguenze occupazionali: Il caso Alfa Romeo," *Economia e politica industriale*, no. 59 (1988): 85.
[a]Figures in parentheses indicate percent of total employees belonging to the unions.

that appears to have benefited both labor and management. How do we account for these differences in patterns of industrial adjustment?

EXPLAINING THE DIVERGENCE

One's first instinct is to attribute these differences to economic factors: because these two firms occupy different market segments, they faced different challenges and thus the processes and outcomes of their respective reorganizations diverged. Although it is true that Alfa and Fiat have traditionally pursued different strategies, it is also true that during the 1970s (with Fiat's acquisition of Lancia in 1969 and Alfa's construction of Pomigliano) their strategies and product ranges began to converge (Volpato 1983: 441–55). If anything, Alfa's financial difficulties were much more serious than Fiat's. Moreover, other foreign companies competing with Fiat in exactly the same market segments appear to have restructured in vastly different ways (Streeck 1987b: 437–62; Turner 1991). Thus, competitive strategy alone can not explain the observed differences.

Another commonly offered explanation focuses on the fact that until 1986 Alfa was a state-owned firm and its management could thus be more relaxed about economic goals like efficiency and sales, permitting it to be "easier" on the union. A 1986 study reviewing management practices at Alfa during these years, however, indicates that Alfa's management was no more benevolent toward the unions than was Fiat's management and, at times, it was even more aggressive (Montini 1986). That labor relations at Alfa continue to be significantly different from those at Fiat, even now that they share the same ownership and management, also casts doubt on this assertion.

My alternative explanation for the divergent patterns of adjustment observed at Fiat and Alfa Romeo focuses on the different sociopolitical networks within which the two firms (and their respective local unions) are embedded. In Chapter 1 I argue that the Italian economy is a composite of very different local economic orders—each with a distinct pattern of associationalism, political representation, and economic governance. These divergent sociopolitical networks create alternative mixes of resources and constraints for local economic actors. These networks not only structure relations among local economic actors, but also provide local actors with very different linkages or channels of communication and representation to outside (national) organized actors and/or policymakers. As a result, different sociopolitical networks shape the understandings, resources, and hence the strategic choices of local firm managers and unionists in very different ways.

Fiat and Alfa are embedded in very different local economies with divergent underlying sociopolitical networks. Fiat is situated in Turin, a more or less one-company town that resembles in many ways the "polarized" ideal type I described in Chapter 1. Polarized local economies are characterized by a small number of parochial and organizationally underdeveloped interest groups and associations clustered together into two opposing camps. Although the ties among organized actors or groups within each camp are quite strong, linkages between the two clusters are often tenuous. Thus, when conflicts arise between actors affiliated with the two opposing camps, they often develop into zero-sum struggles in which the gains achieved by one side are perceived as equivalent losses by the other. Because local secondary associations are also associated with the two competing camps, they are unable to mediate disputes between conflicting actors.

Alfa, on the other hand, is located in Milan, which more closely resembles the "polycentric" local economy outlined in Chapter 1. Polycentric systems are characterized by a dense network of encompassing and open associations and interest groups that are linked to one another through many horizontal ties. In these local economies, interests are well organized and communication among the different groups is frequent. Whenever disagreements or conflicts arise between any two actors, other interest groups or associations within the local network will seek to facilitate negotiations or arbitrate differences between the conflicting parties.

Illustrating the distinctive features of these two local economies is extremely difficult, especially since much of what distinguishes Milan and Turin involves highly qualitative attributes like the "openness" or "parochialism" of particular interest groups and the kinds of linkages (strong vs. weak) that exist among the various local actors. However, there are a few rough indicators that suggest that these two local economies are indeed quite different. In his recent book on regional government in Italy, Robert Putnam employs two indicators in order to assess the varying degrees of "civic sociability" in Italy's various regions: 1) the number of local associations (e.g., social clubs, choral societies, literary circles); and 2) newspaper readership. According to Putnam, regions with greater numbers of associations and well-informed citizens will be more "civic" and hence their regional governments will perform better than regions with fewer associations and less well-informed inhabitants (Putnam 1993).

Using these same rough indicators and the same data source[12] to explore underlying sociopolitical differences between Milan and Turin reveals some very interesting patterns. For example, Milan has twice as many secondary associations as Turin. There are 657 associations operating within the province of Milan and 341 associations in Turin. Even when we control for differences in the population sizes of these two localities, divergences in the vibrancy of associational life remain. There are .35 associations per 100 residents in the province of Turin and .48 associations per 100 residents in Milan. Patterns of newspaper readership are also quite distinct in these two cities. Over 292,000 newspapers are sold each day in Milan, whereas in Turin only 107,039 papers are sold on any given day (ISTAT 1989: 81). Again, when controlled for differences in population size of these two cities, this same pattern holds.[13] These data suggest that associational life is more vibrant in Milan than in Turin and that inhabitants in Milan are better informed, perhaps more engaged in broader societal debates, than their compatriots in Turin.

[12]Mortara 1982. Mortara lists only local associations and not local branches of national organizations like unions and political parties. But another source, the *Guida Monaci*, a directory of all interest groups, political parties, business and labor associations, cultural societies, etc., with and without national affiliations, confirms the basic differences in associational life between Milan and Turin. See *Guida Monaci* 1991.

[13]Dividing total number of daily newspapers in both localities by their populations confirms the overall patterns. In Turin, there are 4.8 newspapers sold for every 100 people, whereas in Milan, the number increases to 7.5 newspapers per 100 residents. Population figures for both localities can be found in Di Nicola 1991: table 7. Newspaper readership figures are reported in ISTAT 1989: 81.

Yet as important, if not more, than general patterns of newspaper readership and the total number of secondary associations present in any given locality are the qualitative features of the various associations and organized interest groups. Again, we can use only very rough and incomplete indicators to assess the strength or openness of associations in different localities. Membership data for various political parties are available and suggest that parties are stronger (i.e., have more members) in Milan than in Turin, but these data are not reliable since it is quite apparent, especially after the recent corruption scandals, that several political parties completely invented their membership lists. Union membership data are also incomplete and subject to inflation, but one data set from the Research Office of the CGIL, Italy's largest union confederation, appears to be sufficiently reliable to serve as a rough indicator of the strength and inclusiveness of at least organized labor in the two localities under consideration.[14] The CGIL data reveal that in 1981 the CGIL organized 23.18 percent of all salaried workers in Milan but only 16.45 percent of these same workers in Turin. During the 1980s, rates of unionization declined in both cities, but still the CGIL continued to organize a greater percentage of eligible workers in Milan than in Turin.[15]

These differences in union strength are not exceptional but seem indicative of more general patterns of associational life in both cities. In his book on Turin, Arnaldo Bagnasco has argued that membership figures in interest groups and participation rates in political movements and/or elections have historically been lower in Turin than in Milan (Bagnasco 1986: 69–81). His evidence is also fragmentary, but the picture that emerges is nonetheless quite consistent: Not only are there more secondary associations in Milan than in Turin, but also these groups in Milan appear to be stronger, more vibrant, perhaps even more representative than they are in Turin.

Beyond overall numbers of associations and the specific attributes of particular groups in the two localities, what also matters is how these

[14]Union membership figures are reported in Di Nicola 1993: 96. I discussed the reliability of the data both with Mr. Di Nicola and with several leading industrial relations scholars at different Italian universities.

[15]In 1990, the respective CGIL unionization rates for Turin and Milan were 14.05 percent and 16.30 percent. I attempted to collect comparable data from the other two major union confederations, the CISL and the UIL, but without any luck. Given that the CISL is much stronger in Milan than in Turin, the CGIL data, if anything, underestimate the differences in unionization rates between these two cities.

different associations relate to one another and how their relations are structured. At a theoretical level one can imagine two localities with equal numbers of associations, but with relations among these different groups structured in very different ways (i.e., the polycentric vs. hierarchical patterns outlined in Chapter 1). The different structures or patterns of interaction would also have significant implications for the ability of various actors within these different localities to share information, pool resources, and form alliances at critical moments.

Because of resource constraints and technical limitations, I was unable to do a rigorous network analysis of the interactions and linkages among different local groups and associations in either Milan and Turin and thus cannot systematically demonstrate the way relationships among various local actors are structured in different ways in these two cities. But I did conduct scores of in-depth interviews with local business, union, and political leaders in both cities (see Appendix A for a list of interviewees). Through these interviews, I tried to learn about the various kinds of ties or relationships that existed among different local actors, and from this information I was able to sketch out the rough contours of the different sociopolitical networks underlying the local economies of Milan and Turin. As diagramed in Figure 4.1, Alfa appears to be embedded in what approximates a polycentric local economy, whereas Fiat is situated in a more polarized setting.

By structuring relations, information flows, and the distribution

Figure 4.1. Schematic representation of sociopolitical networks in Milan and Turin

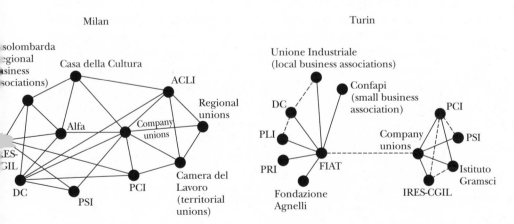

of resources among local actors in different ways, these divergent sociopolitical networks created alternative mixes of incentives and constraints for managers and unionists at the two companies. A reexamination of our two cases illustrates how the distinct local economic orders in which Fiat and Alfa are embedded shaped the contrasting strategies pursued by these actors.

LOCAL PATTERNS OF INDUSTRIAL POLITICS

The development of Fiat along the lines of fordism, and the way in which that development occurred, had significant effects on both the firm and its work force, as well as on the underlying sociopolitical features of Turin (Castronovo 1979; Michelsons 1986). The expansive growth of the firm made it not only the biggest but in many ways the only show in town. Fiat is referred to as "la mamma" by local residents. The local economy has historically revolved around the firm, and most of the local labor force is employed either at Fiat or at one of its numerous suppliers.

Due to its hegemonic position, Fiat was able to dominate local government, control local business and cultural associations, and thus more or less determine the development of the city. Fiat management also cultivated an extremely authoritarian, hierarchical vision of its role and sought to control unilaterally the firm's development (see Castronovo 1977; and Bairati 1983, for more on this). As a result, management promoted pro-business political forces and dominated the local government.

Management also sought to tame the company's work force through a combination of repression and paternalism and undermined all attempts to create alternative bases of power within Fiat's plants. For example, in the immediate postwar period, Vittorio Valletta, then general director of Fiat, destroyed the *consigli di gestione,* comanagement councils that had been established immediately after the war in order to promote workers' participation in production decisions (Lanzardo 1971). During the 1950s, Fiat management also persecuted CGIL union members and engineered the systematic expulsion of CGIL activists from the company's factories (Pugno and Garavini 1974). The impact of this strategy is best illustrated by the results of the elections to Fiat's *commissione interne,* the company's grievance committee (see Table 4.6). Between 1955 and 1957 support for the FIOM, the CGIL's metalworkers federation, fell from about 33,000 to about 12,000 votes. Following the FIM-CISL's 1958 decision to stop colluding with Fiat management in its persecution of CGIL unionists, it too fell victim to company repression. Fiat management engineered the local FIM's split and established its own company union (Gheddo 1980).

Without any significant opposition from the local trade unions, the local government, or any other local interest group or political party, Fiat management was able to shape both Turin's industry and its local labor market into a highly integrated pyramidlike structure with itself at the commanding heights. This particular model of development had a major impact on the local labor movement (Gianotti 1979; Golden 1988a). Local unions were essentially weak organizations with strong ideologies. Antagonism toward the firm combined with a radical vision of politics to create a local labor movement that perceived itself (and at times sought to act) as the vanguard of the Italian labor movement (Rieser 1981). For instance, peculiar to the local labor movement are its spontaneous strike waves, regularly followed by the politicization of industrial relations. This pattern occurred in 1913, when the rank and file supported anarchosyndicalist positions and prevented the local union from negotiating with the firm, and the pattern has recurred throughout the local union's history.

As a result of the particular way in which industry developed in Turin and the peculiarities of the local labor movement, stable relations between Fiat and the unions never developed. The result was a continuous struggle between these actors in which no long-lasting compromises were possible. Defeat by one meant its almost complete subordination to the other. The wounds of past battles were nourished as the loser prepared revenge in the next round of struggles. Thus, since the factory occupations in 1920 and continuing through the rise and fall of fascism, the restoration of private capital in the 1950s, the Hot Autumn struggles in the late 1960s, and the 35-day strike in 1980, labor and management in Turin have been engaged in an all-or-nothing battle.

Furthermore, because of the particular way in which Turin developed, the city was unable to create and/or preserve the sociopolitical resources necessary to mediate the type of conflictual labor relations characteristic of Fiat. Because of the simplicity of Turinese society,

Table 4.6. Election results for the Commissioni Interne at Fiat, 1948–1968

Year	FIM-CISL			UILM-UIL			CGIL-FIOM			Other unions		
	Votes	Percent	Members	Votes	Percent	Members	Votes	Percent	Members	Votes	Percent	Members
1948	9,433	21.4	35	—	—	—	33,420	75.9	98	1,291	2.7	7
1954	13,175	25.4	45	5,889	11.3	13	32,885	63.2	100	76	0.1	2
1955	20,910	40.5	93	11,628	22.5	40	18,937	36.7	55	157	0.3	4
1956	26,000	47.2	111	13,147	23.9	46	15,903	28.8	45	70	0.1	2
1957	28,435	50.0	114	16,200	28.5	57	12,025	21.4	34	201	0.4	—
1958	7,365	12.9	15	16,149	28.3	58	14,454	25.3	36	19,076	33.4	82
1960	10,163	16.4	34	17,007	27.4	58	13,766	22.2	31	21,137	34.0	82
1965	12,554	15.4	33	23,418	28.8	67	17,538	21.6	32	27,773	34.1	70
1968	13,394	13.1	36	28,638	28.1	72	31,932	31.4	56	27,852	27.4	68

Source: Emilio Pugno and Sergio Garavini, *Gli anni duri alla Fiat* (Turin: Einaudi, 1974): 98.
Note: 1968 is the last year of Commissioni Interne elections since they were subsequently replaced by the delegates and factory councils following the Hot Autumn.

which is composed essentially of an industrial bourgeoisie and a prole-
tarian working class,[16] organized interest groups (such as labor unions,
trade associations, and religious groups) and political parties never
fully developed in Turin. Its unions, for example, have historically
behaved more like social movements than organized interest groups,
and their membership rates have always been below the national average (see Golden 1988b: 180 for recent membership figures and 197–
242 for a historical analysis of this phenomenon). The few other
interest groups or associations that exist in Turin are dominated by
either the firm or the union movement. The only institutions that are
autonomous of these two protagonists are the local churches. But
due to their own historical development, even the churches are quite
radical, and they actually exacerbated rather than diminished antago-
nisms between labor and management at Fiat (Berzano et al. 1984).

In sum, by the late 1970s Fiat had developed into a powerful but
extremely hierarchical and inward-looking company, while the unions
had become highly politicized but weak organizations. Moreover, both
Fiat and its unions were embedded in a polarized setting that lacked
potential mediators of industrial conflict. It should come as no surprise, therefore, that during the 1970s repeated attempts at Fiat by
small groups within both the local unions and the firm to construct a
more negotiated and stable system of industrial relations failed and
that the company's adjustment process entailed so much conflict and
social dislocation.

Based on my own interviews with company managers and union
leaders, published memoirs by Fiat managers and local union leaders
(Dealessandri and Magnabosco 1987; Romiti 1988), and several surveys and analytic studies of Fiat workers (Istituto Gramsci 1980; Bonazzi 1984; Carmignani 1984; and Accornero, Carmignani, and
Magna 1985) we can reconstruct the strategies of the different actors
and the events that led to the fall 1980 strike at Fiat. Small groups
interested in building more stable labor relations at Fiat existed within
both the local union and the company. Within the firm, this group
was referred to as the "doves" (in contrast to the "hawks," who were
more traditional, hard-line managers). I have not been able to quantify
the size of this group nor assess its relative power, but there is ample

---

[16] Recent census data indicate that Turin's population consists primarily of industrial
workers, with significantly fewer people employed in commerce or services. The composition of Milan's work force appears much more balanced. See ISTAT 1991.

anecdotal evidence to suggest that this group was sufficiently powerful in the 1970s to promote several initiatives aimed at changing labor relations at Fiat.

It was this group of managers, many of whom had been recruited by the company in the early 1970s specifically to develop modern human resource management practices at Fiat (Contini 1986; Dealessandri and Magnabosco 1987), which had sought to negotiate various shop floor changes aimed at enhancing labor flexibility in the 1970s. This group of managers also had tried to build an antiterrorist coalition with local union leaders in the late 1970s, when the Red Brigades had infiltrated the company's work force, vandalized its factories, and assaulted several company managers and even some workers. Finally, it was this group of more moderate managers who had secretly worked with the union's negotiating committee in early 1980 in order to develop a mutually agreeable restructuring plan for Fiat (Carmignani 1984).

Within the local union movement there was also a significant number of activists who had come to believe that the unions' highly conflictual strategy had run its course and that the unions needed to develop new positions in light of the company's growing financial difficulties. During the 1970s, this group of unionists had sought to renegotiate work rules concerning overtime and internal labor flexibility in order to enhance the company's productivity (Contini 1986; Dealessandri and Magnabosco 1987). They had also organized a number of research projects and conferences on both the company's crisis (Comito 1982) and on the changing political and social attitudes of Fiat's work force (Istituto Gramsci 1980).

The studies and conference proceedings produced by and for this group illustrated clearly that Fiat lagged behind its principal European competitors in terms of plant utilization rates, product quality, and the introduction of new products and thus needed to restructure. This finding was especially powerful given that it emerged from a union-sponsored study. Moreover, one study based on survey research of Fiat's work force showed quite clearly that the local union movement was extremely divided and that a growing number of Fiat employees disagreed with the union's political positions and organizational strategies (Istituto Gramsci 1980). The "collaborative" group of unionists hoped that this information would persuade their colleagues within the local union movement, especially the more militant factory council delegates, to moderate their demands. Otherwise, they argued, the union risked alienating a significant number of Fiat employees and perhaps even driving the company into bankruptcy.

Yet, notwithstanding the existence of more moderate groups within both the local union movement and the company, the qualitative features of both these organizations and the structure of sociopolitical relations in Turin were such that, in the end, these groups had no real chance of promoting an alternative adjustment strategy at Fiat. Because of the polarized structure of sociopolitical relations in Turin, it was difficult for the cooperative forces within the local union movement and the company to communicate, let alone forge a stable and powerful alliance. There were very few points of contact between them and no third parties or autonomous secondary associations that could serve as a bridge and facilitate communication between these two like-minded groups. Moreover, because the local union movement was organizationally weak and parochial, it was unwilling, perhaps even unable, to absorb the new information the various studies and conferences provided. Finally, as things heated up around the reorganization of Fiat, the position of these moderate groups within their respective camps became increasingly tenuous.

Earlier I mentioned that union negotiators and Fiat managers had met secretly in Rome in early 1980 in order to hammer out a mutually agreeable accord over the company's restructuring. When these meetings were discovered (several people I interviewed claimed that the hawks within the company had leaked the information to the press), the more militant faction of the local union movement mobilized and demanded an end to the meetings. The demise of these secret negotiations not only cut off all contacts between union and management moderates, but also discredited both groups within their own camps. As a result, the militants within the local union movement were able to insert a whole set of demands, including more radical language and several nonnegotiable demands (e.g., that the Italian government should develop a plan for the entire automobile sector) within the unions' official bargaining platform. This radicalization of the unions' position, in turn, undermined the doves within the company since it was clear that their efforts had produced few tangible results for the company. As a result, the hard-line managers gained the upper hand and pursued a confrontational strategy with the unions (Romiti 1988). The 35-day strike and the defeat of the local unions soon followed.

The contrast with Alfa is striking. As we have seen, Alfa developed in such a direction that preserved workers' skills and reinforced local union organizations through much of this century. Unlike at Fiat, the unions at Alfa were never seriously repressed during the postwar period. Thus, throughout the 1950s and 1960s, as well as after the Hot Autumn of 1969–72, the unions at Alfa consisted of a sizeable group of disciplined, old-guard unionists who promoted shop floor bargaining. This group was active in all debates over union politics and played a major role in the negotiated restructuring of the firm in the 1980s.[17]

The local unions in Alfa's plants in Milan were always stronger and more complex organizations than their equivalents at Fiat and thus were less subject to the vicissitudes of the kind that troubled the more movement-oriented unions in Turin (Mershon 1986). Moreover, the auto industry is only one of many industries in the Milan area, and, although Alfa has the largest factory there, the metalworkers are not hegemonic in the same way they are in Turin. Textile workers and chemical workers unions, both with much experience in technological innovation and firm restructuring, are also strong in Milan, and they counterbalanced the particular interests or strategies of the more militant wings of the local metalworkers union.

Unlike Turin, Milan possesses strong and well-organized interest groups and political parties that have served historically as mediators between labor and management and thus have helped avoid the development of the zero-sum scenario that exists between labor and management at Fiat (Fumagalli 1982). For example, during the 1980s, when not only Alfa but also many other firms in Milan were being restructured, groups like Italian Catholic Action (ACLI) and the La Casa della Cultura (a left-wing cultural society) organized a series of seminars and conferences aimed at bringing together unionists, managers, politicians, and academics to discuss various issues associated with the changes underway in industry. Participation at these meetings was high, and several union leaders and business managers

[17] Based on interviews with local union leaders at Alfa Romeo, May 1987, and with the national secretaries of the FIOM and FIM, Rome, October 1987. See Appendix for list of interviewees.

I interviewed claimed that these meetings were useful in stimulating information-sharing and developing dialogue among the different groups.

The existence of this network of well-organized and connected groups seems to have played a role in shaping the adjustment process at Alfa. Notwithstanding the existence of a very strong and militant group within the local FIM which actively opposed the May 1987 accord over the restructuring of the company, the other local unions (FIOM, UILM, and FLM), as well as the regional CGIL, CISL, and UIL, all supported the agreement. Not only did these other groups outnumber the opposition but, more important, they were able to build a stable pro-accord coalition that included various local labor organizations, business associations, and even the national metalworkers federation. Thus, when workers voted on whether or not to support the restructuring accord, the majority voted in favor and the radical elements within the FIM were isolated. In other words, because of the different structure of Milanese society, reform-oriented groups within Alfa's unions were able to construct a cooperative coalition and avoid the type of showdown that had occurred with the same managers seven years earlier in Turin.

This chapter has analyzed the alternative adjustment processes of Italy's leading automobile manufacturers: Fiat Auto and Alfa Romeo. During the 1980s, both companies promoted major restructuring efforts: investing in new process and product technologies, rationalizing their supplier networks, and shedding redundant workers. Yet the adjustment strategies pursued at these two firms differed significantly. Whereas Fiat reorganized by reasserting managerial control over the shop floor and repressing the local unions, Alfa experienced a more negotiated process that appeared to produce benefits for both the company and its unions. To account for these divergent outcomes—a divergence that initially appears puzzling given that both companies share the same ownership, their work forces are organized by the same unions, their plants possess similar technologies, and they both operate within the same legal-institutional setting—this chapter elucidates the important role different local contexts played in shaping the strategic choices of company managers and union leaders at the two companies.

Because Fiat and Alfa are embedded in very different local economies, each with a distinct pattern of associationalism and structure of sociopolitical relations, company managers and union leaders at both firms faced alternative mixes of incentives and constraints which shaped their ability to formulate and implement different strategies. Since Fiat is located in Turin, a highly polarized, one-company town lacking a vibrant associational infrastructure, information-sharing and cooperation between moderate groups within both the company and the local union movement proved fleeting. Moreover, because Turin lacked well-organized and relatively autonomous interest groups, secondary associations, and political parties, potential mediators of conflict between the company and its unions simply did not exist. As a result, disagreements over the company's restructuring efforts escalated into an all-out struggle between the local unions and the company and resulted in massive layoffs, the decimation of the local union movement, and major social dislocation, especially among laid-off automobile workers.

Alfa, on the other hand, is situated in Milan, a more cosmopolitan city packed with many well-organized interest groups and secondary associations. These organizations facilitated information-sharing and cooperation between labor and management at Alfa and thus supported negotiations between these two parties over the massive changes under way at the firm. In fact, this dense sociopolitical network permitted cooperative labor, management, and community groups to form a powerful coalition that successfully fought efforts by the radicals within the local FIM to undermine the May 1987 labor-management accord over Alfa's restructuring.

In short, the cases presented in this chapter illustrate that local context matters. Context matters in the sense that different local, sociopolitical networks structure relations, information flow, and the distribution of resources within local economies in very different ways. As a result, they shape the range of possible strategies available to the various economic actors within these different local settings.

This lesson on the importance of a well-developed and vibrant social structure for economic adjustment strategies has not escaped the attention of the principal actors in Turin. In fact, by the mid-1980s, both Fiat and the local union movement were busy constructing an array of new organizations and institutions in and around Turin. The Fondazione Agnelli's efforts to build a network of local high-technology companies through "Tecnocity," the company's efforts to build stronger ties to the local universities and to cooperate with the unions on a variety of research projects and conferences all indicate that the company has come to understand that it must become a more open organization and that Turin must become a more heterogeneous and articulated locality.[18] The unions as well have sought to rebuild their ties to rank-and-file workers and reach out to other groups and associations in Turin in an effort to develop new strategies.

These recent developments are important because they suggest that economic actors are not simply shackled by local historical legacies. As we saw in the cases of Fiat and Alfa Romeo, the particular attributes of the local economy, social structure, and political system are in many ways the product of history. Turin's particular model of development played a major role in shaping the polarized sociopolitical network underlying the local economy. The same was true in Milan, where the city's more heterogenous development process generated a more balanced and complex local economic order. Yet local economic orders and the sociopolitical networks underlying them are not etched in stone and immutable thereafter.

Instead, at critical moments, political struggles among local economic actors with competing strategic choices may produce new kinds of alliances, compromises, and/or power relations that, in turn, may reconfigure the social, political, and institutional contours of the local economy. This does not mean that local economic actors can freely reinvent themselves and their surroundings whenever they find it convenient to do so but rather that, through politics, these actors may recombine legacies of the past in new and different ways, in ways that fundamentally alter the local economic order.

The next chapter on the restructuring of the Biellese textile district seeks to develop this point. Through an in-depth analysis of the reorganization of textile firms in Biella, Italy's most successful district of high-quality, high value-added textile production, I trace the way in which legacies of the past were recombined and modified through periodic political struggles in order to produce fundamentally different local economic orders.

[18] For more on these efforts, see Locke and Negrelli 1989: 87–90.

CHAPTER FIVE

From Economic Backwardness to International Competitiveness: The Biellese Textile District

This chapter examines the reorganization of Italy's textile industry. If any industry is associated with Italian economic success, it is this sector. In the 1980s, "Made in Italy" came to dominate the international fashion industry. Still today, Italy remains a leading exporter of textile and apparel products. Closer examination of how this so-called sunset industry, which was once closely identified with Italian "backwardness" (Frey 1975), was reorganized into a highly competitive sector sheds light on the more general process of industrial adjustment in Italy.

As with the case of the automobile companies examined in the last chapter, Italian textile and apparel firms restructured in very different ways. And like Fiat and Alfa Romeo, these divergent adjustment strategies were shaped by local economic orders with very different sociopolitical relations. Thus, notwithstanding enormous differences between the textile and automobile industries—they differ in terms of their production processes, technologies, firm dimensions, industry characteristics, and labor forces—the strategic choices of managers and union leaders in *both* sectors were nonetheless shaped by their local contexts.

This chapter is divided into three sections. The first section describes the general crisis of the textile industry and how Italian firms reorganized to confront it. Italian textile companies adjusted not in a uniform way but by pursuing a variety of alternative strategies. Some companies decentralized various phases of their production process and formed collaborative relations with other, complementary firms. Others became more integrated and invested heavily in new process technologies. Yet regardless of which strategy individual companies followed, all were shaped by their local settings. In other words, the viability of the alternative strategic choices promoted by local managers and union leaders at individual firms depended as much on the underlying socio-political character of the local economy as on their own core competencies and resources.

The second section shifts the analysis to Biella, Italy's leading woolen textile district, in order to examine in greater detail the adjustment strategies of Italian textile firms. This section begins with a description of the general contours of industrial change in Biella and then examines the specific choices taken by individual firms operating in the area.

In Biella there is a diversity of industrial structures and strategies within the local textile industry. This is the result of how the local industry developed. The emergence of large integrated textile mills did not occur at the cost of either smaller, more artisanal firms nor at the expense of the rather highly skilled local labor force. As a result, a plurality of different industrial structures and strategies continued to exist and later facilitated the reorganization process of the local textile industry.

Industrial restructuring entailed the breakup of large integrated mills producing standardized goods into a network of smaller, more specialized firms working together to produce some of the finest cashmeres and woolens in the world. But different firms made different choices regarding how much or how little to decentralize, which phases of the production process to devolve to outside suppliers and which to maintain and modernize, and what specific product and process innovations to pursue. The range of specific choices available to individual firms was shaped by both the general conditions and characteristics of the industry as a whole and the sociopolitical resources at hand in Biella.

The last section of this chapter analyzes the historical development of Biella's local economic order in order to trace the origins of its various social, political, and institutional features and to illustrate how these historical legacies were periodically recombined and reconfigured through political struggles among the key economic actors.

THE CRISIS OF THE TEXTILE-APPAREL INDUSTRY

Beginning in the 1960s, the textile-apparel industries of most advanced industrial nations began to experience severe crisis. As a result of changing conditions of international competition, increased labor costs and rigidities, higher energy and raw material costs, more restrictive government environmental and safety regulations, and altered consumer tastes, the industry's traditional model of economic development—based on low-wage, semiskilled workers producing large series of low-to-medium quality standardized goods in integrated mills—was rendered inefficient and obsolete in both Western Europe and the United States (OECD 1983; Toyne et al. 1984).

Notwithstanding various attempts at protection from and/or circumvention of these challenges,[1] few nations were spared the disabling consequences these changes held for their domestic textile-apparel industries. In the United States, 282,000 jobs were lost in the textile-apparel industry between 1980 and 1985 (Office of Technology Assessment 1987: 7). Loss in employment was matched by decreases in market share. For example, whereas apparel imports constituted only 2 percent of domestic consumption in 1963, by the late 1980s they had captured over 50 percent of the U.S. market (Dertouzos et al. 1989: 15).

The West German textile-apparel industry also suffered severe dislocation. Between 1970 and 1983, West German textile imports nearly tripled, while the number of domestic textile mills decreased by one-third—from 2,396 in 1970 to only 1,620 in 1980. The reduction in the number of firms was accompanied by a steady decrease in textile employment. Between 1957 and 1980, 350,000 workers lost their jobs in the West German textile industry (Nelson 1987). The situation appeared equally severe, if not worse, in other West European countries (Katzenstein 1984; Cobrin 1990; Dertouzos et al. 1989).[2]

In fact, the crisis of the textile-apparel industry appeared so severe that by the early 1970s scholars and policymakers alike were beginning to theorize about a "new international division of labor" in which "mature" industries like textiles would be ceded to developing countries that possessed an abundance of low-wage, unskilled labor and,

---

[1]See MIT Commission on Industrial Productivity 1989a for a discussion of attempts by the U.S. textile industry to promote protectionism and adopt a "Southern strategy" to circumvent these challenges. For European strategies, see Marchionatti 1987. For an interesting comparison with a non-Western nation that successfully adjusted its industry, see Dore 1986.

[2]The Italian literature on this industry is packed with international comparisons. See, for example, Fornengo 1985; Correale and Gaeta 1983: 145–92; and Federtessile 1986b.

thus, could manufacture labor-intensive products like textiles at lower costs (Froebel, Heinricks, and Kreye 1980; OECD 1983).

The Italian industry was hit particularly hard by this crisis for a variety of reasons, including the high costs of labor and credit, inefficient state intervention, structural weaknesses in the sector's productive structure, and the fragmentation of the industry's distribution networks (Turani 1976; Federtessile 1980). Following the Hot Autumn of 1969 and the severe economic crisis of the 1970s, the cost of both labor and credit (necessary to finance purchases of raw materials and production runs which in this industry take place long before deliveries are made) in Italy were among the highest of all Western nations.[3] These financial constraints were compounded by ill-advised programs of state intervention which purchased and supported failing firms and hence sustained overcapacity in the sector (Adams 1985: 171–201). Finally, the productive structure of the Italian industry— composed of both large, integrated firms and many small shops of suboptimal size—was weak in that large firms produced long series of standardized, low-to-medium quality goods (the first to be captured by Newly Industrialized Countries [NIC] producers) and small firms did not have sufficient resources and contact with the market (often they operated solely as subcontractors for large firms) to develop into autonomous and viable enterprises.

As a result, Italian textile employment experienced a major reduction in the 1970s. For instance, a comparison of the 1971 and 1981 Industry Census reveals a drop in textile employment by 49,485 workers (from 542,908 in 1971 to 493,423 in 1981).[4] During these same years, Italian firms that had once dominated the European market— Lanificio Rossi, Lanificio Rivetti, Marzotto, Lebole, Cantoni, Bassetti— all suffered tremendous financial and organizational problems. Some went bankrupt and were rescued by the state or acquired by competitors.

The crisis of Italy's textile-apparel industry was especially critical given its importance to the national economy. This sector is one of Italy's largest industrial employers. In the 1960s and throughout the 1970s, textile-apparel employment in Italy was significantly above the European Community average (OECD 1983: 15). If one includes the

---

[3] This section draws from Federtessile 1986a.
[4] These figures are from ISTAT, 5th and 6th *Censimento Generale dell'industria, del commercio, dei servizi, e dell'artigianato,* reported in Contarino 1984.

number of undeclared workers employed in the small shops of the "underground economy," employment in this sector is probably much larger (Frey 1975).

The textile-apparel industry is also critical for Italy's balance of payments. Textiles have maintained a trade surplus for most of the postwar period. For a nation that is highly dependent on foreign sources of energy and raw materials, this surplus is very important to the overall health and stability of the nation's economy.

By the end of the 1980s, the situation of the Italian textile industry appeared completely reversed. Far from fulfilling the expectations of those theorizing a new international division of labor, firm-level profitability, productivity, and investment increased dramatically among Italian textile firms over the course of the decade (Confindustria 1990). Both large integrated firms as well as industrial districts of small- and medium-sized companies successfully adjusted to the new terms of international competition. Although employment decreased in the 1980s by about 14 percent, most of that decline occurred during the first half of the decade and employment appeared to stabilize after 1986. Likewise, the use of *cassa integrazione*, which had grown tremendously in the mid-1980s, decreased again by the end of the decade (Confindustria 1990: 80). In fact, by the end of the decade, Italy emerged as one of the industrialized world's leading textile-apparel exporters, with about 10 percent world market share and exports totaling 16.6 billion U.S. dollars in 1988.[5]

How do we account for this reversal of industrial performance? Especially when thinking about Italy, one's first instinct is to assume that lower labor costs and labor "sweating" in the underground economy must be behind the resurgence of Italian textiles. Yet closer examination of the data reveals how misleading this very common assumption actually is. Table 5.1 indicates that hourly earnings in the Italian textile-apparel industry in 1978 were higher than those of most of its European competitors. In Chapter 1 we also saw how Italian wages actually increased over the course of the 1980s. Thus, the revitalization of the Italian textile-apparel industry does not appear to have been at the expense of workers' wages.

[5] Market share data was obtained from United Nations Statistical Office, *International Trade Statistics Yearbook* (New York: United Nations, 1992). Export revenues are reported in Confindustria 1990: 89–90.

Table 5.1. Relative hourly earnings in the textile and clothing industries, 1967 and 1978 (Index numbers, average for manufacturing each year = 100)

Country	Textile industry		Clothing industry	
	1967	1978	1967	1978
Austria	80.1[a]	74.9	75.9	64.4
Belgium	86.4	81.4	73.6	68.7
Canada	74.2	72.7	67.1	70.1
Denmark	82.5	89.2	82.5	85.5
Finland	79.0	77.5	74.3	72.1
France	80.6	84.5	84.0	76.9
West Germany	84.6	83.2	78.3	74.7
Italy	82.5	89.6[b]	74.6	82.1[b]
Netherlands	94.5	92.9	68.9	73.6
Norway	81.7	80.9	78.9	75.8
Sweden	82.6	88.5	78.0	83.8
Switzerland	80.1	82.7	71.8	73.1
United Kingdom	82.0	85.4	67.4	64.0
United States	73.0	69.6	72.0	63.9

Source: OECD, *Textile and Clothing Industries, Structural Problems and Policies in OECD Countries* (Paris: OECD, 1983): 79.

Note: Relative hourly earnings = wages for time worked including time rates, piece rates, shift supplements, overtime supplements and regularly paid bonuses and premiums.

[a]Figure refers to 1977.
[b]Figure refers to 1969.

A second possible explanation focuses on protectionism. Perhaps, as is the case with Japanese automobile imports, Italy possesses a particular trade barrier against imported textiles, above and beyond what other European nations enjoy through the Multi-Fiber Agreement. Again, the data contradict this hypothesis. Over the course of the 1980s, Italian exports increased significantly, but so did imports. Between 1980 and 1986, imports increased 65 percent, from 2.866 to 4.738 billion U.S. dollars (Confindustria 1990: 95). Thus, cheap labor costs and protected markets do not explain the turnaround of Italy's textile industry.

A third possible explanation looks to industrial policy. Perhaps the textile industry benefited from an unusually effective government industrial policy and/or from a well-orchestrated reorganization strategy negotiated by the industry's peak business and labor associations. No doubt, the government tried to reorganize the textile industry, first through the so-called Textile Law (Law 1011 of 1971) and again through the Industrial Restructuring and Reconversion Act (Law 675 of 1977). It also used IRI, ENI, and GEPI to rescue failing private companies.[6]

None of these interventions, however, had a significant impact on the basic structure of the industry or the strategies of individual firms. Like many of the other reforms examined in Chapters 2 and 3, Law 1011 was poorly implemented. Although it reduced textile firms' social security payments by 5 percent for three years, its sectoral reorganization plans went unfulfilled. In ways that foreshadowed the Industrial Restructuring and Reconversion Act, Law 1011 promoted a series of poorly defined and difficult to implement sectoral plans. And, like Law 675, years passed before funds from the Textile Law were disbursed. As a result, many firms simply withdrew their applications for government support, and what funds were eventually released went to finance the adjustment strategies already in progress in several large firms (Piattoni 1986). Thus, like the other cases we have observed, government funding supported the adjustment strategies of individual firms but did not guide the reorganization of the industry as a whole.

Various business and union strategies were equally ineffective. During the latter half of the 1970s, Italy's national textile workers union, Federazione Unitaria Lavoratori Tessile-Abbigliamento (FULTA) also supported sectoral planning as a way of resolving the industry's problems. But the union's proposals were too vague and often combined seemingly contradictory strategies (rationalization of the industry and maintenance of current employment levels). Moreover, the union's ability to implement its strategy varied tremendously in different regions of the country (Contarino 1984) and was sometimes even resisted by local or regional unions. As a result, it was eventually abandoned by the early 1980s.

Interestingly, although Confindustria opposed all government intervention in the industry, including sectoral planning, many of its affiliated textile companies embraced these government and union strategies. As a result, many of these firms took advantage of the

[6]Government bailouts began in 1957, when IRI purchased Maniffature Cotoniere Meridionali (MCM). With 5,000 employees in 1955, MCM was at the time the largest industrial company in the Mezzogiorno. In 1962, ENI purchased Lanerossi and Lebole and, over the next decade, continued to absorb other textile companies. In 1974, it established Tescom, its own financial holding company to manage various textile operations. Between 1971 and 1974, 44 percent of GEPI's funds were dedicated to the textile industry. For more on government bailouts during these years, see Adams 1985: 178–79.

Pirelli Commission's proposed reform of Confindustria and formed their own federation, Federtessile. Throughout the next decade, Federtessile opposed Confindustria's more conservative positions and instead worked closely with local and national unions in facilitating the textile industry's adjustment (Lombardi 1986).

As in the other reform efforts examined in this book, various initiatives to direct the adjustment process *from above* failed. Notwithstanding this failure, or rather because of it, these government-inspired initiatives reinforced adjustment strategies already in progress throughout the industry. Laws 1011 and 675 failed to develop coherent sectoral plans but nonetheless disbursed necessary funds to individual companies struggling to adjust. Likewise, peak-level union and business strategies floundered, but in their wake some very innovative patterns of local-level labor-management cooperation developed (Guidotti 1986; Zoccatelli 1991).

To truly understand the reorganization of the Italian textile industry, we need to look more closely at the adjustment strategies developed by individual firms and clusters of firms (districts). Extensive literature exists on the reorganization of the Italian textile-apparel industry (Camuffo and Comacchio 1990; Canziani 1989; Locke and Antonelli 1990; Roverato 1988; and Zanfei 1985). Essentially, over the course of the last two decades, two very different patterns of adjustment emerged. On the one hand, many previously integrated firms decentralized various phases of their production cycles to smaller nearby firms. Networks of highly specialized and flexible firms developed as a result of this strategy (Belussi 1989; Lazerson 1988; Nardin 1987; Rullani and Zanfei 1988; Trigilia 1989). On the other hand, some large firms increased their degree of integration and invested heavily in new process and product technologies (Camuffo and Comacchio 1990; Confindustria 1990).

Neither one of these strategies, however, was entirely successful everywhere but produced mixed results for companies situated in very different local economies. For example, although textile mills in the Biellese were able to successfully decentralize various phases of their production and develop a strong network of small- and medium-sized firms that collaborated with one another in developing new products, introducing new technologies, purchasing raw materials, training and/or retraining workers, and exhibiting their products, the textile industry in Prato experienced tremendous difficulties in the late 1980s and early 1990s. Once seen as a model of small-scale, flexibly specialized production (Piore and Sabel 1984; Trigilia 1989), by the late 1980s the textile industry in Prato had become so fragmented that many of its local firms lacked the resources to invest in new product and process technologies. As a result, when demand for their traditional products (regenerated woolen fabrics) contracted, these companies were unable to shift quickly into new market niches with new kinds of products (Ritaine 1990; Harrison 1994).

The same was true for the more integrated, large-scale model of adjustment. Some firms (e.g., Marzotto) successfully adapted to changing market conditions by further integrating their production processes, automating their factories, and developing strong ties to large retail chains. Yet other large manufacturers (Lanerossi, Bassetti) failed to rationalize their operations and subsequently went bankrupt or were taken over by their competitors.

After repeated visits to several textile areas throughout Italy, and scores of interviews with local managers, unionists, business association leaders, and local government officials (see the Appendix for a list of interviewees), it became apparent to me that the ability of individual textile firms or even clusters of firms (districts) to successfully adjust along either one of these lines depended upon the qualitative features of the local economy within which the firms were embedded. For example, successful industrial districts relied upon the existence of an underlying network of sociopolitical groups and associations capable of coordinating strategies, diffusing information, and mediating conflicts among the growing number of small- and medium-sized producers. Where this underlying sociopolitical network existed, as in the case of Biella, the increased fragmentation of the local industry did not lead to productive overcapacity and underinvestment in new technologies and/or in the skill-formation of the work force (as was the case in Prato). Instead, the reconfiguration of the local industry was regulated and somewhat offset by various arrangements (territorial collective bargaining) and institutions (Centro Studi Oreste Rivetti) that provided various collective or quasi-public goods (training, marketing advice, technical assistance) to local firms.

However, what mattered was not simply the overall number of local secondary associations—Prato has as many local groups and clubs as Biella—but rather the way relations among these groups were structured. Whereas in Biella, the various associations and interest groups were linked to one another through multiple, relatively equal ties, in Prato relations among the various actors were much more hierarchical. In Prato, certain groups like the local *impannatori* (transformers) possessed much more power than other local actors.[7] As a result, the distribution of resources and the flow of information among local actors was heavily skewed in their favor. This more hierarchical structure of relations had serious implications for the ability of the local industry to adjust. When the impannatori's clients in various export markets reduced their orders, for example, the many local firms which had depended upon the impannatori for their own business experienced tremendous difficulties because they lacked their own, direct ties to these markets and linkages with other market intermediaries. Moreover, their lack of knowledge about changing consumer trends and their limited resources prevented the producers from developing new products for different market niches.

A similar analysis could also be made for the more large-scale, integrated producers. The ability of these firms to implement their adjustment policies also depended upon the kinds of local resources they had at hand (see Camuffo 1993 for a good comparison of Marzotto and Lanerossi). In short, the alternative adjustment strategies pursued by Italian textile firms relied on the existence of particular sociopolitical relations and resources that were present in some local economies, but not in others.

We now turn to an examination of Biella, Italy's leading woolen textile district. Although much of what follows is very specific to Biella, the study nonetheless illustrates the more general argument about the role of local sociopolitical networks in shaping the adjustment strategies of Italian textile firms.[8]

Industrial Crisis and Restructuring in the Biellese

The Biellese, a small area located in the mountainous northwest section of Piedmont, is the birthplace of Italy's industrial revolution.

---

[7]For more on Prato's industrial structure, see Lorenzoni 1980.

[8]The choice of Biella as a case was made after interviewing national, regional, and local business and union leaders throughout Italy, and after visiting numerous textile companies in Busto-Arsizio, Bergamo-Brescia, Carpi, Como, Vincentino, and Prato.

The "Manchester of Italy,"[9] this area consists of eighty-three small towns and villages and about 200,000 residents. Yet, despite its isolation and fragmentation, the Biellese area is a leader in the world's textile industry.[10]

With over 90,000 people active in the labor market, the Biellese area has one of the highest participation rates (45.2 percent vs. the national average of 39.8 percent) in the country. And, with 235 out of every 1,000 residents employed in industry, the Biellese is the most industrial district in all of Italy. The Biellese has over 5,000 firms with approximately 44,000 workers. The vast majority of these firms (3,000) and workers (35,000) are employed in the woolen textile industry. In 1990, the textile industry produced 6,000 billion lire in sales, of which one-third was exported to West Germany, Japan, France, and the United States. Working in close collaboration with textile mills, Biella also has a flourishing textile machinery industry. In 1990 it employed 2,500 workers and generated 450 billion lire in sales. For a sector that is in crisis in almost every advanced industrial nation of the West, this is a notable achievement.

Yet Biella was not always successful. During the 1960s and 1970s the local textile industry was in trouble. Many firms threatened bankruptcy and a number actually shut down. Changing conditions of international competition (NICs with lower labor costs are very strong in the textile-apparel sector) combined with increased labor and energy costs and altered consumer tastes to render traditional integrated textile firms uncompetitive. Only through a massive process of industrial restructuring and technological innovation was the industry restored to health.

The restructuring of the Biellese occurred in two phases. During the first phase in the 1960s, traditional mill owners sought to lower production costs and circumvent labor rigidities by outsourcing various phases of their production processes and investing in some labor-saving technologies. In this initial phase of restructuring, the firms did not have a coherent strategy, nor did they seek to work with

Others have already written about many of these districts. See, for example, Lazerson 1988, and Utili 1989 on Carpi; Contarino 1984, and Magatti 1991 on Busto-Arsizio; Istituto Guglielmo Tagliacarne 1989, and Trigilia 1989 on Prato; and Roverato 1986, Belussi 1989, and Camuffo and Camacchio 1990 on the Vincentino.

[9] This term was taken from Secchia 1960.

[10] These and the following figures are taken from Confindustria 1990: 69; and Unione Industriale Biellese 1987c.

the local unions in resolving the crisis of their traditional system of production. As a result, there was substantial "sweating" of labor and thus, significant conflict between labor and management.

The second phase of restructuring in the Biellese occurred in the late 1960s to early 1970s. Following a massive flood in 1968, which destroyed numerous plants and disrupted production for nearly all the local mills, firms began to decentralize certain phases of their traditional production cycles and introduce new technologies in a systematic way. Unlike in the early 1960s, this second wave of restructuring involved the participation of the local labor movement. Moreover, the breakup of large firms and the development of a network of smaller, more specialized enterprises resulted in the overall upgrading of production, increased coordination and cooperation among local firms, and a territorial collective bargaining agreement that protected all workers in the industry regardless of their employer's dimensions.

A more careful examination of this two-phase process is interesting because it allows us to refine traditional views of industrial adjustment. For instance, the Biella case allows us to update some of the claims regarding economic backwardness often associated with the decentralization of production that took place in Italy (and elsewhere) during these years. Moreover, the story of the Biellese illustrates how equally efficient but divergent adjustment strategies can coexist within the same sector.

The crisis of the Biellese textile district preceded the more general downturn of the industry in the 1970s. It was triggered by the transformation of the textile industry's distribution network in the 1960s. In the 1940s and 1950s, textile mills produced cloth for a fragmented market consisting of either wholesalers or intermediaries who, in turn, sold the cloth to individual customers: tailors, dressmakers, and private individuals. Textiles were considered consumer goods and each firm's identity was clearly associated with its products (Scanziani 1986).

Beginning in the 1960s, with the development of the apparel industry, this original distribution network was transformed. Textile mills no longer manufactured consumer goods for direct consumers. Instead they produced semifinished products for apparel firms which, in turn, transformed the cloth into clothing and sold it to their own customers. Thus, beginning in the 1960s, textile mills no longer dealt with a myriad of smaller customers but with only a few major clients who acquired ever greater amounts of material and thus, increased power vis-à-vis the textile mills. Whereas in the 1940s and 1950s textile mills could impose their products on the market, they now confronted a stronger and more demanding clientele. To satisfy these new clients' demands, the Biellese mills were forced to continue to produce high quality goods, but at lower prices. This resulted in decreased profits which, in turn, hindered investments and furthered the dependence of these mills on their apparel industry clients.

The renewal of the national contract for the textile industry in 1962 further aggravated the situation for the Biellese mills. Like elsewhere in Italy, this round of contract negotiations elicited major labor conflicts and strikes. Essentially workers demanded a share in the fruits of Italy's economic miracle of the late 1950s and early 1960s. Thus, with the renewal of this contract, labor costs increased by 23 percent in just one year. As a result, mill owners began to invest in new automatic looms that required fewer workers to operate. Through these capital investments (which did not, however, effect the general organization of the firms) 1,700 workers were expelled from this sector (Frey 1975: 295; Ciochetti and Ramella 1964).

Yet the situation did not improve for the local industry. Due to Italy's economic downturn between 1963 and 1967, domestic demand (then, Biella's largest market) for textiles stagnated and certain local firms began to falter. During this period, approximately 7,000 workers were expelled from the industry (Frey 1975: 296), most of them previously employed in large, integrated mills (e.g., Lanificio Rivetti), which were forced to close.

Many firms began to dismantle and decentralize certain phases of production in these years. Yet the results appeared uncertain. For instance, although many small firms were established during this period (see Table 5.2), general levels of employment, investment, and average income faltered. In fact, whereas the Biellese was one of the ten most affluent areas in Italy in the 1950s and early 1960s, its standing slipped significantly between the mid-1960s and early 1970s.[11] Thus, when Luigi Frey and his associates conducted their famous study on decentralized production in Italy during this period, they included Biella as one of the cases illustrating the growth of

[11] For more on the divergent and uncertain strategies of this period, see CERPI 1971.

Table 5.2. Employment by firm size in the Biellese, 1965–1969

Firm size (By # of employees)	1965				1969			
	Firms		Employees		Firms		Employees	
	Number	Percent	Number	Percent	Number	Percent	Number	Percent
1–10	281	42.6	970	2.6	540	57.6	1,942	5.3
11–50	228	34.5	5,606	15.2	251	26.8	6,416	17.5
51–100	80	12.1	5,401	14.6	68	7.3	4,685	12.8
101–500	59	8.9	13,551	36.8	67	7.1	14,414	39.2
501–1000	5	0.8	3,250	8.9	8	0.9	5,761	15.7
1000+	7	1.1	8,084	21.9	3	0.3	3,480	9.5

Source: Luigi Frey, ed. *Lavoro a domicilio e decentramento dell'attivita produttiva nei settori tessili e dell'abbiglianeto Italia* (Milan: Franco Angeli, 1975): 298.

exploitative relations between large-scale enterprises and low-paid workers producing at home or in small shops.

The flood of 1968 marked a turning point in Biella's process of industrial restructuring. In many ways, the flood was a blessing in disguise. Although it caused widespread devastation, it also unleashed substantial sums of state aid (primarily subsidized credit) to reorganize and rebuild the industry. The flood also changed the psychology and/or identity of the mill owners, according to the numerous mill owners I interviewed. Previously, these owner-managers had been very "privatistic" or "isolationist" (their own words) in their attitudes and approaches to their problems. Rather than band together to develop a common strategy to confront their problems in the 1960s, they competed against and undermined one another in desperate attempts to satisfy their apparel industry clients. Following the flood, things began to change as these entrepreneurs began to develop a collective identity and increasingly sought to cooperate among themselves.[12] In addition, with the introduction of new technologies, firms began to specialize in particular phases of the production cycle and to coordinate their production with other, complementary firms.

Relations between mill owners and the local unions also began to change after the flood. Workers and their unions became increasingly

[12]Based on interviews with several local manufacturers, including: Alberto Brocca, president of the Unione Industriale Biellese, May 22, 1987; Paolo Botto, president, Lanificio Giuseppe Botto & Figli, Biella, July 17, 1987; and Paolo Ferla, Lanificio Egidio Ferla, S.p.A, Ponzone, May 22 and May 27, 1987.

involved in the restructuring process of the local industry. Sometimes, workers were given plant equipment and start-up capital to open their own, more specialized shops. As a result, they continued to perform their previous jobs as employees, but within their own smaller businesses.

In short, with the flood of 1968, the restructuring process in the Biellese textile district changed dramatically. In this second phase of restructuring, the organization of production, the type of technologies implemented, and the world views of the different organized actors all changed to promote the successful adjustment of the local industry.

For most firms, restructuring occurred through the simultaneous modernization of the weaving shops and the decentralization of traditionally labor-intensive jobs like mending, dyeing, and various processes associated with spinning. Within the weaving shops, new, automatic looms (Sulzers) were introduced. These looms increased productivity, since they were faster and more reliable, and thus managers could assign more machines to each worker. They also improved product quality and variety. The looms were more flexible in that they could work with different yarns, in different patterns, with fewer mistakes or imperfections. Internally companies preserved only those phases of production in which they were most specialized and/or which most distinguished their products. They decentralized the other, typically labor-intensive tasks to nearby shops.

This particular process of restructuring changed the overall industrial geography of the area. For example, in 1970 there were six woolen mills employing between 500 and 1,000 workers and one mill with more than 1,000 employees. By 1979, only one firm employing between 500 and 1,000 employees remained in the area, and there were none with more than 1,000 workers (Ferla 1981). The reorganization process also spawned the development of many new, smaller firms specializing in specific phases of the production process like dyeing and finishing (see Table 5.3).

Increased specialization promoted innovations in product and process technologies for both the original and newly established firms. Products evolved away from traditional, heavy woolens and increased in both quality and creativity through the use of new fibers and/or new ways of weaving or finishing traditional fibers (e.g., "Cool Wool"). Economics of scale were achieved in two basic ways: 1) weaving mills were able to efficiently produce smaller batches of woolens using

Table 5.3. Industrial and artisanal textile-apparel firms in the Biellese, by productive activity

	1962	1965	1968	1973	1978
Spinning and weaving	187	145	130	131	123
Combed wool spinning	181	169	182	242	294
Twisting	82	73	91	131	152
Dyeing	18	18	20	15	15
Finishing	18	18	20	15	15

Source: Elaboration of data presented in Sergio Scanziani, "Profili di analisi del sistema tessile biellese," Tesi di Laurea, Facoltà di Economia e Commercio, Università Commerciale Luigi Bocconi, Milan, 1986: 202–5.

more flexible, universal looms; and 2) dyeing, finishing, and mending contractors were able to aggregate large volumes of work from several different client textile firms.

A network emerged among the different firms engaged in the various processes of production. Cooperation developed not only between the original weaving mills and their dyeing or finishing subcontractors, but also among mills that employed the same suppliers. In other words, increased collaboration between the mills and their new subcontractors led to greater cooperation among competitors as well.[13] This, in turn, further promoted product and process innovations as firms exchanged experiences and techniques with new machines, new fibers, and new finishing processes.

Several owner-managers I interviewed explained that before buying a new machine or initiating a new process, they visited other local plants in the area which had already installed these innovations and conducted tests with their own products.[14] Biellese managers exchanged information and shared experiences with new techniques and technologies during visits to the local Rotary club, business association (Unione Industriale Biellese), and to certain *trattorie* (local restaurants).

New market strategies also emerged from this reorganization process. Most firms changed to produce specialized products for specific market niches. Moreover, while Biellese textile firms continued to remain competitive with one another and very protective of their

[13]For more on the diffusion of innovation between users and suppliers and also among competitors, see von Hippel 1988; and his essay, "Cooperation between Rivals: Informal Know-How Trading," *Research Policy* 16 (1987): 291–302.

[14]Interview with Ferla 1987 and with Pier Luigi Loro Piana and Sergio Loro Piana, copresidents of Lanificio Ing. Loro Piana & Co., S.p.A, Quarona Sesia, June 10, 1987.

individual firm autonomy, they nonetheless united both to buy raw materials (setting up purchasing cartels) and to sell their finished goods (organizing international trade fairs like "IdeaBiella" and "Pitti Filati," at which they exhibit their latest products). They also organized training programs for managers and workers, established a research facility for textile technology and product development, built an airport, rebuilt existing roads, and carried out a wide range of lobbying activities in Rome to enhance government support of their area.[15] By the late 1980s, the industrial landscape of the Biellese was consolidated with local firms thriving and employment once again stable (Unione Industriale Biellese 1987c).

The transformation of the Biellese area illustrates the limits of the traditional literature on the decentralization of production. Normally, this process is described as entailing the outsourcing of production from large firms to smaller shops so as to reduce costs and increase savings. Often, an element of exploitation is involved in this process. Yet, the evolution of the Biellese textile district indicates that this characterization is not entirely accurate.

Although exploitation and backwardness certainly did exist in textile districts like Biella during the 1960s and early 1970s, they are only half the story. The other half is one of dramatic industrial change and the promotion of major organizational and technological innovation during the last two decades.

During this second period of restructuring, the transformation of industry in the Biellese entailed the reorganization of production so that it was no longer structured in a rigid sequential line, but rather through highly specialized, complementary phases.[16] As described above, this process entailed the decentralization of successive phases of the production cycle and, then, the development of a network of smaller firms, specializing in particular jobs previously handled internally by the large, integrated mills.

Along with this change, an evolution in the type of technology used by the Biellese mills also occurred. More flexible and universal machines supplanted technologies dedicated exclusively to one product. New shuttleless looms, for example, could work on several differ-

[15]This section draws on data and documents obtained during an interview with Brocca 1987, and Arnaldo Cartotto, Unione Industriale Biellese, Biella, May 22, June 10, 1987.
[16]This section draws on multiple interviews and plant visits in the Biellese during the spring and summer of 1987. See Appendix for a complete list of those interviewed.

ent fibers (cotton, wool, and silk) and thus could produce a broader range of products.

The reorganization of production by phases also reduced stocks and increased plant utilization rates. Previously, when almost all firms were integrated and possessed the entire production cycle, many shops (dye shops) were active at most only three to four hours a day. The newly reorganized firms, however, were able to work two to three shifts per day, which permitted them not only to utilize their plant's capacity better but also to invest more easily in new technologies, since the more efficient utilization of these machines dramatically reduced their payback period. Hence, a virtuous cycle developed in which firms were increasingly capable of producing higher quality products more efficiently and, thus, better able to respond to the ever-greater volatility of demand and the decreases in product life cycles characteristic of this industry.

My examination of the restructuring of the Biellese textile district casts doubt on another misleading assumption common to the literature. In Biella we find not one predominant pattern of industrial organization but three basic groups of firms following slightly different strategies.[17]

One group consists of firms like Lanificio Ferla, which produce in quasi-artisanal ways extremely high-quality and high-fashion textiles for exclusive clothing boutiques and high-quality manufacturers (Louis of Boston, Hickey Freeman of New York). A second group of Biellese firms, like Lanificio Ing. Loro Piana and Cerruti, employ the latest technologies to manufacture high-fashion, high-quality woolens for top industrial apparel firms like Gruppo Finanziario Tessile of Turin and Hart and Shaftner and Marx of Chicago. Finally, a small group of still-integrated firms employing the latest labor-saving technologies compete by manufacturing medium-high quality goods for industrial apparel firms with whom they have long-standing relations. These integrated firms have invested heavily in new process technologies in order to render their production extremely efficient. Moreover, they, too, rely on some subcontracting in order to enhance their own flexibility and, thus, better respond to their clients' needs without disrupting or altering their own internal production system.

[17]See note 16. This section also draws on interviews with Donatella Canta, regional secretary, Filtea Piedmont, Turin, October 20, 1987; and Ezio Becchis, IRES-CGIL Piemonte, Turin, October 20, 1987. For a similar analysis of the situation, see Gaeta 1987.

In short, within the Biellese one finds three different groups of firms employing different mixes of technology, organization, and skills to manufacture more or less the same goods competitively. Their competitiveness, however, rests on slightly different strategies. Thus, although Ferla may emphasize design and small batch production, Loro Piana competes through the use of new technologies and high-quality raw materials. Botto remains competitive by using both modern looms and integrated production methods to produce medium-high quality goods at lower prices and by establishing close links with several large clients.

A better picture of these different strategies can perhaps best be provided through sketches or vignettes of a number of individual firms. These sketches are not comprehensive, nor are they complete. They are based on interviews and plant visits and are intended only to provide an idea of the range of choices textile firms in the Biellese pursued during the recent wave of restructuring.

A Few Vignettes

Lanificio Egidio Ferla[18] is a small, artisan-style woolen mill that manufactures high-quality, high-priced woolens for specialty boutiques and customized clothiers. In many ways, the history of Lanificio Ferla is characteristic of that of most other firms in the area. Founded in the mid-nineteenth century in Pollone, a small village in the mountains above Biella, Lanificio Ferla developed over the nineteenth and twentieth centuries into a horizontally integrated textile mill.

However, following the crisis of the textile industry in the 1960s, particularly severe for firms with this type of organizational structure, Lanificio Ferla began to restructure. Like all firms in crisis, the company cut its work force, from 150 in the 1960s to 75 by the late 1980s. At the same time, it reduced the number of operations performed within its own plant and entered into close collaboration with other smaller, more specialized enterprises to provide needed services like finishing and dyeing.

Most important, Ferla changed its product line, moving upscale to produce higher quality fabrics. The firm produces hundreds of different types of cloth to be transformed into tailored men's suits

[18]Based on information gathering during an interview with Paolo Ferla 1987.

and jackets. Lanificio Ferla also reorganized its marketing structures. In the past, the firm employed seven sales agents who traveled abroad; following the reorganization of the 1970s, the owner-manager himself travels to Paris, Frankfurt, and New York and maintains close contacts with designers and his principal clients. Paolo Ferla also spoke of attending fashion fairs and visiting other local and nonlocal firms (such as Benetton), to see new machinery in operation and of trying out his own samples on this equipment. My visits to other factories in the area revealed that this was standard practice among the Biellese mills.

Lanificio F.lli Piacenza operates in a similar market niche and with analogous technologies and organizational structures.[19] Established in 1733, Lanificio Piacenza manufactures among the most beautiful and expensive cashmeres and mohairs in the world for women's clothing. In the 1960s, Piacenza, like Ferla, was a horizontally integrated firm. Yet, in the early 1970s, the firm constructed a new plant and simultaneously changed its organizational structure. It retained only the dyeing, weaving, and finishing phases of the production cycle within the firm. Spinning and other related processes were subcontracted out to smaller, independent firms with which Piacenza has long-term relations. This reorganization of production reflected the firm's decision to increase specialization in those phases of production most important to the identity of the firm and the quality of its products.

The firm is owned and run by three brothers and employs about 200 workers. After the introduction of new labor-saving looms in 1973, employment fell by about one-third. However, it remained stable throughout the 1970s and increased slightly in the early 1980s as a result of the firm's successful growth. Like Ferla, Lanificio Piacenza maintains certain ancient machines, such as cards, alongside its modern looms and computers in order to finish high-quality woolens in artisanal fashion.

Relying on external designers for assistance, the firm produces each year four collections consisting of about 370 to 430 separate articles. It renews about 10 to 12 percent of its product range annually and exports around 40 percent of its production yearly, mostly to Japan. In 1987 sales amounted to 30.5 billion lire. The affiliated businesses

[19]This section relies heavily on information available from the Osservatorio Tessile Biellese coordinated by IRES-CGIL Piemonte in Turin, and on Ferla 1981.

of this and similar firms are indicative of its strategies. Aside from a small apparel firm that transforms about 3 percent of its own production into clothing for a small number of exclusive designers, Lanificio Piacenza also owns PAL, a small airplane company. PAL grew as a result of the textile mill's own marketing needs. Used primarily by the owner-managers to travel abroad to sell their products, the planes are also hired by other Biellese firms for similar purposes and by the local business association (Unione Industriale Biellese) to fly local mail to Switzerland in order to expedite affiliates' correspondence with foreign markets.

Lanificio Ing. Loro Piana & Co.[20] of Quarona Sesia, another tiny village in the Italian pre-Alps, operates in the same market segment, but with radically different methods. Founded in 1924 by the current owner-managers' grandfather, the firm developed a product-oriented strategy. During the 1970s, however, this product-driven strategy proved unable to adapt to changing market conditions, and the firm was threatened with bankruptcy. At the same time, however, the two grandsons of the founder, recent graduates of Bocconi University in Milan, entered the firm and began to modernize its structures and adapt its strategy.

The two brothers, Sergio and Pier Luigi Loro Piana, reorganized production away from a wide range of different products for different markets and toward a highly specialized market niche of high-quality, high-priced woolens and woolen mixes. In order to do this, they invested heavily in marketing and in new technologies (spinning machines, weaving looms, computer-assisted design) which enhanced productivity and product quality. In contrast to many other firms in the area, they also began to integrate various phases of the production cycle. Previously, the company was solely a weaving firm. With the new strategy, in which product quality and firm identity were key, the firm began to develop its own spinning, dyeing, and finishing phases of production. It also established a policy to buy each year's prize-winning raw cashmere at international auctions.

Their strategy succeeded. In 1975 Lanificio Loro Piana manufactured 300,000 meters of cloth with 350 workers, generating 3.5 billion lire in sales. In 1985, annual production rose to 1.8 million meters produced by 370 workers, and sales grew to 84 billion lire. The firm

[20]Based on information gathered in an interview with Pier Luigi and Sergio Loro Piana 1987.

is now the world's leader in cashmere production and has opened plants in Latin America, Asia, and even Connecticut. It produces eight yearly collections consisting of about 140 different products. Consistent with the logic of this firm's strategy, products are designed internally, without recourse to outside specialists.

Characteristic of many of the Biellese firms is the way Loro Piana involves its work force in the process of technological innovation and in general firm strategy. Industrial relations at the firm are handled by one of the Loro Piana brothers. With the continuous introduction of new technologies—looms, spinning machines, and a computerized stock room—production workers and managers are retrained to work with the new technologies or in other areas of the plant. Workers and managers meet regularly to discuss product quality and potential improvements in the manufacturing process, and the entire firm meets yearly to discuss firm strategy. Unionization rates are high, and relations between management and the unions are "correct," according to Sergio Loro Piana. This impression was validated both through my own interviews and multiple visits to the firm, as well as by a detailed study of the company by the regional textile union, Filtea-CGIL Piemonte (Becchis and Montani 1988).

Located in the same market niche as, and perhaps serving as a model for, Loro Piana is Lanificio Ermenegildo Zegna.[21] Established in Trivero by its namesake in 1910, Lanificio Ermenegildo Zegna began as a weaving firm seeking to outcompete the then British leaders of the market. Zegna did this by producing extremely high-quality products but in shorter pieces, thus reducing the risk of unsold stock for their clients. Product quality was the principal ingredient of the firm's strategy, and firm managers traveled worldwide to ensure the firm a steady supply of the very best raw materials.

Zegna also began to label its textiles and required its clients, even when they transformed the cloth into clothing, to keep the label attached to the final product. As a result, by the 1930s, Zegna had established name recognition and presence in over forty markets abroad. To ensure the quality of its products, Zegna developed its own spinning, dyeing, and finishing processes in the 1930s. By the 1950s, Lanificio Ermenegildo Zegna was one of the most horizontally

---

[21] Based on information gathered in an interview with Pier Giorgio Colombo, general manager, Lanificio Ermenegildo Zegna, Trivero, July 16, 1987. For more on the community in which Lanificio Zegna is located, see CENSIS 1983.

integrated firms in the industry. It even internalized the "combing" phase of the production cycle, something only industry giants like Marzotto and Lanerossi in Veneto did.

With the crisis of the Biellese industry in the 1960s, Zegna restructured in two opposing ways. First, it decentralized certain phases of production (spinning and mending) to local artisans. It retained other phases (weaving and finishing) which were important for the identity of the firm's products and where the value added was greatest. Second, in response to the growth of the apparel industry, Zegna began to integrate vertically by opening its own factory for formal men's clothing. Over the course of the 1960s and 1970s, Zegna opened other apparel and accessory plants, both in Italy (Novara) and abroad (Spain and Switzerland). It also established commercial affiliates throughout Europe, the United States, and even Japan in order to ensure the increased internationalization of its sales. In the late 1980s, Zegna employed about 2,500 workers worldwide and generated about 300 billion lire in annual sales.

According to Pier Giorgio Colombo, general manager of the firm, despite its evolution, Zegna continues to follow a small batch/market niche strategy aimed at an extremely elite clientele. As a result, its production does not rely primarily on new technologies but rather on experienced and highly skilled workers to manufacture its products. This approach entails continuous training and retraining of personnel and the decentralization of the firm's decision-making. Moreover, Zegna is continuously seeking to improve both the quality of its products and the productivity of its operations. For instance, Zegna's textile division sells cloth both to its own apparel affiliates and to other, competing apparel firms in order to stimulate product innovation and efficiency through competition and cross-pollination of new ideas. The firm is also engaged in various "Quick Response" experiments in order to reduce production and delivery times.

No longer concentrating solely on textiles for men's formal wear, Zegna now manufactures textiles, knitwear, and accessories for both men's and women's sportswear. According to General Manager Colombo, Zegna was able to broaden its product range quite easily. Because its machinery was not specialized and its work force highly skilled, the same plant was easily reorganized to produce a variety of different products.

Lanificio Giuseppe Botto & Figli is unlike the other firms discussed so far in that it is both horizontally and vertically integrated.[22] Founded in 1876 as an integrated textile mill, Lanificio Botto did not decentralize any of its production in the turbulent 1970s. Instead, following the flood of 1968, which devastated the original plant, Lanificio Botto invested heavily in new technologies aimed at enhancing productivity and product quality. It also concentrated production in a market segment (medium-high quality standardized textiles for use by industrial apparel firms) appropriate to this technologically driven strategy and sought to guarantee this niche by developing long-term relations with its clients.

The firm employs 480 people and produces about 4 million meters of cloth a year. It also relies on a large sales network, composed both of firm employees and external agents, in order to preserve and expand its markets. During the 1970s, the firm was able to increase exports from 20 percent of total production in 1975 to over 60 percent in 1988. The firm has purchased interests in various knitwear and apparel companies. In 1987 sales amounted to over 160 billion lire.

As the above anecdotal accounts suggest, within the more general restructuring process that occurred in the Biellese, individual firms pursued a variety of strategies. Although most firms decentralized various phases of their production cycles, some did not. The same holds true for the introduction of new technologies: some firms completely revamped their plants while others were more selective about which technologies they appropriated. Relying on a variety of different local resources, textile companies in Biella were able to adapt through different mixes of organizational change, technological innovation, and human resource management policies.

Labor Relations in Biella

Equally interesting is the role unions played in these developments. Although most (but not all) restructured firms reduced their work forces, the transition from integrated to specialized production was usually negotiated with the union.[23] The union had a say in who was

---

[22]Based on information obtained in an interview with Paolo Botto, president of Lanificio Giuseppe Botto & Figli, Biella, July 17, 1987. See also Andersen 1981: 82–98 for more on Lanificio Giuseppe Botto.

[23]Based on data and documents obtained in an interview with Renzo Giardino, secretary general, Camera del Lavoro, Biella, June 10, 1987. Documents obtained include: Ufficio Economico Filtea Nazionale 1983; Ufficio Economico Filtea Nazionale 1984b and 1984a.

let go or put in Cassa Integrazione and was consulted on plans to innovate plants and introduce new technologies. In 1987, for instance, Biella's Chamber of Labor negotiated a restructuring plan with Lanificio Cerrutti, one of the area's oldest and most successful firms. In this plan, put forth by the local union, the firm guaranteed to maintain employment at the current level in exchange for enhanced labor flexibility after the restructuring process.

During the local industry's reorganization, the local union negotiated territorial collective bargaining agreements with the local business association in order to extend union strength in certain firms to other weaker sectors of the work force.[24] Not only did these territorial agreements protect workers, they also strengthened the unions by preventing whipsawing, enhancing workers' solidarity, and extending union agreements in large firms to the newly formed smaller firms.[25] As a result, the productive decentralization that took place in this area did not undermine union strength. Workers who remained within the restructured firms were often retrained in the use of new process and product technologies, while many who exited the firms set up their own small businesses, buying old machines from and often working as subcontractors for their original bosses.[26]

After 1985, with much of the local industry's reorganization completed, firm-level agreements supplanted these territorial accords. Indicative of the local union's continued strength, over 140 new firm-level contracts covering almost half of the area's industrial work force (in large and small firms alike) were negotiated within two years of this shift in bargaining structure. Firm-level contracts covered wage increases, flexible work time regimes, and retraining programs (Garavini, Calistri, and Cilona 1988: 66).

Labor relations were not always so tranquil in the Biellese. During the 1960s and 1970s, there were a number of strikes and even a few factory occupations. The local union is militant and factory owners are far from complacent about it. Although the workers are primarily

---

[24] For a good description of these territorial agreements, see Camera del Lavoro Territoriale Biellese 1987.

[25] This is also based on interviews with various union leaders at different levels of the union hierarchy, including Giardino 1987; Canta 1987; Mario Agostinelli, regional secretary, CGIL Lombardia, Sesto San Giovanni, June 11, 1987; Agostino Megale, national secretariat, Filtea-CGIL, Rome, October 13, 1987; Gianni Amoretti, national secretary, Filtea-CGIL, Rome, October 13, 1987.

[26] For more on this, see Paolo Ferla 1981: 59; and Giardino 1984.

Table 5.4.   Employment by industrial sector in the Biellese, 1976–1986

Year	Textile-apparel		Mechanical engineering		Others		Total	
	Number	Percent	Number	Percent	Number	Percent	Number	Percent
1976	33,086	73.4	5,828	12.9	6,166	13.7	45,080	100.0
1977	32,631	73.2	5,836	13.1	6,102	13.7	44,569	100.0
1978	32,301	73.0	5,837	13.2	6,121	13.8	44,259	100.0
1979	33,303	73.2	5,932	13.0	6,216	13.7	45,501	100.0
1980	32,983	71.9	6,732	14.7	6,131	13.4	45,846	100.0
1981	32,131	71.6	6,503	14.5	6,223	13.9	44,857	100.0
1982	30,239	71.5	6,207	14.7	5,827	13.8	42,273	100.0
1983	28,835	72.1	5,731	14.3	5,452	13.6	40,018	100.0
1984	29,270	71.9	5,758	14.2	5,661	13.9	40,689	100.0
1985	30,504	72.2	6,002	14.2	5,749	13.6	42,255	100.0
1986	30,109	71.3	6,212	14.7	5,887	13.9	42,208	100.0

Source: Unione Industriale Biellese, *Economia biellese: 1986* (Biella: Unione Industriale Biellese, 1987): 25.

supporters of various left-wing parties (Rifondazione Comunista, Partito Democratica della Sinistra), most business leaders support the rightist Liberal party (PLI). The point, however, is that radical industrial change was negotiated by management and the unions. Although both sides recognize their different interests and express very different ideologies, they nevertheless bargained and reached accords regulating the adjustment of the local industry. As one local business leader put it, the unions and the managers united in a "pact for development" in order to save the local industry and preserve jobs.[27] Interestingly enough, the major confrontations between labor and management occurred not in restructured firms but rather in those businesses that did not restructure and thus were forced to close (see Massazza Gal 1987).

Following the major reorganization efforts of the 1980s, cooperation continued between local unions and business leaders. Joint efforts emerged to promote research and development, technical education and job retraining, and improved infrastructures—all aimed at enhancing the competitiveness of the local industry. The results have been positive. Record sales and profit rates for firms have been matched by high rates of employment—people actually commute into the Biellese area to work (see Unione Industriale Biellese 1981). Union membership rates are above the national average and local political parties are ex-

[27] Interview with Ferla 1987.

tremely active in this politically competitive electoral district. For an area only 75 kilometers from Turin, the contrast is striking.

Unlike at Fiat, in Biella firm managers and union leaders cooperated to promote the successful adjustment of the area's industry. In fact, in many ways this cooperation served as a safety net that allowed the firms to experiment with alternative industrial structures and strategies. Since the workers were protected and involved in one way or another in the reorganization of the local industry, it really did not matter which particular mix of skills, technology, and organization any particular firm adopted.

To better understand this pattern of industrial politics in the Biellese area, the next section of this chapter will explore the origins and development of these more cooperative patterns of relations and how their continuity contributed to the successful reorganization of the local industry in the 1970s and 1980s.

Local Patterns of Industry and Industrial Relations in the Biellese

The particular pattern of industrial development in the Biellese had significant effects on the structures and strategies of the local textile mills, the worldviews of their managers and workers, and the underlying sociopolitical character of the local economy. In essence, Biella industrialized in a way that preserved a reserve of highly skilled workers with artisanal traditions and a network of small, specialized firms. During the 1960s, industrial sociologists pointed to these characteristics as feudal vestiges destined to disappear with modernization. However, the existence of these two "backward" vestiges greatly facilitated the adjustment process of the local textile industry in the 1970s and 1980s.

In order to better understand how these historical legacies shaped recent strategies, a synoptic account of the development of Biella's textile industry and labor movement follows. This account is not comprehensive. It is intended merely to highlight certain critical conjunctures in which the contours of the local economic order were shaped.

The three periods that I describe are: 1) the initial industrialization of the Biellese and the uneasy coexistence of the first factories with preindustrial social relations; 2) the consolidation of the factory system and the role of "backwardness" in the development of the local industry during the first half of the twentieth century; and 3) the breakdown of this model of development and the reorganization of the textile industry in the 1960s and 1970s. In all three periods, struggles between firm managers and local unionists as well as between mill owners and apparel clients, small vs. large firms and so on, resulted in the consolidation of certain organizational, social, and political attributes and in the transformation of others. Regardless of their precise form, these elements of the local economic order, in turn, shaped the strategic choices of the actors throughout their histories and during the most recent wave of industrial restructuring.

The Uneasy Coexistence of Industrial Production and Preindustrial Social Relations

The history of the Biellese in the nineteenth century is in many ways the history of the difficult coexistence of industrial patterns of production with preindustrial social relations. Although these relations were forced to change over the course of the century, they evolved in ways that promoted bargaining relations between labor and management. In fact, notwithstanding the transformation of these original social relations, the local labor movement developed various institutions that permitted it to preserve power and identity.

Moreover, due to the intense struggles between skilled workers and mill owners which marked much of this period, many small producers continued to exist alongside the newly formed, integrated factories, despite successive attempts to concentrate or rationalize the local industry.

In short, during these years, two "traditional sectors"—a reserve of skilled workers and artisans and a network of small specialized firms—successfully resisted their elimination or expropriation by the emerging industrial system of production. As a result, certain peculiar characteristics of both the local industry and its work force emerged during this period. Although aspects of these features changed over time, the legacies of these patterns nonetheless continued to color the strategic choices of the local industrial actors throughout this century and into the current era.

Industrialization began in the Biellese during the eighteenth century. Previously, lanaioli (wool traders) distributed raw wool to be transformed into yarn, and later yarn to be woven into cloth, to a network of artisans working in their homes. These lanaioli relied on still other workers to perform other jobs like finishing, dyeing, and mending.[28]

With the introduction of the first mechanical looms in the late eighteenth century, however, the first factories were established in the Biellese. Although these factories internalized various phases of the production cycle, they nevertheless continued to rely heavily on outside artisans to perform significant portions of their spinning and weaving. Moreover, this industrialization process remained somewhat limited due to external, governmental constraints. The expansion of the local industry was severely curtailed, first, by the corporatist policies of the Savoy monarchy in Turin and, later, by the mercantilist trade policies of Napoleon.[29]

Following the defeat of Napoleon and the restoration of the Savoy monarchy in 1814, a 30-year period of protectionism ensued. Although the protectionist policies of the Piedmont monarchy safeguarded the textile industry from foreign competition and permitted it to develop (by 1850 there were 1,100 looms and 7,000 workers employed in the Biellese industry), this policy skewed the industrialization of the area by maintaining many small artisanal shops and, thus, preventing the concentration of the industry and the diffusion of new technologies.

Change occurred only later, following the unification of Italy and the implementation of Cavour's free trade policies, which forced firms to experiment with and promote innovation in order to withstand foreign competition from better developed rivals in England, France, and Germany.[30] For the Biellese, this translated into a substantial development

---

[28] This section relies on Scanziani 1986: chap. 1.

[29] At first a reactionary monarchy in Turin feared the growth of a powerful industrial bourgeoisie in nearby Biella and thus sought to restrict and severely regulate the expansion of the textile industry. Later, during the Napoleonic era, the French government sought to promote French textiles at the expense of the nascent Italian industry and planned to transform all of Italy into an agricultural breadbasket for France. In accordance with this policy, the Napoleonic regime blocked the transfer of mechanical looms from either France or Belgium (the Continental blockade also hindered British imports) and discouraged all investments in the industry. For more on these policies, see Secchia 1960: chap. 2.

[30] Unification also created a national market that further promoted the development of this industry. Previously, Italy was plagued by hundreds of different trade barriers, transportation taxes, tithes, etc., by the numerous principalities, papal territories, and small states. Between 1870 and 1890, the Italian state built thousands of miles of road and railroad, hundreds of schools and postal offices, and reformed its trade policy (1878) in order to provide some protection to its nascent industries. As a result, Italy

of the local industry. For instance, in 1861, the Biellese counted 94 woolen mills with 2,166 looms and 6,500 workers. By 1882, there were 178 woolen mills with 3,000 looms and 12,000 workers (Secchia 1960: chap. 3). Moreover, by this time, 62 percent of all textile firms in the area were horizontally integrated. These firms employed 89 percent of all local textile workers and possessed 75 percent of all active spindles and 90 percent of total looms in the Biellese.[31]

Yet, this industrialization process was shaped by the particular strategies of the local industrialists as well as by peculiarities of the local labor force. For instance, the Biellese mill owners sought to compete with foreign industries and compensate for the high cost of energy and their complete dependence on foreign machinery and chemical products by paying their workers low wages and working them long hours. As a result, the Biellese mill owners lagged behind in the use of newer, more advanced technologies but oddly enough, this backward strategy allowed textile workers to preserve both their skills and many of their preindustrial artisanal traditions.

Moreover, many smaller producers continued to exist next to the integrated mills. Although these shops generally manufactured lower quality goods for different markets, they had an ambiguous relationship with the larger, integrated manufacturers. On the one hand, they served as buffers for these integrated manufacturers, producing for them during moments of peak demand and absorbing redundant labor during cyclical downturns. But the small shops also posed a potential threat to these mills since they could both move upscale and invade the markets of the integrated mills and provide skilled textile workers with an alternative source of employment (hence, giving these workers greater bargaining power with the larger mill owners).

Although many of these smaller shops vanished with the mechanization of the industry at the end of the century, some continued to operate through the remainder of the nineteenth and into the twentieth century. Their continued existence throughout these years permitted the Biellese industry to preserve its development model based on low wages, high skills, and little or no technological innovation.

---

experienced its first economic "takeoff." For more on this process, see Gerschenkron 1976, 1985. For more on Cavour, see Mack Smith 1985.

[31] Scanziani 1986: chap. 1. For more on the history of the Biellese, see Castronovo 1964.

Biella's industrialization was also colored by an atypical working class that was tightly linked both to the land and to various community traditions that ran counter to mainstream patterns of industrial development (technological innovation, deskilling of workers, increased scale of production, etc.). As a result of the incomplete expropriation of its preindustrial bases of subsistence, the local working class was able to negotiate both its place and working conditions within the newly established textile factories of this period. Thus, industrialization in the Biellese did not result in the deskilling of the local labor force or in their substitution by machines. Rather, through various working class struggles, textile workers were able to preserve their preindustrial skills and status and contribute to the industrial development in the Biellese.

The local working class in the Biellese was unusually militant and well organized given its embeddedness in a strong local community and its ownership of the land. Tight integration into the rather complex local community is best illustrated by the numerous mutual aid societies, cooperatives, wine circles, and so on, that these workers developed throughout the Biellese. For instance, by 1884 there were sixty-four mutual aid societies with 9,789 members in forty-two of the ninety-three villages and towns of the Biellese. At the same time, there were about 800 "wine circles," which were essentially small taverns created by and for workers as places where they could relax, gather, and organize.[32]

Land ownership not only guaranteed subsistence and credit (power and autonomy) for these workers, but also contributed to preserving their identity as artisans, as producer-citizens. For instance, textile workers did not work their own land but rather hired day laborers to do so, seeing such work as beneath their status as artisans. Mill owners recognized and respected this identity. When state troops attempted to arrest and exile striking textile workers during the strike waves of 1877–78, mill owners like Quintino Sella intervened, arguing that such treatment, although appropriate for "migrants or brigands of the South" was unacceptable for the Biellese textile workers who, after all, were artisans and landowners.[33]

---

[32] For more on these societies and cooperatives, see Neiretti 1987.

[33] This section relies heavily on Berta 1979. Interestingly, this type of artisanal-republican ideology was expressed by other worker movements elsewhere during the same phase of industrialization. For more on this in America, see Wilentz 1984; Gutman 1977; and Dawley 1976. For expressions of this ideology elsewhere in Europe, see Stedman Jones 1983; and Sewell 1980.

Thus, during this initial phase of Biella's industrialization, textile workers managed to preserve their skills and identity as artisans. Even when textile manufacturers managed to expropriate some workers of their artisanal professionalism, they never succeeded at removing them from their land. As a result, they had to contend with a work force capable of waging very long and militant strikes. Beginning in the 1850s, but continuing through the 1860s and late 1870s, strikes in the Biellese were always among the most militant in all of Italy and attracted the attention of several parliamentary commissions and numerous scholars.

The Biellese strikes appeared enigmatic to these observers since the area did not possess the features normally associated with industrial unrest—large-scale plants and lack of direct contact between mill owners and workers. Moreover, conflicts in the Biellese were often not over wages but over the organization of production, and they were often settled through the negotiation of territorially based collective agreements. For instance, the strike of 1861 was settled with an accord that gave workers control over existent apprenticeship programs. This, in turn, provided workers with substantial power in the local labor market while simultaneously safeguarding their skills. The agreement also regulated working conditions and work hours within the factories (Berta 1979).

In short, during most of the nineteenth century, Biellese workers were able to rely on preindustrial patterns of land tenure and community organization to protect their skills and preserve their identities as artisans. Paradoxically, Biella's first mill owners were also able to rely on these same premodern features to develop the textile industry. Since most textile workers had alternative sources of subsistence and were highly skilled, the local industrialists could get by with paying them lower wages and reducing their work hours during cyclical downturns. Highly skilled workers also allowed local mill owners to compete without investing in expensive new technologies.

The Consolidation of the Factory System and the Development of "Reformism"

With the electrification of the area at the turn of the century, the Biellese continued to grow as an industrial center. According to the 1901 census, out of a total population of 164,000 in the Biellese,

83,918 were actively employed, of which 44.7 percent were in the textile industry (see Neiretti 1987). And yet, the extensive emigration from the area—21,367 emigrants between 1879 and 1900 and 52,262 between 1901 and 1914—indicates that with the consolidation of the factory system, traditional patterns of landholding and work were being undermined and thousands of ex-artisans/small landowners were forced to leave the Biellese.[34]

During this period, the local labor movement also began to change. For most of the nineteenth century, the Biellese working class expressed an artisanal-republican ideology and was organized into local mutual aid societies and strong territorially based "resistance leagues" (Berta 1979). Yet, by the turn of the century, this ideology was increasingly supplanted by various forms of socialist and even anarchist thought, and the resistance leagues became transformed, into full-fledged trade unions. In 1901, the local Chamber of labor, (*Camera del Lavoro*) was established in an attempt to coordinate and centralize the various labor organizations of the area (Neiretti 1987).

Although this period witnessed various internal struggles within the local labor movement (i.e., between reformist Social Democrats and anarchists, and between the territorial chamber of labor and the various individual craft unions) the victorious union structures and ideology that emerged from these struggles nevertheless contributed to the consolidation of Biella's particular model of economic development. For instance, although reformist socialists replaced the original republican artisans as leaders of the local labor movement, their particular brand of Marxist positivism merely encouraged local mill owners to develop their industry along traditional lines.

Believing that the concentration of industry, like technical progress, followed certain historical laws and trajectories that would eventually lead to socialism, local union leaders discouraged workers from struggling against such developments. Yet, because these local union leaders also encouraged textile workers to develop their technical skills and negotiate the particular forms of industrial change, the Biellese labor movement *in practice* continued to strike against any changes that threatened the professional skills or autonomy of local workers.

Illustrative of this particular brand of Marxist positivism are the words of Pietro Secchia, leader of the Biellese workers' movement

[34]For a discussion of this process, see Ramella 1983.

and later a national figure in the PCI (Italian Communist party). According to Pietro Secchia:

> Biellese workers are not opposed to technological development, to the introduction of new machines. They do not oppose progress. First of all, because such opposition would be useless and would not impede the objective laws of history from taking their course. Second, because technical progress, like the concentration of industry, creates the material bases for the future socialist society where machines, expropriated from capital, will serve the workers.
>
> Workers are not contrary to technical progress, but they know that if they do not struggle to defend their wages, their right to work; if they do not react with the most militant and organized struggles against their exploiters, technical progress can bring about a deterioration of their living conditions. Therefore, workers know that with every introduction of new machines or new methods, they must generate new demands and new struggles in order to realize a corresponding progress in social conditions.[35]

Thus, although theoretically not opposed to technical change, local textile workers *in practice* continued to block most technical innovation in the local industry. As a result, they reinforced the mill owners' traditional model of economic development based not on new product or process innovations but on low wages and long work hours. Notwithstanding the continuation of artisanal methods of production, the local industry grew. As a result, textile workers maintained not only their skills but also their jobs and remained firmly rooted in their local community. Saved by the blocked technical development of the local industry, many smaller shops also continued to operate.

The embeddedness of the textile workers in their local communities was also promoted by the organizational features of the Biellese union movement. Put simply, the organizational struggles between the territorial chamber of labor and the individual craft unions which took place during this period resulted in a compromise in which the craft unions maintained considerable political autonomy, but the territorial chamber of labor acquired strategic control over all subsequent collective bargaining.

In essence, although certain organizational and ideological features of the local labor movement changed at the turn of the century, many

---

[35]Secchia 1960: 200. My translation.

of the legacies of the earlier artisanal system were preserved, perhaps even reinforced. These historical and ideological legacies continued to survive throughout the twentieth century, notwithstanding the repressive policies of the fascist regime and the turmoil surrounding both World Wars.[36] Similarly, the factory system became consolidated during this period, but Biella's basic model of industrial development remained more or less in tact. It continued along these lines until the mid-1960s, when the local industry entered into crisis as a result of the growth of the apparel industry and the increase in labor costs and worker militance.

The Demise of the Mass Production Model and the Restructuring of the Textile Industry in the 1970s and 1980s

Many Italian scholars claim that the workers' struggles in the Biellese during the early 1960s were in certain ways a precursor and model for the Hot Autumn struggles of the late 1960s. In these struggles, highly skilled Biellese workers joined forces with recently arrived unskilled immigrants from the surrounding countryside and the Veneto region to demand increased wages and improved working conditions. It was in reaction to this wave of worker militance that the Biellese mill owners finally began to modernize their plants by introducing new labor-saving technologies (Ciochetti and Ramella 1964).

Yet, as we saw earlier in this chapter, mill owners initially reorganized their firms in limited and makeshift ways. The purpose of this first wave of restructuring was to circumvent labor rigidities and preserve the old regime of industrial production and administration. Only after the flood of 1968 did local entrepreneurs embark on a completely new industrial strategy.

This is not to suggest that the old system would have remained in place had it not been for a natural disaster, but rather that the devastation of old factories and the reconfiguration of the local economic order in the wake of the flood greatly facilitated the reorganization of the local industry. That this reorganization occurred also during the years of strong worker militancy following the Hot Autumn may also help explain why firm managers embarked on the strategies they did. In other words, caught in a situation in which they suddenly

[36] For more on this period, see Moranino 1987; Perona 1987; and Giardino, n.d.

found themselves with devastated plants and strong unions, these managers reformulated their strategies to take advantage of the skilled workers and small shops they inherited from the past. These two external factors served as the carrot and stick to influence industrial change in the Biellese, but the particular strategies pursued by local mill owners were shaped by the local resources at hand.

External constraints (increased power of the union movement, changing conditions of international competition, etc.) combined with already existing local characteristics (the continued existence of highly skilled workers, the survival of many small specialized shops, a dense network of local institutions and secondary associations, etc.) to transform Biella from a site of economic backwardness into a center of highly competitive industrial firms.

In a strange irony of history, it was precisely the backwardness of the Biellese model of industrial development which formed the basis for the industrial reorganization of the 1970s and 1980s. Because the industry developed by exploiting low-wage labor rather than mechanizing production, it retained a large pool of skilled workers. Moreover, because the local industry never fully modernized, a myriad of premodern vestiges, such as small specialized production shops, were able to survive and compete alongside larger firms throughout the nineteenth and twentieth centuries. As a result, the development of an extensive network of small-scale, specialized firms operated by highly skilled ex-factory workers, often using the original machinery of the ex-integrated mills, was greatly facilitated.

Finally, because the local labor movement had historically been able to protect its skills and organizational strength and maintain its links to the local community, it possessed the ideological predisposition and organizational capacity to negotiate the restructuring processes of the 1970s and 1980s. The continuation of its tradition of territorial collective bargaining, for example, greatly facilitated the transformation of the area into an industrial district during these years.

In sum, the particular pattern of industrial development had a significant impact on subsequent patterns of industry and industrial relations in the area. The struggles between the various industrial actors during the three periods just examined resulted in the consolidation of certain organizational features of the local economic order and the reconfiguration of others. For example, following the 1968 flood and the Hot Autumn struggles of the early 1970s, relations between organized labor and business, as well as among the individual firms, changed dramatically. Whereas in the early 1960s, individual firm managers were suspicious of one another and antagonistic toward the local unions, by the mid-1970s, relations both among the individual textile companies and between managers and local labor leaders had become increasingly more collaborative.

The switch from a fragmented and somewhat polarized sociopolitical setting to a more balanced, heterogenous, and collaborative local economic order did not occur overnight. It took many years to achieve, but it was facilitated by the presence of a strong but moderate local labor movement, an open-minded and progressive territorial business association, and the continued existence of numerous local interest groups, secondary associations, and social organizations. These sociopolitical resources, in turn, shaped the flow of information and resources and, hence, the range of possible strategies available to local firm managers and union leaders during the reorganization of Biella's textile sector in the 1970s and 1980s.

I have argued in this chapter that the particular restructuring pattern of the Biellese textile industry was the result of the peculiarities of its industrial development and the impact of this development on the strategic choices of the various industrial actors. In other words, over the course of the last two centuries, various industrial actors (mill owners, skilled workers, subcontractors) developed particular worldviews and organizational attributes that shaped the range of possible strategies available to them. The political struggles between these industrial actors over their competing worldviews consolidated certain of these original features and, thus, structured the subsequent patterns of industry and industrial relations in the Biellese.

At the same time, this case study on the textile industry illustrates some of the more general trends underlying Italy's recent industrial turnaround. Industries that were indeed once backward in the sense of sweating labor and employing obsolescent technologies were reorganized along completely new lines. Government policy and peak-level bargaining between the social actors did not direct but unwittingly supported this process. Yet this process of reorganization took on different forms in different regions of the country. Divergent strategies were shaped by the regional industrial orders in which local firms and unions were embedded.

Closer examination of how Italian textile firms restructured also raises questions concerning some of our most commonly held assumptions regarding industrial change. One lesson of this chapter is that societies that want to produce industrial goods competitively are not restricted to a single organizational structure or pattern of relations. Instead, production can be organized in several different ways, using different mixes of technology, skills, and organization. In the Biellese, this plurality of different patterns coexists within the same industry because of certain organizational and ideological features peculiar to the area.

We now turn to a discussion of the main findings of this book and their implications for how we understand industrial change more broadly.

CHAPTER SIX

Conclusion:
Beyond Italian Exceptionalism

> We thus encounter, at the most basic level, political identification
> and allegiance that is local rather than national. Parochialism, while
> strongly evident in the traditional South, is also amazingly present
> in the North, where localizing influences of the city-states and inde-
> pendent duchies are still very much in influence.
> —Joseph La Palombara, *Interest Groups in Italian Politics*

This book has told a somewhat unconventional story about the
Italian economy. Unlike writers of popular accounts which portray
Italy as the "sick man" of Europe, I have tried to tell a more nuanced
and differentiated tale, one that recognizes not simply the country's
many political-economic problems but also its impressive rates of economic growth, productivity, savings, and exports. To reconcile these
two apparently contradictory images of Italy and make some sense of
contemporary developments, I have argued that the Italian economy
should be viewed *not* as a coherent "national system" but rather as a
somewhat incoherent composite of diverse subnational patterns that
coexist (often uneasily) within the same national territory.

These divergent, more localistic economic orders are characterized
by alternative patterns of associationalism and intergroup relations
that, in turn, shape the strategic choices of local economic actors in
very different ways. This accounts for both the diversity of economic
patterns currently manifest within Italy as well as some of the country's
current maladies.

This argument was developed incrementally. The first part of the
book analyzed Italy's failed institutional reform process. Like many

American and European social scientists writing at the time, Italy's political and economic elite became convinced that their country's political problems stemmed from its lack of a strong and coherent national model. Thus, they embarked on a major reform effort aimed at remaking Italian institutions in the image of other, apparently more stable and efficient nations. With few exceptions, none of these efforts to build a new Italy succeeded. In fact, certain backward features of the Italian system (multiple and competing centers of political and economic power, decentralized decision-making, regional socioeconomic disparities, etc.) were reinforced as a result of this failed reform process and the inter- and intraorganizational struggles it spawned.

Failed institutional reform and radical change in the structure and strategy of industry combined to shift industrial politics to the micro-level of Italy's political economy. But this shift was in no way synonymous with a return to laissez-faire marketism. Beneath Italy's facade of institutional chaos lies a dense network of regulation. This regulation does not emanate from the central government in Rome, but rather from the array of different local economic orders that coexist within Italy. Thus, during the recent wave of industrial restructuring, Italian firms did not simply reinvent themselves de novo. Instead, they were shaped in both their understandings of the changes underway and their range of strategic options by the local economic orders in which they were embedded.

The second part of this book illustrated the importance of the local economic orders by analyzing the politics of industrial adjustment in the Italian automobile and textile industries. Notwithstanding tremendous differences between these sectors—differences in production processes, technology, average firm size, and the composition of their respective work forces—in both industries, the strategic choices of company managers and local union leaders were shaped by the local economic orders in which they were situated. Economic actors embedded in local economic orders possessing dense but relatively egalitarian sociopolitical networks were able to share information, form alliances, build trust, and hence negotiate the process of industrial adjustment, whereas company managers and local union leaders situated in more fragmented and polarized sociopolitical settings often engaged in highly conflictual struggles over the changes underway in their industries.

In short, given the very different sociopolitical features underlying

Italy's various local economic orders, failed institutional reform and increased decentralization had radically different consequences for different areas of the country. For some localities, it proved to be a blessing in disguise. But for others, the shift to the local level only exacerbated already persistent problems.

Perhaps the most striking example of this divergence is the continuing (perhaps even growing) disparity between Italy's north-central regions and the Mezzogiorno. Table 6.1 shows that in 1990, various economic indicators like per capita product, consumption, and bank deposits were significantly lower in the South than in the North. Today, youth unemployment is three times greater in Italy's southern regions than in the rest of the country. Crime, corruption, poverty, and joblessness are standard features of Italy's Mezzogiorno (see Trigilia 1992 for more on the differences between Italy's North and South).

Notwithstanding continuing government support for economic development in the South, economic differences between Italy's North and South actually widened over the last decade. For example, although the North's share of the nation's total unemployment decreased from 42 percent in 1980 to 31.3 percent in 1990, the South witnessed a reverse trend, with its share of unemployment rising from 44.3 percent to 52.3 percent (CENSIS 1992: 340). This is especially alarming given that the North was particularly hard hit by the recent wave of industrial restructuring.[1]

Likewise, public services and welfare state provisions in the South also seem to have fallen further behind over the course of the last decade. For instance, although the level and quality of education (from elementary schools to universities) in the South has always been below the national average, it slipped even further over the course of the 1980s (CENSIS 1992: 871).

Interestingly enough, not all parts of the South have suffered. A few localities have experienced significant economic growth and even impressive rates of performance of their administrative structures (Piattoni, in progress; Putnam, Leonardi, Nannetti, and Pavoncello 1983). Thus, even within the South, islands of prosperity, possessing particular organizational and sociopolitical features, are beginning to appear in what more or less continues to be a sea of despair.

In telling this alternative tale about Italy, this book also develops a

[1] For more on these disparities, see Wollieb and Wollieb 1991.

Table 6.1. Disparity between Italy's Messogiorno and the Center-North (Index=100=Center-North)

Selected economic indicators	Disparity
Per capita product	55.6
Per capita consumption	70.0
Youth unemployment, 14–21 year-olds	301.3
Labor market participation	87.7
Savings deposits	26.6

Source: CENSIS, *25 Rapporto sulla situazione sociale del paese 1991* (Milan: Franco Angeli, 1992): 194.

different, micropolitical approach to the study of comparative political economy. In contrast to accounts that focus on national institutional arrangements to explain differences in economic performance and/ or behavior across nations, I look instead at the microlevel, at the strategic choices of economic actors, to understand diverse patterns of industrial politics *within* the same nation, same industry, and even the same firm. Moreover, rather than deduce industrial behavior from a variety of structural factors, my approach stresses the role of politics in shaping the alternative conceptions and strategies of local economic actors. The micropolitical approach advocated here has significant implications both for how we understand industrial change and how we go about doing research in comparative political economy. We now turn to a discussion of these two themes.

RETHINKING INDUSTRIAL CHANGE

Two basic assumptions—reductionism and evolutionism—dominate the traditional literature on industrial change. Reductionism[2] assumes that the interests, consciousness, and hence the strategic choices of various economic actors stem from their place in the division of labor. In other words, it assumes that all people employed either within the same sectors (manufacturing vs. public services, or export-oriented vs. sheltered sectors) or possessing the same level of skills, or even working on the same assembly line, share the same interests and thus will react in similar ways to the same set of challenges.

[2]This section draws on Sabel 1982: 5–9.

Peter Gourevitch's study of economic policy-making in the advanced industrial states (Gourevitch 1986) and Gary Marks's book on union politics in Britain, Germany, and the United States (Marks 1989) both exemplify reductionist-based analyses of industrial change. Gourevitch's sectoral-coalition argument for why some nations pursue free trade while others support protectionism has many layers and includes intermediary variables like state structure, ideology, and interest group politics. But these many layers all rest on the basic assumption that the interests of social actors can best be understood by examining their place within the economy, by whether the sector these actors are situated in will gain or lose from these alternative policy choices. In other words, the interests of economic actors can be read off the fate of the sectors in which they are employed.

Gary Marks's account of the remarkably similar policies of printing and coal mining unions in three very different countries is also layered and examines a variety of factors, including variations in legal environments and the effects of the "organizational revolution" (the rise of national unions) on industrial relations patterns. Yet he too builds these other explanatory variables around the basic idea that workers employed in a particular sector share the same interests, identity, and labor market power. These factors not only distinguish the workers from others employed in different sectors, but also affect the ways they understand and react to the changes underway in their own industries.

The findings presented in the case study on the Italian automobile industry challenge this reductionist assumption. Chapter 4 compared the alternative strategic choices of company managers and local union leaders at two companies—Alfa Romeo and Fiat Auto. Both companies shared the same ownership, were organized by the same unions, and employed similar work forces to produce analogous products with more or less identical technologies. But the politics of industrial adjustment at these two companies was radically different. Whereas at Fiat, company managers restructured the firm by reasserting control over the shop floor and decimating the local union, at Alfa, managers and local union leaders negotiated a restructuring plan that appeared to produce positive results for both sides.

Thus, observed differences in the politics of adjustment at these two companies do not appear to be explained through the structural variables on which reductionist analyses build. Instead, I argued that the divergent strategic choices pursued by industrial actors at the two firms were best explained through closer examination of the local economic orders in which these two firms were embedded.

Because Fiat and Alfa are embedded in very different local economies, each with a distinct pattern of associationalism and structure of sociopolitical relations, company managers and union leaders faced alternative mixes of incentives and constraints that shaped their ability to formulate and implement different strategies. Fiat is located in Turin, a highly polarized one-company town lacking a vibrant associational infrastructure. As a result, information-sharing and cooperation between moderate groups within both the company and the local union movement was difficult to sustain, and potential mediators of conflict between the company and its unions simply did not exist. As a result, disagreements over the company's restructuring efforts escalated into an all-out struggle between the local unions and the company.

Alfa, however, is situated in Milan, a more policentric local economic order teaming with well-organized interest groups and secondary associations. These organizations facilitated information-sharing, compromise, and cooperation between labor and management at Alfa and thus supported negotiations between these two parties over the massive changes underway at the firm. In short, economic actors who otherwise possessed identical or relatively similar structural attributes nonetheless reacted to comparable challenges in very different ways. This was due to the way the divergent local contexts shaped both their understandings of the challenges they faced and the range of viable strategic responses available to them.

Evolutionism,[3] the second common assumption in the literature on industrial change, rests on the idea that there exists a single "best practice" and/or optimal organizational solution for manufacturing industrial goods competitively. Underlying this assumption is a view of industrial change as a Darwinian process of adaptation and competitive selection.

The most recent work on "lean production" in the automobile industry rests on this assumption (Womack, Jones, and Roos 1990). According to these authors, the emergence of a highly successful Japanese system of production plus increased international competition

---

[3]My understanding of this problem is shaped by Friedman 1988: chap. 1.

have rendered it increasingly difficult for less efficient (i.e., U.S.) mass production and craft-based (i.e., European) firms to compete in world markets. Only by reorganizing their structures and strategies along the more efficient Japanese pattern can (only a few) of these Western manufacturers hope to survive.

The case of Biella (Chapter 5) challenged this assumption by illustrating that a plurality of different organizational structures and strategies have historically coexisted alongside one another and that they have evolved over time through continuous interaction with each other. Firms that want to produce industrial goods competitively are not restricted to a single organizational structure or a specific pattern of relations with workers, suppliers, and customers. Instead, production can be organized in several different ways, using different mixes of technology, skills, and organization. In the Biellese textile district, this plurality of different patterns exists within the same area because of the peculiarity of the local economic order. But divergent patterns of equally competitive industrial organization can be observed in a variety of different industries throughout Italy.[4]

Of course, major economic and technological constraints restrict the range of viable options available at any one moment. Not everything is possible and, certainly, industries with different types of technology and product markets possess different degrees and types of choices. Nonetheless, within this (albeit) narrow range of possibilities, options still remain. As the case study of Biella illustrates, economic actors pursue alternative strategic choices based on the local sociopolitical resources they inherit.

Although historical legacies shaped the original organizational attributes of the various local orders, patterns of industrial politics in these localities were not simply set in stone at the beginning and immutable thereafter. Instead, legacies of the past could be reconfigured through periodic political struggles. In Biella, for example, we saw how various features of the local economic order which for centuries had been organized in ways that sustained one model of industrial development (the dominance of large integrated firms, low-paid workers, etc.) were

[4]In textiles, for example, both highly integrated and decentralized systems coexist and compete with one another. Similar patterns can be observed in ceramic tiles (within the area of Sassuolo), machine tools (compare Comau in Turin with various smaller producers in and around Modena), steel (the minimills around Brescia compete successfully with integrated steel plants in Taranto). Nor is this just an Italian phenomenon. See, for instance, Herrigel 1994; Friedman 1988; Dertouzous et al. 1989.

recombined to support a completely different one (a network of medium-sized firms employing a well-organized, highly skilled, and well-paid work force).

Thus, instead of reducing industrial behavior to a narrow set of responses or deducting it from a variety of structural variables, the approach advanced in this book celebrates the wide range of alternative strategies pursued by various economic actors. And rather than treat national systems as the basic unit of analysis and macroinstitutional features as the source of divergent patterns of industrial change, this book focuses on microlevel developments and the politics of strategic choice to explain variation *within* states, within industries, sometimes even within the same company. We now examine the implications of this alternative, micropolitical approach for future research and theory in comparative political economy.

COMPARATIVE POLITICAL ECONOMY IN A CHANGING WORLD

The dominant paradigm in comparative political economy focuses on the institutional arrangements and/or patterns of state-society relations of different nation-states to explain divergent patterns of industrial politics. According to this view, national institutional arrangements are important because they shape the goals that organized interest groups like unions and business associations can pursue. National institutional arrangements structure not only the strategic interaction among economic actors but also their access to government policy making (Immergut 1992). As a result, scholars working within this tradition emphasize the institutional context of industrial politics, including the organizational characteristics of unions and business, the legal framework of industrial relations, the alternative systems of financial intermediation, and the linkages to the state.[5] Because scholars working within this tradition are interested in showing how nationally distinctive institutional configurations mediate the effects of common international pressures very differently, they often assume a certain degree of homogeneity within different nation-states.

A good example of this approach is Lowell Turner's *Democracy at Work*. Based on a series of rich, company-level case studies of industrial

[5]See, for example, Streeck 1992; Thelen 1991; and Turner 1991.

restructuring in the German and American automobile industries as well as an insightful analysis of the institutional frameworks of both these countries, Turner uncovers substantial differences in the ability of American and German unions to participate in industrial restructuring. Because labor's rights at the shop floor are institutionalized through legislation in Germany, German unions were able to negotiate the introduction of new technologies and the reorganization of work in their industries. In the absence of these same formal, guaranteed rights in the United States, American unions faced a more uncertain situation. Although some American unions were able to negotiate the changes underway in their plants, other unions with less organizational power and/or less benevolent managers were given no significant voice in the restructuring process.

This book also analyzed divergent patterns of industrial politics but focused instead on the alternative adjustment strategies present *within* the same country. Rather than analyze systematic differences that exist across countries, I instead stressed the internal heterogeneity manifest within a single national economy. And rather than focus on the organizational attributes of national interest groups and/or particular features of different institutional arrangements, I concentrated on the strategic choices of microlevel actors and the underlying sociopolitical features that shape these choices.

Like Turner, I too believe that national institutional arrangements and legal frameworks shape economic behavior. These institutional arrangements, as with various market and technological factors, constrain the range of possible strategies that economic actors can pursue in particular national and sectoral contexts. But even within these constraints, there still exists a range of possibilities open to economic actors. This book has sought to understand the logic guiding the alternative strategic choices pursued by company managers and union leaders situated in otherwise similar industrial and institutional settings by examining the way local sociopolitical networks influence the understandings, resources, and strategic possibilities available to these actors.

Although present within the same country, local economic actors are embedded in very different local economies that are, in turn, characterized by alternative patterns of associationalism and sociopolitical relations. Firms and industries situated in localities with particular sociopolitical attributes (e.g., dense but relatively egalitarian networks of well-developed associations and interest groups) adjusted to changing world markets in a more negotiated manner, whereas companies embedded in localities with more limited local resources experienced more conflict. Figure 6.1 describes the salient differences between the micropolitical approach advocated in this book and the more traditional, national models account.

This book explains the divergent patterns of industrial adjustment observed in the Italian automobile and textile industries by showing how local economic orders possessing divergent underlying sociopolitical networks shaped the strategic choices of local economic actors in alternative ways. Three ideal-typical local economic orders were described in Chapter 1. The three ideal-types, which I labeled hierarchical, polarized, and policentric, differed along three critical dimensions: the structure of intergroup relations, patterns of associationalism, and linkages to central policymakers. The case studies presented in the second part of this book sought to illustrate how these divergent underlying characteristics shaped the strategic choices of company managers and local union leaders in very different ways. Of course, these ideal-typical local economic orders do not exist in pure form in either one of the industries we examined, and they cannot possibly capture the rich detail of any of the industrial cases we analyzed. But they do nonetheless help us organize what might initially appear to

Figure 6.1. Two images of adjustment

	National models	Micro-political approach
Key actors	National governments, national business associations, and labor unions.	Microlevel actors: firm managers, local union leaders, secondary associations, and local interst groups.
Level of analysis	Primary national-level.	Primarily subnational.
View of the national economy	As a system—different pieces fit together with more or less coherence; relatively homogeneous.	As a composite of differentiated local patterns.
Noneconomic factors influencing industrial adjustment strategies	Government policies (industrial, monetary, labor legislation); organizational capacities of interest groups; institutional architecture of different nation-states.	Underlying sociopolitical features of local context.

be an endless variety of local arrangements and to see how particular contextual features shape economic behavior in clearly distinct ways. The point, in short, is that a variety of different subnational patterns of industrial politics coexist within Italy and that these localistic patterns are worthy of study.

But this is not only an Italian phenomenon. To the extent that other national governments also appear to have lost macroeconomic control over their economies and given that today, countries as diverse as Sweden, Germany, and the United States—national models Italians once sought to emulate—are beginning to resemble Italy in terms of institutional fragmentation and economic decentralization, the Italian case may indeed provide more general lessons for students of comparative political economy.

The first part of this book focused on two policy areas—economic policy and industrial relations—to illustrate the problems Italians faced in constructing a new, apparently more efficient and homogeneous system in an era of continuous industrial change and economic turbulence. Yet Italy was not alone in confronting these problems, nor were its eventual solutions so unique. In recent years, for example, industrial relations systems in other advanced nations have faced challenges similar to those described in Italy. New patterns of international competition and technological change have prompted firms to reorganize their structures and strategies in ways that transcend traditional union practices. And increased diversity within the labor force has provoked a growth of new demands by "new workers" which run counter to conventional organizing strategies.

To meet these challenges, industrial relations systems in countries as diverse as Germany (Kern and Sabel 1991), Sweden (Ahlen 1989; Martin 1991; Pontusson and Swenson 1992), Belgium (Hancke 1991), and the United States (Kochan, Katz, and McKersie 1986) have, like the Italian system, become more decentralized and heterogeneous.

Similarly, the plurality of patterns of industrial organization described in Italy appears in other national economies as well. Gary Herrigel (1995) has described alternative patterns of industrial order in the German mechanical engineering industry, Annalee Sexenian (1994) has done the same for the American semiconductor sector, and Michael Porter (1990) has described these patterns for a variety of other industries in several advanced industrial nations.

Thus, although local patterns of industrial politics may appear to be more pronounced in Italy given the country's peculiar process of political-economic development, they nonetheless exist in other countries with very different institutional arrangements and historical traditions. In other words, what is happening in Italy is *not* exceptional but rather indicative of more general trends sweeping across all advanced industrial nations.

This book has tried to show that these subnational patterns are worthy of study and should not be so quickly dismissed as outliers or exceptions to the dominant (national) model. In the same way that I have sought to identify ideal-typical patterns of industrial politics within Italy and to analyze the key variables underlying these different local orders, new research in comparative political economy must begin to compare seemingly analogous subnational patterns across nations. This would allow us to better grasp the underlying sociopolitical factors shaping the strategic choices of local economic actors in these apparently similar subnational systems. Once we better understand the determinants and consequences of each of these microlevel patterns, we can then analyze the different mixes or distribution of these subnational orders *within* nations. This second step would allow us to see whether or not, and if so how, national institutions shape the various interactions among and distributions of local economic orders across countries. Extrapolating once again from the cases presented in this book, one can imagine, for example, that the three ideal-typical patterns described in Chapter 1 could exist in very different countries, say the United States and Germany. However, because of institutional and regulatory differences among these three countries, the distribution of these three patterns within these three nation-states would vary (see Figure 6.2).

Only if one or a particular set of economic patterns emerges as dominant in a given country should we return to the convention of comparing industrial politics in terms of national models. *If* such a model or set of models is identified, we will be on our way toward reconstructing national models that highlight rather than obscure the dynamic relationship that exists between microlevel strategies and national regulatory institutions. If not, we must construct completely new typologies, based perhaps on more local patterns of industrial politics, to guide further comparative research and theorizing.

The shift in industrial politics is not simply a theoretical issue. Nor is it just a question of privileging a different level of the political

Figure 6.2.   Hypothetical cross-national distribution of three ideal-typical economic orders

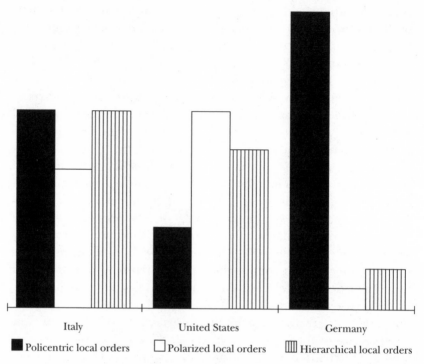

| Italy | United States | Germany |

■ Policentric local orders   □ Polarized local orders   ▥ Hierarchical local orders

economy. As the various cases in this book make clear, boundaries and/or distinctions that we used to assume as given—among different levels of the political economy (international, national, local); between firms and their local environments; between different functions or jobs within firms; and among different levels of union, company, and government hierarchies—have all become more porous and plastic in recent years. This, in turn, has led to a shift not only in the locus of industrial politics, but also in its basic features. Even the identities of the various actors and the structural characteristics of the institutions normally involved in industrial adjustment have changed.

The blurring of previously established boundaries and roles, combined with a proliferation of diverse subnational patterns of industrial politics, creates a number of new challenges for firms, unions, and governments. For example, the reconfiguration of industrial relations in favor of the local or firm level not only creates opportunities for unions to become more responsive to local needs but also poses several risks for the labor movement as a whole. How does the labor movement prevent whipsawing or the exploitation of workers in firms with weaker local unions? How do unions (with or without allied political parties) reaggregate the increasingly divergent interests of their rank and file (and of the majority of workers who do not belong to unions) into an organizationally coherent labor movement capable of protecting social standards and promoting political reforms at the national level? Maintaining unity amid the increasing diversity of the labor movement will not be easy. But it will be essential, especially when unity of the labor movement could determine its future viability in the advanced industrial nations.

The problem of recognizing, perhaps even embracing, internal diversity while still maintaining some semblance of coherence of the whole is equally great for business and government. The development and implementation of successful corporate strategies has become extremely difficult at a time when markets are becoming simultaneously globalized and segmented. Firm structures and strategies used to be shaped by the industries and markets in which they competed. Moreover, the capabilities and responsibilities among the different levels of the corporate hierarchy were clearly delineated and accepted. Career trajectories matched these corporate ladders.

In the current era, when international competition and technological change have redefined both the underlying features of many industries and the shape of markets, previously successful large corporations are struggling to reorganize along completely new lines—ones that blur distinctions and emphasize linkages among different geographic markets, corporate functions, manufacturing operations, and levels of the corporate hierarchy (Bartlett and Ghoshal 1989).

Finally, although political factionalism (Cohen and Rogers 1992) and fragmentation (Tarrow, Katzenstein, and Graziano 1978; Dente 1985) have always troubled central governments, the very nature and intensity of the current shift renders ineffective most traditional solutions to these challenges. Etatist practices, for example, may have been successful at promoting industrial development in a previous era of more stable, domestic-centered markets, limited international competition, and incremental technological change. But they appear to experience tremendous difficulties managing industrial change in the current period of radical technological change and globalized markets (Zysman 1977; Ziegler 1989; Levy 1994). And when the state relies on societal actors to compensate for its own deficiencies, it appears merely to add problems of equality and representation to its previous economic troubles (Keeler 1981; Hall 1986).

Neocorporatist solutions, on the other hand, depend upon the stability and internal coherence of the various peak-level interest groups involved in the policy-making process. Yet these conditions have been undermined by the increased fragmentation of national economies and the growth of diversity *within* social groups and not just between them. Although countries like Italy and the United Kingdom may have never (or only occasionally) possessed the organizational features necessary for neocorporatism (Regini 1984), it now appears that even in Sweden and the Netherlands, countries that were once paragons of this model, these same underlying characteristics are disappearing as well (Hammerich 1992; Martin 1991; Pontusson and Swenson 1992). The neoliberal path is also not viable given that it would exacerbate rather than resolve the current problems challenging the advanced industrial states. The current economic and social disarray in both the United States and the United Kingdom—two countries most closely associated with this model—speaks for itself (Albert 1993).

Thus, even if institutional tinkering and/or borrowing were a possibility for the advanced industrial nations, it does not appear that established national models would provide much help. In fact, it is hard to imagine that any one organizational solution or public policy response could adequately deal with the incredible variety of scenarios present within any of the advanced industrial economies.[6]

Remaking the Italian economy—like the economies of the other advanced industrial nations—promises to be an extremely arduous and complicated process, one which will be heavily determined by the legacies of the past and how these are reconfigured to meet the challenges of the future. Whether or not this process is possible cannot yet be answered. If this book has been at all convincing, you will think that it is worthwhile to try.

[6]For more on these scenarios, see Boyer 1988: 268–73.

Selected List of Persons Interviewed

Aris Accornero, professor of sociology, University of Rome

Umberto Agnelli, vice president, Fiat S.p.A.

Mario Agostinelli, regional secretary, CGIL Lombardia, Sesto San Giovanni.

Angelo Airoldi, national secretary, FIOM-CGIL, Rome

Gianni Alasia, PCI parliamentary deputy from Turin, Turin.

Bruno Alcaro, Associazione Laniera Italiana, Milan.

Mr. Alessio, director of purchasing, Fiat Auto, Turin.

Gianni Amoretti, national secretary, Filtea-CGIL, Rome.

Alfredo Anastasio (Uilcea-UIL), local chemical workers union leader, Mestre, Venice.

Cesare Annibaldi, director of external relations, Fiat S.p.A., Turin.

Cristiano Antonelli, professor of economics, University of Turin.

Mr. Aquadro, Research office, Associazione Laniera Italiana, Milan.

Alberto Archetti, president, Gruppo Tessile Niggeler and Kupfer, Capriolo (Brescia).

Vittorio Argento, Unione Industriale Pratese, Prato.

Valerio Astolfi, secretary general, Associazione Cottoniero Italiana, Milan.

Arnaldo Bagnasco, professor of sociology, University of Turin.

Salvatore Barone, provincial secretary, Filtea-CGIL, Como.

Bianca Beccalli, professor of labor sociology, University of Milan.

Ezio Becchis, IRES-CGIL Piemonte, Turin.

Cleto Benucci, director, Tessile di Como, Como.

Carlo Bessusso, director, Organization of Production, Fiat S.p.A., Turin.

Patrizio Bianchi, professor of economics, University of Bologna; Research Director, NOMISMA, Bologna.

Mr. Bigagli, president, Bigagli, S.p.A.

Guido Bolaffi, FIOM-CGIL, National Coordinating Committee for Autos, Rome.

Giuseppe Bonazzi, professor of sociology, University of Turin.

Lorenzo Bordogna, professor of sociology, Univeresity of Brescia.

Mr. Borsero, director of industrial policy (Marketing and Commerce), Fiat Auto, Turin, Italy.

Bruno Bottliglieri, Fondazione Giovanni Agnelli, Turin.

Anna Botto, Istituto Tecnotex, Città Degli Studi, Biella.

Paolo Botto, president, Lanificio Giusepppe Botto & Figli, Biella.

Virginia Brancadoro, Ufficio Studi, Montedison, Milan.

Mr. Brovia, Associazione Abbigliamento, Milan.

Donatella Canta, regional secretary, Filtea-CGIL, Turin.

Mr. Paolo Cantarelli, general director, Fiat Auto (former general director of COMAU, Fiat's Machine Tool Division), Turin, Italy.

Fabrizio Carmignani, CesPe, Rome.

Sergio Carpini, Promotrade, Prato.

Gianpiero Carpo, IRES-CGIL Piemonte.

Antonio Cavaliere (CGIL) and Alfredo Anastasio (UIL), local union leaders at Porto Marghera, Mestre.

Francesco Cecchinato, Relazione Esterne, Nouvo Pignone-SMIT, Schio, Vicenza.

Gianprimo Cella, professor of industrial relations and sociology, University of Brescia.

Cesco Chinello, provincial secretariat, PCI Venezia.

Francesco Ciaffaloni, Camera del Lavoro-CGIL, Turin.

Mr. Ciampini, secretary general, Federtessile, Milan.

Mario Coda, general manager, Tessiana, S.p.A., Adorno Mica, Biella.

Sergio Cofferati, national secretary, Filcea-CGIL, Rome.

Ada Collidà, Sinistra Indipendente parliamentary deputy, Rome.

Pier Giorgio Colombo, general manager, Lanificio Ermenegildo Zegna, Biella.

Cesare Cosi, FIOM-CGIL, Provincia di Torino.

Cesare Damiano, provincial secretary, FIOM-CGIL Torino, Turin.

Orlando De Toni, general secretary, Flerica-CISL Venezia, Mestre.

Tom Dealessandri, CISL, Provincia di Torino, Turin.

Bruno Dente, professor of political science, University of Bologna.

Enrico Di Giorgi, director of personnel, Montedipe, (ex-personnel director at both the Ferrara and Porto Marghera plants), Milan.

Director of personnel, Altissimo-ITT, Turin.

Aldo Dutto, ex-delegate at Fiat Mirafiori, Turin.

Factory Council group interview, Altissimo-ITT, Turin.

Paolo Ferla, Lanificio Egidio Ferla, Ponzone, Biella.

Michele Figurati, director of industrial relations, External Relations, Fiat S.p.A., Turin.

Graziella Fornengo, Laboratorio di Economia Politica, Università degli Studi di Torino.

Sergio Gambarelli, general manager, Leglertex S.p.A., Ponte San Pietro, Begamo.

Mr. Gambilara, secretary general, Uilcea-UIL, Mestre, Venice.

Francesco Garibaldo, director, Istituto di Ricerche Economiche e Sociali, Rome. (former regional secretary, FIOM-CGIL [metalworkers union], Emilia-Romagna.

Piero Gastaldo, Fondazione Giovanni Agnelli, Turin.

Mr. Gaude, factory delegate, ITT-Altissimo.

Mr. Gavagnin, chemical engineer, Montedison-Porto Marghera plant, Mestre.

Ms. Giardini, personnel office, Gruppo GFT, Turin.

Marco Giatti, FIOM-CGIL, Provincia di Torino, ex-member of the FLM Coordinating Committee on Autos.

Mr. Giugliani, director of personnel, Himont, Marghera, Venice.

Oliviero Godi, sales representative, Marzoli, Palazuolo Sull'Oglio.

Franco Grassini, professor of political science, LUIS, Rome (ex-general director of GEPI).

Dino Greco, provincial secretary, Filtea-CGIL, Brescia.

Group interview with Alfa Romeo Factory delegates, Milan.

Flavio Iano, Agenzia Industriale Italiana, Turin.

Loradana Legabue, director of CITER—Centro Informazione Tessile Emilia Romagna, Carpi.

Luciano Locatelli, plant manager, SOMET, Colzate, Bergamo.

C.G. Lovera, general manager, SOMET, Colzate, Bergamo.

Dr. Maestri, director of personnel, Montedipe-Porto Marghera, Venice.

Pierpaolo Pollari Maglietta, Associazione Italiana Industriali Tintori, Stampatori e Finitori Tessili, Milan.

Maurizio Magnabosco, director of industrial relations, Fiat Auto.

Mr. Mairano and Ms. Pinto, industrial relations, Fiat Auto, Turin.

Bruno Manghi, provincial secretary, CISL.

Aldo Marchetto, FIOM-CGIL, Provincia di Torino.

Pier Franco Marzoli, sales manager, Marzoli, Palazuolo Sull'Oglio, Brescia.

Agostino Megale, national secretariat, Filtea-CGIL, Rome.

Stefano Micoli and Paolo Lombardi, Associazione Magliacalze, Milan.

Vito Milano, regional secretary, CISL Lombardia, Milan.

Giacinto Militello, president of INPS, Milan.

Giancarlo Monti, general secretary, ACIMIT—Italian Textile Machinery Association, Milan.

Raffaele Morese, national secretary, FIM-CISL, Rome.

Mr. Ongaro, plant manager, Leglertex, Crespi Ada, Bergamo.

Enrico Ottolino, director, Centro Tessile Cottoniero, Busto-Arsizio. President of Istituto Tecnico Industriale Statale, Busto-Arsizio.

Corrado Paracone, Fondazione Giovanni Agnelli, Turin.

Mr. Parenti, president, Unione Industriale Pratese, Prato.

Mr. Parodini, provincial secretary, Filtea-CGIL, Busto-Arsizio (Varese).

Franco Perazio, president, Tessiana, Biella.

Paolo Perulli, professor of urban sociology, University of Venice.

Pier Luigi Loro Piana and Sergio Loro Piana, co-presidents, Lanificio Ing. Loro Piana and Co., S.p.A., Quarona Sesia, Biella.

Gian Maria Gros-Pietro, director, Istituto di Ricerca Sull'Impresa E Lo Sviluppo, CNR, Turin.

Mr. Pinna, personnel director, Gruppo Tessile Niggeler and Kupfer, Capriolo, Brescia.

Andrea Pinto, general manager, Krizia, Milan.

Evelina Codacci Pisanelli, manager, Strategic and Market Analysis, Montedison, Milan, Cambridge.

Claudio Poli, general director, ISVOR-Fiat (Fiat's Training Division), Turin, Italy.

Mr. Pollaro, Associazione Piccole e Medie Imprese, Turin.

Mr. Raccanella, Raccanella S.r.L., Palazuolo Sull'Oglio, Brescia.

Giorgo Rampa, director of strategic planning, Fiat Auto, Turin.

Pippo Ranci, professor of economics, Catholic University, Milan; director of Istituto di Ricerca Sociale (IRS), Milan.

Bruno Ravazio, regional secretary, Filtea-CGIL Lombardia, Milan.

Ida Regalia, IRES-Lombardia, Milan.

Marino Regini, professor of industrial sociology, University of Trento and President IRES- Lombardia.

Gloria Regonini, professor of political science, University of Milan.

Marco Ricchetti, research office, Federtessile (Textile Business Association), Milan, Italy.

Mr. Riva, provincial secretary, FIOM-CGIL Milan, Sesto San Giovanni.

Marco Rivetti, president, Gruppo Finanziario Tessile, Turin.

Matteo Rollier, ex-delegate at Fiat Mirafiori.

Guido Romagnoli, professor of sociology, University of Trento.

Mr. Rossi, factory delegate, Niggeler-Kupfer, Capriolo, Brescia.

Dr. Rubino, controller, Montedipe-Porto Marghera, Venice.

Giuseppe Ruzzioni, provincial secretary, CGIL, Ferrara (former head of the Factory Council, Montedison-Ferrara).

Claudio Sabattini, national secretary, CGIL, Rome.

Michele Salvati, professor of economics, University of Milan.

Ettore Santi, research director, CESOS, Rome (now deceased).

Gaetano Sateriale, national secretariat, CGIL, ex-regional secretary, Filcea-CGIL Emilia Romagna, Rome.

Nicola Schiavone, Fondazione Giovanni Agnelli, Turin.

Maria-Teresa Schütt, director, Research Office, Fiat Auto.

Gastone Sclavi, Montedison manager (ex-national secretary, Filcea-CGIL), Milan.

Mr. Signorini, senior vice-president for business development and management, Fiat Auto, Turin.

Giancarlo Sivornino, director of Women's Division, Gruppo GFT, Turin.

Chemistry Teacher, Istituto Tecnico Industriale Statale Di Setificio Paolo Carcano, Como.

Ferruccio Tinghi, director, GFT-USA, Turin.

Lorenzo Tossarelli, director of marketing, Gruppo GFT, Turin.

Mr. Tramontana, CEO, Alfa Romeo, Arese.

Giancarlo Trapparo, PSI representative in the regional government, Turin.

Carlo Trigilia, professor of political science, University of Palermo.

Giuseppe Volpato, professor of industrial economics, University of Venice.

References

Accornero, Aris. 1973. *Gli anni '50 in fabbrica.* Bari: De Donato.
——. 1976. "Introduzione." In *Annali della Fondazione Giacomo Feltrinelli, problemi del movimento sindacale in Italia, 1943–1973.* Milan: Feltrinelli.
——. 1981. "Come si riproduce un'avanguardia." In Aris Accornero and Vittorio Rieser, eds., *Il mestiere dell'avanguardia: Riedizione di "Fiat Confino."* Bari: De Donato.
——. 1988a. "Recent Trends and Features in Unemployment." Paper presented at the Political Economy Seminar Series, Center for International Studies, MIT. November 8.
——. 1988b. "Torino da laboratorio a caso limite." *Politica ed economia* 1, January.
——. 1991. *La parabola del sindacato.* Bologna: Il Mulino.
Accornero, Aris, Alberto Baldissera, and Sergio Scamuzzi. 1980. "Ricerca di massa sulla condizione operaia alla Fiat." *Bollettino Cespe* 2, February.
Accornero, Aris, and Fabrizio Carmignani. 1986. *I paradossi della disoccupazione.* Bologna: Il Mulino.
Accornero, Aris, Fabrizio Carmignani, and Nino Magna. 1985. "I tre tipi di operai della Fiat." *Politica ed economia* 5: 33–47.
Accornero, Aris, and Paolo Ceri. 1987. *Opinioni e attegiamenti nell'area di Torino su industria, innovazione, lavoro.* Turin: Istituto Universitario di Studi Europei.
Accornero, Aris, and Vittorio Rieser. 1981. *Il mestiere dell'avanguardia: Riedizione di "Fiat Confino."* Bari: De Donato.
Adams, Pamela. 1985. "Government-Industry Relations in Italy: The Case of Industrial Policy." Diss., Department of Political Science, Yale University.
Agosti, Aldo, and Gian Maria Bravo. 1979. *Storia del movimento operaio del socialismo e delle lotte sociali in Piemonte.* Bari: De Donato.
Agostinelli, Mario. 1983. "Innovazione e tecnologia/occupazione e condizioni di lavoro." In *fabbrica e idee,* supplemento al Bolletino Filtea-CGIL 13, October 10.

REFERENCES

Agostinelli, Mario, and Mauro Beschi. 1988. "Sistemi dei turni e utilizzo degli impianti nel settore tessile-cotoniero della Lombardia." *Quaderni di rassegna sindacale* 88, January–February.

Ahlen, Kristina. 1989. "Swedish Collective Bargaining under Pressure: Inter-Union Rivalry and Income Policies." *British Journal of Industrial Relations* 27, no. 3, November: 330–46.

Alasia, Giorgio, et al. 1981. "Cultura e sindacato a Torino sul finire degli anni '50." *Quaderni della Fondazione Vera Nocentini*, 1, June.

Albert, Michel. 1993. *Capitalism against Capitalism*. London: Whurr.

Allum, Percy A. 1973. *Italy—Republic without Government?* New York: W. W. Norton.

Altshuler, Alan, et al. 1984. *The Future of the Automobile: The Report of MIT's International Automobile Program*. Cambridge: MIT Press.

Amin, Ash. 1985. "Restructuring in Fiat and the Decentralization of Production into Southern Italy." In R. Hudson and J. Lewis, eds., *Uneven Development in Southern Europe: Studies of Accumulation, Class, Migration, and the State*. London: Methuen.

———. 1989. "Specialization without Growth: Small Footwear Firms in Naples." In Edward Goodman, Julia Bamford, and Peter Saynor, eds., *Small Firms and Industrial Districts in Italy*. London: Routledge.

Amoretti, Aldo. 1984. "L'iniziativa sindacale nell'impresa tessile artigiana: Note per una discussione." *Quaderni di rassegna sindacale*. 108–9, May–August.

Anderlini, Fausto, and Cesco Chinello. 1986. *Operai e scelte politiche: Il caso delle zone bianche a economia diffusa del Veneto*. Milan: Franco Angeli.

Andersen, Arthur, and Co. 1981. *Scelte imprenditoriali ed organizzazione: Il caso di quattro aziende Biellesi*. Biella: Unione Industriale Biellese.

Anderson, Perry. 1979. *Lineages of the Absolutist State*. London: Verso.

Antonelli, Cristiano. 1986. *L'attività innovativa in un distretto tecnologico*. Turin: Fondazione Giovanni Agnelli.

———. 1987. "The Determinants of the Distribution of Innovative Activity in a Metropolitan Area: The Case of Turin." *Regional Studies* 21, no. 2: 85–94.

Antonelli, Cristiano, ed. 1986. *Structural Impacts of Telematics on the Automobile and Textile and Clothing Industries*. Brussels: Commission of the European Communities.

Antonelli, Cristiano, et al. 1987. "Technological Diffusion and Firm's Investment Behavior: The Case of the Textile Industry." Unpublished paper. Turin.

Armstrong, Philip, Andrew Glyn, and John Harrison. 1984. *Capitalism since World War II*. London: Fontana.

Azzolini, Riccardo. 1980. "La politica della Confindustria da Carli a Merloni." *Politica ed economia* 1.

Azzolini, Riccardo, Giuseppe Dimalta, and Riccardo Pastore. 1979. *L'industria chimica tra crisi e programmazione*. Rome: Editori Riuniti.

Baglioni, Guido. 1968–69. "L'istituto della commissione interna e la questione della rappresentanza dei lavoratori nei luoghi di lavoro." *Annuario del Centro Studi CISL*. 8: 35–64.

——. 1974. *L'ideologia della borghesia industriale nell'Italia liberale.* Turin: Einaudi.

——. 1975. *Il sindacato dell'autonomia.* Bari: De Donato.

Baglioni, Guido, ed. 1980. *Analisi della CISL,* vol. 2. Rome: Lavoro.

Baglioni, Guido, Marina Camonico, and Ettore Santi, eds. 1988. *Le relazioni industriali in Italia: Rapporto 86–87.* Rome: Lavoro.

Baglioni, Guido, and Rinaldo Milani, 1990. *La contrattazione collettiva nelle aziende industriali in Italia.* Milan: Franco Angeli.

Baglioni, Mirella. 1989. *Regions and Business Interests: The Italian Case.* Parma: Istituto di Scienze Economiche, Università degli Studi di Parma.

Baglioni, Mirella, and Ezio Tarantelli. 1980. "Il paradigma economico nell'azione e nella cultura della CISL." In Guido Baglioni, ed., *Analisi della CISL,* vol. 2. Rome: Lavoro.

Bagnasco, Arnaldo. 1977. *Le Tre Italie.* Bologna: Il Mulino.

——. 1986. *Torino: Un profilo Sociologico.* Turin: Einaudi.

——. 1988. *La costruzione sociale del Mercato.* Bologna: Il Mulino.

Bairati, Piero. 1983. *Valetta.* Turin: UTET.

——. 1986. *Sul filo di lana: Cinque generazioni di imprenditori: I Marzotto.* Bologna: Il Mulino.

Balconi, Margherita. 1991. *La siderugia italiana (1975–1990).* Bologna: Il Mulino.

Baldissera, Alberto. 1981. "Le immagini del terrorismo tra gli operai della Fiat." *Politica ed economia* 12, no. 9: 33–40.

——. 1984. "Alle origini della politica della disuguaglianza nell'Italia degli anni '80: La marcia dei quarantamila." *Quaderni di sociologia* 31, no. 1: 1–78.

Balestri, Andrea, ed. 1988. "La ricerca di nuovi sentieri di sviluppo nei distretti industriali: Note sull'evoluzione del tessile pratese." Unpublished manuscript. Prato.

Balestrini, Nanni. 1971. *Vogliamo tutto.* Milan: Feltrinelli.

Balliano, Piera. 1985. "Crisi e ristrutturazione del settore automobilistico negli anni ottanta." In Angelo Michelsons, ed., *Tre incognite per lo sviluppo.* Milan: Franco Angeli.

Banfield, Edward. 1967. *The Moral Economy of a Backward Society.* New York: Free Press.

Barberis, Guido, and Bruno Bottiglieri. 1980. *Crisi industriale e governo regionale: Il caso del Piemonte.* Turin: Eda.

Barca, Fabrizio, and Marco Magnani. 1989. *L'industria fra capitale e lavoro.* Bologna: Il Mulino.

Barkin, Solomon, ed. 1975. *Worker Militancy and Its Consequences, 1965–75.* New York: Praeger.

Barnes, Samuel. 1977. *Representation in Italy: Institutionalized Tradition and Electoral Choice.* Chicago: University of Chicago Press.

Barrattieri, Vittorio. 1984. "La ristrutturazione del settore chimico in Italia: Una analisi dei principali avvenimenti dal 1977 al 1983." *Rivista di politica economica* 3, March.

Bartolini, Stefano. 1982. "The Politics of Institutional Reform in Italy." *West European Politics* 5, no. 3, July: 203–21.

Beales, Derek. 1981. *The Risorgimento and the Unification of Italy*. London: Longman.

Becchis, Ezio. 1985. "Il ruolo del lavoro umano negli impianti automatizzati." *Sisifo* 6, December.

Becchis, Ezio, and Gianni Montani 1988. "Loro Piana," unpublished report for the Osservatorio Tessile Piemontese, Filteo—CGIL Piemonte.

Bell, Daniel. 1976. *The Coming of Post-Industrial Society*. New York: Basic Books.

Bellandi, Marco. 1989. "The Role of Small Firms in the Development of Italian Manufacturing Industry." In Edward Goodman, Julia Bamford, and Peter Saynor, eds., *Small Firms and Industrial Districts in Italy*. London: Routledge.

Belussi, Fiorenza. 1983. "La Lanerossi tra risanamento e imobilitazione." *Oltre il ponte*, 2: 20–45.

———. 1989. "Benetton Italy: Beyond Fordism and Flexible Specialization to the Evolution of the Network Firm Model." In Susan Mitter, ed., *Information Technology and Women's Employment: The Case of the European Clothing Industry*. Berlin: Springer Verlag.

Bendix, Reinhard. 1964. *Nation-Building and Citizenship*. New York: John Wiley and Sons.

Benenati, Elisabetta, and Claudio Sabattini. 1986. *Sindacato e potere contrattuale*. Rome: Ediesse.

Bergamaschi, Myriam, Emilio Zanette, Ernesto Matini, eds. 1980. *Salari contrattuali e piattaforme rivendicative dei metalmeccanici, 1948–79*. Milan: Franco Angeli.

Berger, Suzanne. 1972. *Peasants against Politics: Rural Organization in Brittany 1911–1967*. Cambridge: Harvard University Press.

Berger, Suzanne, ed. 1981. *Organizing Interest Groups in Western Europe*. New York: Cambridge University Press.

Berger, Suzanne, and Michael Piore. 1980. *Dualism and Discontinuities in Industrial Societies*. New York: Cambridge University Press.

Berta, Giuseppi. 1978. "Dalla manifattura al sistema di fabbrica: Razionalizzazione e conflitti di lavoro." In *Storia d'Italia*, Annali 1. Turin: Einaudi.

———. 1979. "La formazione del movimento operaio regionale: Il caso dei tessili (1860–1900)." In Aldo Agosti and Gian Maria Bravo, eds., *Storia del movimento operaio, del socialismo, e delle lotte sociali in Piemonte*, vol. 1: Bari: De Donato.

Berta, Giuseppe, and Sergio Chiamparino. 1986. "Lavoro industriale e azione politica." *Sisifo* 7, April.

Berzano, Luigi, et al. 1984. *Uomini di frontiera: "Scelta di classe" e transformazioni della coscienza cristiana a Torino dal Concilio ad oggi*. Turin: Cooperativa di Cultura Lorenzo Milani.

Best, Michael. 1990. *The New Competition*. Cambridge: Harvard University Press.

Bianchi, Gianfranco, and Giorgio Lauzi, eds. 1981. *I metalmeccanici: Documenti per una storia della FIOM*. Bari: De Donato.

Bianchi, Patrizio. 1983. "Component Technology and the Automobile Production Process." In Jean Pierre Barbier, et al., *Automobile Components Industry Study: Final Report*. Berlin: Wissenschaftszentrum.

———. 1984. *Divisione del lavoro e ristrutturazione industriale*. Bologna: Il Mulino.

——. 1987. "The IRI in Italy: Strategic Role and Political Constraints." *West European Politics* 10, no. 1, January: 269–90.

——. 1988. "Privatization of Industry: The Alfa Romeo Case." In Raffaella Y. Nanetti, Robert Leonardi, and Piergiorgio Corbetta, eds., *Italian Politics: A Review,* vol. 2. London: Pinter.

——. 1990. "Ripensare la programmazione." *Il Mulino* 39, no. 4, July–August: 607–39.

Bianchi, Patrizio, and Gaetano Sateriale. 1983. "Contratti di solidarietà: L'esempio di Ferrara." *Prospettiva sindacale* 49, September: 178–85.

Bianchi, Patrizio, Pino Foschi, and Gaetano Sateriale. 1986. "Organizzazione della produzione, del lavoro e nuove relazioni industriali." *Cds documentazione* 1–4.

Bianchi, Patrizio, Sabino Cassese, and Vincent della Sala. 1988. "Privatization in Italy: Aims and Constraints." *West European Politics* 11, no. 1, January.

Bigazzi, Duccio. 1986. "Management Strategies in the Italian Car Industry 1906–1945: Fiat and Alfa Romeo." In Steven Tolliday and Jonathan Zeitlin, eds., *The Automobile Industry and Its Workers.* Oxford: Polity Press.

——. 1988. *"Il Portello: Operai, tecnici e imprenditori all'Alfa-Romeo 1906–1926.* Milan: Franco Angeli.

Bignami, Francesca. 1992. "The Resurgence of Old Patterns of Representation in Contemporary Italy: The Engine Drivers' Movement." M.S. Thesis, Faculty of Social Studies, University of Oxford.

Binder, Leonard, et al. 1971. *Crises and Sequences of Political Development.* Princeton: Princeton University Press.

Blackmer, Donald L. M., and Sidney Tarrow, eds. 1975. *Communism in Italy and France.* Princeton: Princeton University Press.

Blim, Michael L. 1990. "Economic Development and Decline in the Emerging Global Factory: Some Italian Lessons." *Politics and Society* 18, no. 1, March: 143–63.

Bognetti, Giuseppe. 1981. "Il sistema delle partecipazioni statali negli anni '70," In Emilio Gerelli and Giuseppe Bognetti, eds., *La crisi delle partecipazioni statali: Motivi e prospettive.* Milan: Franco Angeli.

Boltho, Andrea, ed. 1982. *The European Economy: Growth and Crisis.* Oxford: Oxford University Press.

Bonazzi, Giuseppe. 1984. "La lotta dei 35 giorni alla Fiat: Un'analisi sociologica." *Politica ed economia* 11: 33–43.

——.1986. "Spontaneita ed assistenza nello sviluppo cooperativo: Una ricerca in un'area metropolitana in crisi occupazionale." *Quaderni di sociologia* 32, no. 6: 94–132.

——. 1988. "La sociologia e il gioco della produzione." *Politica ed economia* 1, January.

——. 1990. "Lasciare la fabbrica." In Arnaldo Bagnasco, ed., *La citta dopo Ford.* Turin: Bollati Boringhieri.

Bordogna, Lorenzo. 1989. "Il caso del Petrolchimico Montedison di Ferrara." In Marino Regini and Charles F. Sabel, eds., *Strategie di riaggiustamento industriale.* Bologna: Il Mulino.

Bower, Joseph L. 1986. *When Markets Quake: The Management Challenge of Restructuring Industry.* Boston: Harvard Business School Press.

REFERENCES

Boyer, Robert. 1988. "The Search for New Wage/Labor Relations." In Robert Boyer, ed., *The Search for Labor Market Flexibility*. Oxford: Clarendon Press.

Brancadoro, Virginia, and Giovanni Schieppati. 1983. "Le strategie industriali per gli anni '80: Il settore chimico di base." *Economia e politica industriale* 39: 173–91.

Brandini, Pietro Merli. 1975. "Italy: Creating a New Industrial Relations System from the Bottom." In Solomon Barkin, ed., *Worker Militancy and Its Consequences, 1965–75*. New York: Praeger.

Cacciari, Massimo. 1975a. "Ciclo chimico e lotte operaie: Porto Marghera 1972–74." *Classe* 11, November.

——. 1975b. "Struttura e crisi del 'modello' economico-sociale Veneto." *Classe* 11, November.

Cacioppo, Maria, Luciano Pero, and Anna Tempia. 1987. *Ritagliare il tempo: L'orario di lavoro nel settore tessile*. Rome: Lavoro.

Cainarca, Giancarlo. 1984. "L'evoluzione del tessile-abbigliamento." *Quaderni di rassegna sindacale* 106: 117–24.

Calmfors, Lars, and John Driffil. 1988. "Bargaining Structure, Corporatism, and Macroeconomic Performance." *Economic Policy* 3, n.1, April: 13–61.

Camera del Lavoro Territoriale Biellese. 1987. *Ricerca sul sistema industriale biellese*. Biella.

Cameron, David R. 1984. "Social Democracy, Corporatism, Labor Quiescence, and the Representation of Economic Interest in Advanced Capitalist Society." In John H. Goldthorpe, ed., *Order and Conflict in Contemporary Capitalism*. Oxford: Clarendon Press.

Cammett, John M. 1967. *Antonio Gramsci and the Origins of Italian Communism*. Stanford: Stanford University Press.

Campetti, Loris. 1986. "Separati fuori casa: Inchiesta sulla periferia del sindacato: La ex Flm di Torino." *Il Manifesto*, September 12.

Camuffo, Arnaldo. 1993. "L'evoluzione del Gruppo Marzotto: Imprenditorialità e Management." Unpublished manuscript. Universiti Cà Foscari, Venice.

Camuffo, Arnaldo, and Anna Comacchio. 1990. *Strategia e organizzazione nel tessile—abbigliamento*. Padua: CEDAM.

Canta, Donata. 1981. "Mutamenti tecnologici e lavoro a isole nell'esperienza piemontese." *Quaderni di rassegna sindacale* 88, January–February.

Canziani, Aznaldo, ed. 1989. *Il settore cotoniero italiano*. Milan: EGEA.

Carbognin, Maurizio. 1980. "I comunisti sono tutti zucconi." In Maurizio Carbognin and Luigi Paganelli, eds., *Il sindacato come esperienza: La CISL nella memoria dei suoi militanti*. Rome: Lavoro.

Cardaci, Roberto. 1985. "Gli effetti sociali della ristrutturazione: La cassa integrazione a Torino dopo il 1980." In Angelo Michelsons, ed., *Tre incognite per lo sviluppo*. Milan: Franco Angeli.

Carmignani, Fabrizio. 1984. "Il 'sindacato di classe' nella lotta dei 35 giorni alla Fiat." *Politica ed economia* 11: 43–48.

Carniti, Pierre. 1977. *L'autonomia alla prova*. Milan: Coines Editore.

——. 1985. *Remare controcorrente*. Rome: Lavoro.

Carocci, Gianpiero. 1975. *Storia d'Italia dall'unità ad oggi*. Milan: Feltrinelli.

Cartocci, Roberto. 1987. "Otto risposte a un problema: La divisione dell'Italia in zone politicamente Omogenee." *Polis* 1, no. 3, December: 481–514.

Cassese, Sabino. 1981. "Il controllo delle partecipazioni statati." In Emilio Gerelli and Giuseppe Bognetti, eds., *La crisi delle partecipazioni statali: Motivi e prospettive*. Milan: Franco Angeli.

——. 1987. "Stato ed economia: Il problema storico." In Peter Lange and Marino Regino, eds., *Stato e regolazione sociali: Nuove prospettive sul caso italiano*. Bologna: Il Mulino.

——. 1992. "Oltre lo Stato: I limiti dei governi nazionali nel controllo dell'economia." In *Nazioni senza ricchezza, ricchezze senza nazione*. Bologna: Il Mulino.

Castronovo, Valerio. 1964. *L'industria laniera in Piemonte nel secolo XIX*. Turin: Einaudi.

——. 1977. *Giovanni Agnelli: La Fiat dal 1899 al 1945*. Turin: Einaudi.

——. 1979. *Impresa ed economia in Piemonte dalla "grande crisi" ad oggi*. Turin: UTET.

——. 1987. *Torino*. Bari: Editori Laterza.

Catena, Carlo, ed. 1975. *La piccola e la media industria nella crisi dell'economia italiana*, vol. 2. Rome: Editori Riuniti.

Cazzola, Franco. 1992. *L'Italia del pizzo: Fenomenologia della tangente quotidiana*. Turin: Einaudi.

Celata, Gianni. 1980. "Sviluppo tecnologico ed economico nel tessile." *Quaderni di rassegna sindacale* 84–85 January–February: 105–12.

Cella, Gianprimo. 1987. "Criteri di regolazione nelle relazioni industriali italiane: Le istituzioni deboli." In Peter Lange and Marino Regini, eds., *Stato e regolazione sociale*. Bologna: Il Mulino.

——. 1989. "Criteria of Regulation in Italian Industrial Relations: A Case of Weak Institutions." In Peter Lange and Marino Regini, eds., *State, Market, and Social Regulation: New Perspectives on Italy*. New York: Cambridge University Press.

Cella, Gianprimo, and Tiziano Treu, eds. 1989. *Relazioni industriali: Manuale per l'analisi della esperienza italiana*. 2d ed. Bologna: Il Mulino.

CENSIS. 1983. *Il caso Trivero: Demografia, occupazione, qualità e stili di vita in un comune montano industrializato*. Biella: Unione Industriale Biellese.

——. 1992. *25 Rapporto sulla situazione sociale del paese 1991*. Milan: Franco Angeli.

CER-IRS. 1986. *Quale strategia per l'industria?* Bologna: Il Mulino.

——. 1989. *Mercato e politica industriale*. Bologna: Il Mulino.

CERPI. 1971. *Ricerca su alcune linee di ristrutturazione dell'industria tessile biellese*. Milano: CERPI.

CESOS. 1983. *La CISL nel settore tessile, 1948–1954*. Rome: CESOS.

——. 1990. *Le relazioni sindacali in Italia: Rapporto 1988/89*. Rome: Lavoro.

——. 1991. *Le relazioni sindacali in Italia: Rapporto 1990*. Rome: Lavoro.

CGIL. 1985. *Innovazione tecnologica e occupazionale nel tessile-abbigliamento: Aspetti della contrattazione e nuove relazioni industriali*. Rome: Ediesse.

Chiesi, Antonio M. 1981. *Il sistema degli orari*. Milan: Franco Angeli.

——. 1987. "L'organizzazione degli interessi imprenditoriali in un caso di ristrutturazione settoriale." *Studi organizzativi* 3–4.

Chiesi, Antonio M., and Alberto Martinelli. 1987. "La rappresentanza degli interessi imprenditoriali come meccanismo di regolazione sociale." In Peter Lange and Marino Regini, eds., *Stato e regolazione sociale*. Bologna: Il Mulino.

REFERENCES

Chiesi, Antonio M., and Alberto Martinelli. 1989. "The Representation of Business Interests as a Mechanism of Social Regulation." In Peter Lange and Marino Regini, eds., *State, Market, and Social Regulation: New Perspectives on Italy*. New York: Cambridge University Press.

Chinello, Cesco. 1975. *Storia di uno Sviluppo capitalistico: Porto Marghera e Venezia: 1951–1973*. Rome: Editori Riuniti.

———. 1977. "Ristrutturazione e integrazioni produttive nell'area chimica Montedison del nord e verteze di gruppo." *Rinnovamento Veneto* 21, July–August.

———. 1984. *Classe, movimento, organizzazione: Le lotte operaie a Marghera/Venezia: I percorsi di una crisi, 1945–55*. Milan: Franco Angeli.

Chubb, Judith, and Maurizio Vannicelli 1988. "Italy: A Web of Scandals in a Flawed Democracy." In Andrei Markovits and Mark Silverstein, eds., *The Politics of Scandal*. New York: Holmes-Meier.

Ciborra, Claudio, Tullio Colombo, and Claudio Roveda. 1981. "Dimensione d'impresa, innovazione tecnologica ed effeti organizzativi nel tessile." *Quaderni di rassegna sindacale* 88, January–February.

Ciborra, Claudio, and Gian Franco Lanzara, eds. 1985. *Progettazione delle nuove tecnologie e qualità del lavoro*. Milan: Franco Angeli.

Ciciotti, Enrico. 1986. *Natalità delle imprese e diffusione delle innovazioni di processo in un distretto tecnologico*. Turin: Fondazione Giovanni Agnelli.

Cilona, Ornella, and Maria Luisa Righi. 1986. *Cent'anni di storia dei lavoratori chimici*. Rome: Ediesse.

Ciochetti, Clemente, and Franco Ramella. 1964. "Una rivoluzione tecnologica nel biellese." *Quaderni Rossi* 4.

Clark, Martin. 1977. *Antonio Gramsci and the Revolution That Failed*. New Haven: Yale University Press.

Cobrin, Steven Howard. 1990. "Two Paths of Industrial Adjustment to Shifting Patterns of International Competition: The Political Economy of Flexible Specialization and Mass Production in British Textiles." Diss., Department of Government, Harvard University.

Cohen, Cathy J., and Michael C. Dawson. 1993. "Neighborhood Poverty and African American Politics." *American Political Science Review* 87, no. 2, June: 286–302.

Cohen, Joshua, and Joel Rogers. 1992. "Secondary Associations and Democratic Governance." *Politics and Society* 20, no. 4, December: 393–472.

Cohen, Steven. 1969, 1977. *Modern Capitalist Planning: The French Model*. Berkeley: University of California Press.

Cole, Robert E. 1989. *Strategies for Learning*. Berkeley: University of California Press.

Coleman, James. 1988. "Social Capital in the Creation of Human Capital." *American Journal of Sociology* 94, supplement: S95–S120.

Collidà, Ada Becchi. 1989. "Le associazioni imprenditoriali." In Gianprimo Cella and Tiziano Treu, eds., *Relazioni industriali: Manuale per l'analisi della esperienza italiana*. Bologna: Il Mulino.

Collidà, Ada Becchi, and Serafino Negrelli. 1986. *La transizione nell'industria e nelle relazioni industriali: L'auto e il caso Fiat*. Milan: Franco Angeli.

Comito, Vicenzo. 1982. *La Fiat tra crisi e ristrutturazione*. Rome: Editori Riuniti.

Commissione Carniti. 1988. *I salari in Italia negli anni ottanta*. Venice: Marsilio.

Confindustria. 1988. *X Rapporto CSC: Squilibri commerciali e aggiustamento produttivo nei paesi industriali*. Rome: Confindustria.

———. 1990. *Previsioni dell'economia italiana: Il settore tessile—abbigliamento*. Rome: Confindustria.

Consolati, Luciano, and Alberto Riva. 1989. "Crescita e riposizionamento della grande industria italiana negli anni '80 (1981–1986)." In Pier Carlo Padoan, Andrea Pezzoli, and Francesco Silva, eds., *Concorrenza e concentrazione nell'industria italiana*. Bologna: Il Mulino: 119–72.

Contarino, Michael. 1984. "The Politics of Industrial Change: Textile Unions and Industrial Restructuring in Five Italian Localities." Diss., Department of Government, Harvard University.

Contini, Giovanni. 1985. "Politics, Law and Shop Floor Bargaining in Postwar Italy." In Steven Tolliday and Jonathan Zeitlin, eds., *Shop Floor Bargaining and the State: Historical and Comparative Perspectives*. Cambridge: Cambridge University Press.

———. 1986. "The Rise and Fall of Shop Floor Bargaining in Fiat, Turin: 1969–1980." In Steven Tolliday and Jonathan Zeitlin, eds., *The Automobile Industry and Its Workers*. Cambridge, UK: Polity Press.

Correale, Giacomo, and Raffaele Gaeta. 1983. "Mutamenti strutturali nell'industria tessile-abbigliamento mondiale: Posizione competitiva e strategie internazionali delle aziende italiane." *Economia e politica industriale* 38: 145–92.

Costa, Giovanni, and Claudio Gradara. 1984. *Impresa e relazioni industriali: Alfa Romeo, Italsider e Olivetti*. Padua: CEDAM.

Costantini, Silvio. 1980. "La formazione del gruppo dirigente della CISL (1950–1968)." In Guido Baglioni, ed., *Analisi della CISL*, vol. 1. Rome: Lavoro.

Cotula, Franco. 1984. "Financial Innovation and Monetary Control in Italy." *Banca Nazionale del Lavoro Quarterly Review* 37: 219–56.

Cristofoli, Maria Cristina, and Martino Pozzobon. 1981. *I tessili milanesi: Le fabbriche, gli industriali, i lavoratori, il sindacato dall'Ottocento agli anni '30*. Milan: Franco Angeli.

Dawley, Alan. 1976. *Class and Community: The Industrial Revolution in Lynn*. Cambridge Mass: Harvard University Press.

Dealessandri, Tom, and Maurizio Magnabosco. 1987. *Contrattare alla Fiat*. Rome: Lavoro.

De Cecco, Marcello. 1989. "Keynes and Italian Economics." In Peter Hall, ed., *The Political Power of Economic Ideas: Keynesianism across Nations*. Princeton: Princeton University Press.

De Cesaris Benedetto. 1971. "La scuola CISL di Firenze negli anni '50." *Quaderni di rassegna sindacale* 10, no. 37, July–August: 80–94.

Della Porta, Donatella. 1992. *Lo scambio occulto: Casi di corruzione politica in Italia*. Bologna: Il Mulino.

Della Sala, Vincent. 1988. "The Italian Budgetary Process: Political and Institutional Constraints." *West European Politics* 11, no. 3, July: 110–25.

REFERENCES

Dellavalle, Claudio. 1979. "La classe operaia piemontese nella guerra di Liberazione." In Aldo Agosti and Gian Maria Bravo, eds., *Storia del movimento operaio, del socialismo, e delle lotte sociali in Piemonte*, vol. 2. Bari: De Donato.

Dente, Bruno. 1985. *Governare la frammentazione: Stato, regioni ed enti locali in Italia*. Bologna: Il Mulino.

De Rosa, Luigi, and Ennio Di Nolfo, eds. 1986. *Regionalismo e centralizzazione nella storia di Italia e Stati Uniti*. Florence: Leo S. Olschki Editore.

Dertouzos, Michael L., Richard K. Lester, Robert M. Solow, and the MIT Commission on Industrial Productivity. 1989. *Made in America: Regaining the Productive Edge*. Cambridge: MIT Press.

Dickens, William T., and Jonathan S. Leonard. 1985. "Accounting for the Decline in Union Membership." *Industrial and Labor Relations Review* 38, no. 3, April: 323–34.

Dina, Angelo. 1985. "Innovazione, lavoro, e organizzazione: Il caso Fiat." *Sisifo* 6, December.

Di Nicola, Patrizio. 1991. *Sindacalizzazione e rappresentanza negli anni ottanta*. Rome: Ires Materiali, no. 3.

Di Nicola, Patrizio ed. 1993. *Oltre la crisi: I futuri possibili della rappresentavita dei sindacati*. Rome: Ires Materiali.

Di Palma, Giuseppe. 1980. "The Available State: Problems of Reform." In Peter Lange and Sidney Tarrow, eds., *Italy in Transition*. London: Frank Cass.

Dirrheimer, Manfred J., and Thomas Hubner. 1983. "Economic Consequences of Different Component and Car Producer Relations." In *Automobile Components Industry Study: Final Report*. Berlin: Wissenschaftszentrum.

Dore, Ronald. 1986. *Flexible Rigidities: Industrial Policy and Structural Adjustment in the Japanese Economy, 1970–1980*. Stanford: Stanford University Press.

Drago, Franco, et al. 1971. *Movimento sindacale e contrattazione collettiva, 1945–1970*. Milan: Franco Angeli.

Dunlop, John T. 1958. *Industrial Relations Systems*. New York: Holt.

Economist, The. 1992. "The Tangle in Italy." February 20: 3–4.

Enrietti, Aldo. 1983. "Industria automobilistica: La 'quasi integrazione verticale' come modello interpretativo dei rapporti tra le imprese." *Economia e politica industriale* 38: 39–71.

———. 1985a. "L'impatto occupazionale dell'automazione." *Sisifo* 6, December.

———. 1985b. "L'innovazione di processo in Fiat." In Angelo Michelsons, ed., *Tre incognite per lo sviluppo*. Milan: Franco Angeli.

———. 1986. "La caduta dell'occupazione alla Fiat." *Ex macchina* 1.

———. 1988. "Gli economisti guardano nel motore." *Politica ed economia*. 1, January.

Enrietti, Aldo and Massimo Follis. 1983. "Il settore dei componenti per autoveicoli." *Politica ed economia* 14: 37–45.

Enrietti, Aldo, et al., eds. 1980. *La ristrutturazione nell'industria metalmeccanica: Il caso dell' auto e dei componenti*. Milan: Franco Angeli.

Epstein, Gerald, and Juliet Schor. 1989. "The Divorce of the Banca d'Italia and the Italian Treasury: A Case Study of Central Bank Independence." In Peter Lange and Marino Regini, eds., *State, Market, and Social Regulation*. New York: Cambridge University Press.

Fardin, Giorgio, Massimo Casoli, and Luigi Cerato. 1986. *I nuovi sistemi produttivi: Tecnologie, organizzazione e nuove professionalita.*" Turin: Fondazione Giovanni Agnelli.

Farnetti, Paolo. 1985. *The Italian Party System.* London: Pinter.

Federazione Regionale CGIL-CISL-UIL Piemonte. 1980. "Riflessioni sulla vicenda Fiat per il Rilancio dell'iniziativa sindacale." November 17.

Federchimica. 1987. *Rapporto sullo stato dell'industria chimica in Italia: Anno 1986.* Milan: Federchimica.

Federmeccanica. 1985. "Impresa e lavoro." *Rivista Italiana di diritto del lavoro* 2.

Federtessile. 1980. *Il settore tessile e abbigliamento in Italia.* Milan: Franco Angeli.

———. 1986a. *L'industria tessile: Sua evoluzione dal 1950 ai Giorni nostri.* Milan: Federtessile.

———. 1986b. *Problemi dell'industria tessile nei confronti di un quadro internazionale.* Milan: Federtessile.

Ferla, Paolo. 1981. "Progresso tecnico e nuove forme organizzative nel comparto laniero biellese: Analisi empirica di alcuni casi significativi." Tesi di Laurea, Facolta di Economia e Commercio, Universita Degli Studi di Torino.

Ferraris, Pino. 1965. "Giornali politici nelle fabbriche del biellese." *Quaderni Rossi* 5, April.

Ferrera, Maurizio. 1984. *Il Welfare State in Italia.* Bologna: Il Mulino.

———. 1987. "Politica, aspetti isituzionali e governo dell'industria." In Peter Lange and Marino Regini, eds. *Stato e regolazione sociale.* Bologna: Il Mulino.

———. 1989. "Politics, Institutional Features, and the Government of Industry." In Peter Lange and Marino Regini, eds., *State, Market, and Social Regulation: New Perspectives on Italy.* New York: Cambridge University Press: 111–28.

Fiat. 1989. *Relazioni e bilancio al 31 dicembre 1988.* Turin.

Fiat. 1990. "Libro bianco: Il caso Alfa Romeo." Turin: Internal Company Document.

Fiat Relazioni Industriali. 1989. "Retribuzione—Costo del lavoro: Confronti internazionali e competitività." Turin: Fiat Internal Company Document.

FILCEA-CGIL Regione Lombardia. 1981. *Vertenza chimica: Analisi e problematiche per l'iniziativa del sindacato.* Milan: CGIL.

FIM-CISL. 1986. *Alfa Romeo: Tutti gli accordi aziendali, 1968–1985.* Milan: FIM-CISL.

FIM-CISL Milano. 1982. "Documentazione sulla situazione Alfa Romeo per tutti i lavoratori operai, imipiegati e capi." Milan: FIM-CISL.

FIM-CISL Torino. 1983. *La FIM-CISL di Torino.* Turin: CISL.

FIOM-CGIL Piemonte, and Istituto piemontese di scienze economiche e sociali Antonio Gramsci, eds. 1985. *Tornio 1945–1983: Memoria FIOM: Parlano alcuni protagonisti.* Milan: Franco Angeli.

Flanagan, Robert J., David W. Soskice, and Lloyd Ulman. 1983. *Unionism, Economic Stabilization, and Income Policies: European Experience.* Washington, D.C.: Brookings Institution.

Flerica-CISL Venezia, and CISL Venezia. 1984. *Per l'innovazione della chimica a Porto Marghera e per la difesa delle prospettive occupazionali.*

Follis, Massimo. 1979. "Mercato del lavoro e piccole-medie imprese dell'indotto auto." *Quaderni di rassegna sindacale* 78–79: 141–51.

REFERENCES

Fornengo, Graziella. 1985. "Innovazione e internazionalizzazione nell'industria tessile-abbigliamento." In Angelo Michelsons, ed., *Tre incognite per lo sviluppo.* Milan: Franco Angeli.

——. 1986. "Le politiche di ristrutturazione e salvataggio." In Franco Momigliano, ed., *Le leggi della politica industriale in Italia.* Bologna: Il Mulino: 33–90.

Fornengo, Graziella, and Enzo Rullani, eds. 1980. *L'industria dell'auto e dei componenti: Integrazione e internazionalizzazione produttiva.* Milan: Franco Angeli.

Foschi, Pino, et al. 1985. "Il caso Montedison: Esperienze di organizzazione della produzione per fasi di lavoro integrate." *Cds documentazione* 1–2.

Frey, Luigi, ed. 1975. *Lavoro a domicilio e decentramento dell'attività produttiva nei settori tessile e dell'abbigliamento in Italia.* Milan: Franco Angeli.

Frey, Marco. 1988. "Ristrutturazione ritardata e conseguenze occupazionali: Il caso Alfa Romeo." *Economia e politica industriale.* 59, September: 51–96.

Fried, Robert C. 1963. *The Italian Prefects: A Study in Administrative Politics.* New Haven: Yale University Press: chap. 2.

Friedman, David. 1988. *The Misunderstood Miracle.* Ithaca: Cornell University Press.

Froebel, Folker, Juergen Heinrichs, and Otto Kreye. 1980. *The New International Division of Labor: Structural Unemployment in Industrialized Countries and Industrialization in Developing Countries.* Cambridge: Cambridge University Press.

FULC. 1980. *Professionalità, responsabilità giuridiche e nuove organizazzione del lavoro: L'esperienza delle fabbriche chimiche,* special issue of *Quaderni Fulc* 1, October.

——. 1981a. *Conferenza di produzione della Montedison di Ferrara: Relazioni, interventi, e documentazione,* special issue of *Quaderni Fulc* 2, February.

——. 1981b. *Politica industriale e contrattazione aziendale: Il Piano Chimico,* special issue of *Quaderni Fulc.* 3, July.

——. 1981c. *Vertenze e riconversione nel settore chimico,* special issue of *Quaderni Fulc.* 4, November.

——. 1982a. *La II conferenza di produzione della Montedison di Ferrara: Il ruolo di un petrolchimico nel tessuto economico regionale,* special issue of *Quaderni Fulc.* 5, February.

——. 1982b. *Programmazione nazionale e territoriale, intervento pubblico, controllo sociale.* Rome: FULC.

——. 1982c. *Ristrutturazione, innovazione e livelli occupazionali nel settore chimico,* special issue of *Quaderni Fulc.* 6, May.

——. 1982–83. *La terza fase della vertenza chimica,* special issue of, *Quaderni Fulc* 7, July 1982–January 1983.

——. 1983. *L'industria delle materie plastiche tra ristrutturazione e innovazione,* special issue of *Quaderni Fulc* 8, September.

Fumagalli, Amelia. 1982. "Lo sviluppo dell'area metropolitana milanese." In R. Mainardi and C. Tombola, eds. *Grandi citta e aree metropolitane,* vol. 1. Milan: Franco Angeli.

Gaeta, Raffaele. 1987. "La segmentazione strategica di un settore industriale: La filatura e la tessitura pettinata biellese." Unpublished paper. Milan.

Galli, Giorgio, and Alessandra Nannei. 1976. *Il capitalismo assistenziale*. Milan: SugarCo.

Gallo, Maurizio. 1973. "L'organizzazione Fiat nel secondo dopoguerra: Caratteristiche e sviluppo." Fiat Internal Company Document. Divisione Organizzazione. Turin.

Gallo, Riccardo, ed. 1986. *Risanamento e riordino delle partecipazioni statali*. Milan: Franco Angeli.

Garavini, Roberto, Franco Calistri, and Ornella Cilona. 1988. *La quarta Italia*. Rome: Ediesse.

Garrett, Geoffrey, and Peter Lange. 1986. "Performance in a Hostile World: Domestic and International Determinants of Economic Growth in the Advanced Capitalist Democracies." *World Politics* 38.

Garrona, Paolo, and Elena Pisani, 1986. "Italian Unions in Transition: The Crisis of Political Unionism." In Richard Edwards, Paolo Garonna, and Franz Todling, eds., *Unions in Crisis and Beyond: Perspectives from Six Countries*. Dover, Mass.: Auburn House.

Gavagnin, Gianpietro, Costantino Grillo, and Carlo Mulas. 1988. *Porto Marghera: Storia di una crescita*. Venice: Marsilio Editori.

Genco, Pietro. 1979. "Fattori di crisi e problemi di riorganizzazione del settore delle materie plastiche." In Pippo Ranci and Sergio Vacca, eds., *L'industria petrolchimica in Italia: Anatomia di una crisi*. Milan: Franco Angeli.

Gerelli, Emilio, and Giuseppe Bognetti, eds. 1981. *La crisi delle participazioni statali: Motivi e prospettive*. Milan: Franco Angeli.

Geroldi, Gianni, and Antonio Nizzoli. 1987. *L'Alfa Romeo: Il mercato, la struttura, le risorse d'azienda, le prospettive*. Milan: FIM-CISL.

Gerschenkron, Alexander. 1976. *Economic Backwardness in Historical Perspective*. Cambridge: Harvard University Press.

——. 1985. "Notes on the Rate of Industrial Growth in Italy 1881–1913." *Journal of Economic History* 15, no. 4, December.

Gheddo, Franco. 1980. *La FIM e CISL a Torino*. Rome: Lavoro.

Ghezzi, Giorgio. 1981. *Processo al sindacato: Una svolta nelle relzioni industriali*. Bari: De Donato.

Gianotti, Renzo. 1979. *Trent'anni di lotte alla Fiat (1948–1978)*. Bari: De Donato.

Giardino, Renzo. n.d. "Il movimento operaio nel biellese." Unpublished manuscript.

——. 1984. "Ristrutturazione e professionalità diffusa (il settore tessile)." In Enrico Taliani, ed., *Processo produttivo e professionalità emergente*. Rome: Carucci Editore.

Giavazzi, Franco, and Luigi Spaventa. 1989. "Italy: The Real Effects of Inflation and Disinflation." *Economic Policy* 4, no. 1, April 133–71.

Gilder, George F. 1989. *Microcosm: The Quantum Revolution in Economics and Technology*. New York: Simon and Schuster.

Ginsborg, Paul. 1990. *A History of Contemporary Italy: Society and Politics 1943–1988*. London: Penguin Books.

Girardi, Giulio, ed. 1980. *Coscienza operaia oggi*. Bari: De Donato.

Giugni, Gino. 1957. "Bargaining Units and Labor Organizations in Italy." *Industrial and Labor Relations Review* 10, no. 1, April: 424–39.

REFERENCES

——. 1985. "Concertazione sociale e sistema politico in Italia." *Giornale di diritto del lavoro e di relazioni industriali* 25.

Golden, Miriam Anna. 1983. "Austerity and Its Opposition: Italian Working Class Politics in the 1970s." Diss., Department of Government, Cornell University.

——. 1988a. "Historical Memory and Ideological Orientations in the Italian Workers' Movement." *Politics and Society* 16, no. 1, March: 1–34.

——. 1988b. *Labor Divided: Austerity and Working Class Politics in Contemporary Italy.* Ithaca: Cornell University Press.

Goldthorpe, John H. 1984a. "The End of Convergence: Corporatist and Dualist Tendencies in Modern Western Societies." In John H. Goldthorpe, ed., *Order and Conflict in Contemporary Capitalism.* Oxford: Clarendon Press.

Goldthorpe, John H., ed. 1984b. *Order and Conflict in Contemporary Capitalism.* Oxford: Clarendon Press.

Goodman, Edward. 1989. "Introduction: The Political Economy of the Small Firm in Italy." In Edward Goodman, Julia Bamford, and Peter Saynor, eds., *Small Firms and Industrial Districts in Italy.* London: Routledge.

Goodman, John B. 1992. *Monetary Sovereignty: The Politics of Central Banking in Western Europe.* Ithaca: Cornell University Press: chap. 5.

Gourevitch, Peter. 1978. "Reforming the Napoleonic State: The Creation of Regional Governments in France and Italy." In Sidney Tarrow, Peter Katzenstein, and Luigi Graziano, eds., *Territorial Politics in Industrial Nations.* New York: Praeger.

——. 1986. *Politics in Hard Times.* Ithaca: Cornell University Press.

Gramsci, Antonio. 1971. *Selections from the Prison Notebooks of Antonio Gramsci,* ed. Quintin Hoare and Geoffrey Smith. New York: International Publishers.

Granaglia, Elena. 1989. "Public Intervention and Health Policy: An Analysis of Tendencies in Progress." In Peter Lange and Marino Regini, eds., *State, Market, and Social Regulation.* New York: Cambridge University Press.

Granovetter, Marc. 1973. "The Strength of Weak Ties." *American Journal of Sociology* 78, no. 6, May: 1360–80.

——. 1982. "The Strength of Weak Ties: A Network Theory Revisited." In Peter V. Marsden and Nan Lin, eds., *Social Structures and Network Analysis.* Newbury Park, Calif.: Sage Publications.

——. 1985. "Social Structures and Economic Action: The Problem of Embeddedness." *American Journal of Sociology* 91, no. 3, November: 481–510.

Grassini, Franco A. 1979. "Le imprese pubbliche." In Franco A. Grassini and Carlo Scognamiglio, eds., *Stato e industria in Europa: L'Italia.* Bologna: Il Mulino.

——. 1981. "The Italian Enterprises: The Political Constraints." In Raymond Vernon and Yair Aharoni, eds., *State-Owned Enterprise in the Western Economies.* New York: St. Martin's Press.

Grassini, Franco A., and Carlo Scognamiglio, eds. 1979. *Stato e industria in Europa: L'Italia.* Bologna: Il Mulino.

Graziano, Luigi. 1978. "Center-Periphery Relations and the Italian Crisis: The Problem of Clientalism." In Sidney Tarrow, Peter Katzenstein, and Luigi Graziano, eds., *Territorial Politics in Industrial Nations.* New York: Praeger.

Graziano, Luigi, and Sidney Tarrow, eds. 1979. *La crisi italiana*, vol. 1. Turin: Einaudi.

Greco, Anthony. 1976. "Trade Unionism and Politics: The Evolution of Catholic Labor in Italy." Diss., Department of Political Science, Columbia University.

Grilli, Enrico, Giorgio La Malfa, and Paolo Savona. 1985. *L'Italia al bivio*. Bari: Laterza.

Gros Pietro, Gian Maria, Franco Onida, and Carlo Scognamiglio. 1986. *L'industria metalmeccanica italiana*. Bologna: Il Mulino.

Guidi, Gianfranco, A. Bronzino, and L. Germanetto. 1974. *Fiat: Struttura aziendale e organizazzione dello sfruttamento*. Milan: Mazzotta Editore.

Guidotti, Daniela. 1986. *Strategia generale e azione decentrata: I precontratti dei tessili in Lombardia nel 1983*. Milan: Franco Angeli.

Guiotto, Luigi. 1979. *La fabbrica totale*. Milan: Feltrinelli.

Gutman, Herbert G. 1977. *Work, Culture, and Society in Industrializing America*. New York: Vintage Books.

Hall, Peter. 1986. *Governing the Economy*. Oxford: Oxford University Press.

Hall, Peter, ed. 1989. *The Political Power of Economic Ideas: Keynesianism across Nations*. Princeton: Princeton University Press.

Hancké, Bob. 1991. "The Crisis of National Unions: Belgian Labor in Decline." *Politics and Society* 19, no. 4, December: 463–87.

Harrison, Bennett. 1994. *Lean and Mean: The Changing Landscape of Corporate Power in the Age of Flexibility*. New York: Basic Books.

Harvard Business School. 1984. *Montedison, S.p.A.* Case no. 0-385-065. Boston: Harvard Business School Press.

Hellman, Stephen. 1975. "The PCI's Alliance Strategy and the Case of the Middle Classes." In Donald L. M. Blackmer and Sidney Tarrow, eds., *Communism in Italy and France*. Princeton: Princeton University Press.

——. 1987. "The Emergence of the Modern Italian State." In Mark Kesselman and Joel Krieger, eds., *European Politics in Transition*. Lexington, Mass.: D. C. Heath.

——. 1988. *The Rise and Fall of the Historical Compromise in Turin*. Oxford: Oxford University Press.

Hemerijck, Anton. 1992. "The Historical Contingencies of Dutch Corporation." Diss., Balliol College, University of Oxford.

Hennesy, Josselyn, Vera Lutz, and Giuseppe Scimone. 1964. *Economic "Miracles": Studies in the Resurgence of the French, German, and Italian Economies since the Second World War*. London: André Deutsch.

Herrigel, Gary. 1990. "Industry and Politics: The German Case." Diss. in progress, Department of Political Science, M.I.T.

Herrigel, Gary B. 1989. "Industrial Order and the Politics of Industrial Change: Mechanical Engineering in the Federal Republic of Germany." In Peter Katzenstein, ed., *Toward a Third Republic? Industry, Politics, and Change in West Germany*. Ithaca: Cornell University Press.

——. Forthcoming, 1995. *Reconceptualizing the Sources of German Industrial Power*. New York: Cambridge University Press.

Hildebrand, George. 1965. *Growth and Structure in the Economy of Modern Italy*. Cambridge: Harvard University Press.

REFERENCES

Holland, Stuart. 1972a. "The National Context." In Stuart Holland, ed., *The State as Entrepreneur*. London: Weidenfeld and Nicholson.

Holland, Stuart, ed. 1972b. *The State as Entrepreneur*. London: Weidenfeld and Nicholson.

Holland, Stuart. 1974. "Europe's New Public Enterprises." In Raymond Vernon, ed., *Big Business and the State—Changing Relations in Western Europe*. Cambridge: Harvard University Press, 1974: 25–42.

Imazio, Alberto, and Carlo Costa. 1975. *L'organizzazione del lavoro alla Fiat*. Padua: Marsilio Editore.

Immergut, Ellen M. 1992. *Health Politics: Interests and Institutions in Western Europe*. New York: Cambridge University Press.

Inzerilli, Giorgio. 1990. *The Italian Alternative: Flexible Organization and Social Management*, special issue of *International Studies of Management and Organization*. 20, no. 4, Winter.

IRES, 1985. *Analisi della domnada di beni di investimento e di servizi da parte dei principali complessi industriali della regione*, vol. 2. Turin: Quaderni di ricerca IRES 33, October.

IRES-CGIL Piemonte. 1986. *Delegati in Piemonte: Una ricerca di cento fabbriche*. Milan: Franco Angeli.

ISTAT. 1989. *Statistiche Culturali*. Rome: ISTAT: 81.

——. 1991. *Settimo censimento generale dell'industria e dei servizi*. Rome: ISTAT.

Istituto Guglielmo Tagliacarne. 1986. *Localismi e nuove strategie d'impresa*. Milan: Franco Angeli.

——. 1989. *Localismi e nuove strategie d'impresa: I casi di Bari. Padova e Prato*. Milan: Franco Angeli.

Istituto Piemontese di scienze economiche e sociali Antonio Gramsci. 1980. *Ricerca di massa sulla condizione dei lavoratori Fiat*. Turin: Gramsci Institute.

Jacobi, Otto, et al. 1986. *Technical Change, Rationalization, and Industrial Relations*. London: Croom Helm.

Johnson, Chalmers. 1982. *MITI and the Japanese Miracle: The Growth of Industrial Policy. 1925–1975*. Stanford: Stanford University Press.

Katz, Harry, and Charles Sabel. 1985. "Industrial Relations and Industrial Adjustment: Diverging Responses in the World Automobile Industry." *Industrial Relations* 24, no. 3, Fall: 295–315.

Katzenstein, Peter J. 1984. *Corporatism and Change*. Ithaca: Cornell University Press.

——. 1985. *Small States in World Markets*. Ithaca: Cornell University Press.

——. 1989. "Conclusion: Stability and Change in the Emerging Third Republic." In Peter J. Katzenstein, ed., *Industry and Politics in West Germany: Toward the Third Republic*. Ithaca: Cornell University Press.

Katzenstein, Peter J., ed. 1978. *Between Power and Plenty*. Madison: University of Wisconsin Press.

Keeler, John T. S. 1981. "Corporatism and Official Union Hegemony: The Case of French Agricultural Syndicalism." In Suzanne D. Berger, ed., *Organizing Interests in Western Europe*. New York: Cambridge University Press.

Kemeny, Pietro. 1990. "Le politiche di concertazione: Storia di una rinuncia." *Prospettiva sindacale* 21, no. 77, September.

Kemp, Tom. 1981. *Industrialization in Nineteenth-Century Europe*. London: Longman.

Kendall, Walter. 1972. "Labor Relations." In Stuart Holland, ed., *The State as Entrepreneur*. London: Weidenfeld and Nicholson.

Kern, Horst, and Charles F. Sabel. 1991. "Trade Unions and Decentralized Production: A Sketch of Strategic Problems for the West German Labor Movement." *Politics and Society* 19, no. 4, December: 373–402.

Kesselman, Mark, and Joel Krieger, eds. 1987. *European Politics in Transition*. Lexington, Mass.: D. C. Heath.

Kindelberger, Charles P. 1967. *Economic Growth in Europe: The Role of Labor Supply*. Cambridge: Harvard University Press.

Knoke, David. 1990. *Political Networks: The Structural Perspective*. New York: Cambridge University Press.

Kochan, Thomas A., ed. 1985. *Challenges and Choices Facing American Labor*. Cambridge: MIT Press.

Kochan, Thomas, Harry Katz, and Robert McKersie. 1986. *The Transformation of American Industrial Relations*. New York: Basic Books.

Krafcik, John F. 1988. "Comparative Analysis of Performance Indicators at World Auto Assembly Plants." M.S. Thesis, Sloan School of Management, MIT.

Kramer, Jane. 1992. "Letter from Europe." *New Yorker*, September 21: 108–24.

Kreile, Michael. 1983. "Public Enterprise and the Pursuit of Strategic Management: Italy." In Kenneth Dyson and Stephen Wilkes, eds., *Industrial Crisis— A Comparative Study of the State and Industry*. New York: St. Martin's Press: 208.

Lanaro, Silvio. 1984. "Geneologia di un modello." In *Storia d'Italia: Le regioni: Il Veneto*. Turin: Einaudi.

Lange, Peter. 1975. "The PCI at the Local Level: A Study of Strategic Performance." In Donald L. M. Blackmer and Sidney Tarrow, eds., *Communism in Italy and France*. Princeton: Princeton University Press.

——. 1986. "The End of an Era: The Wage Indexation Referendum of 1985." In Robert Leonardi and Raffaella Y. Nanetti, eds., *Italian Politics: A Review*, vol. 1. London: Pinter.

Lange, Peter, and Marino Regini, eds. 1987. *Stato e regolazione sociale*. Bologna: Il Mulino.

Lange, Peter, and Marino Regini, eds. 1989. *State, Market, and Social Regulation*. New York: Cambridge University Press.

Lange, Peter, George Ross, and Maurizio Vannicelli. 1982. *Unions, Change, and Crisis: French and Italian Union Strategy and the Political Economy, 1945–1980*. London: George Allen and Unwin.

Lange, Peter, and Maurizio Vannicelli. 1982. "Strategy under Stress: The Italian Union Movement and the Italian Crisis in Developmental Perspective." In Peter Lange, George Ross, and Maurizio Vannicelli, eds., *Unions, Change, and Crisis*. Boston: George Allen and Unwin: 95–206.

Lanzardo, Dario. 1979. *La rivolta di piazza statuto: Torino, luglio 1962*. Milan: Feltrinelli.

REFERENCES

Lanzardo, Liliana. 1971. *Classe operaia e partito comunista alla Fiat.* Turin: Einaudi.

La Palombara, Joseph. 1955. "The Political Role of Organized Labor in Western Europe." *Journal of Politics* 17, No. 1, February: 59–81.

——. 1956. "Trade Union Education as an Anticommunist Weapon in Italy." *Southwest Social Science Quarterly* 37, No. 2, June: 29–42.

——. 1957. *The Italian Labor Movement: Problems and Prospects.* Ithaca: Cornell University Press.

——. 1964. *Interest Group Politics in Italilan Politics.* Princeton: Princeton University Press.

——. 1966. *Italy: The Politics of Planning.* Syracuse: Syracuse University Press.

——. 1987. *Democracy, Italian Style.* New Haven: Yale University Press.

La Palombara, Joseph, and Myron Weiner, eds. 1966. *Political Parties and Political Development.* Princeton: Princeton University Press.

Lazerson, Mark H. 1988. "Organizational Growth and Small Firms: An Outcome of Markets and Hierarchies?" *American Sociological Review* 53, No. 3, June: 330–42.

Leon, Paolo, and Ettore Masucci. 1981. "Gli sviluppi del settore tessile-abbigliamento in Europa." *Quaderni di rassegna sindacale.* 88, January–February.

Levi, Fabio, Paride Rugafiori, and Salvatore Vento. 1977. *Il triangolo industriale: Tra ricostruzione e lotta di classe: 1945–1948.* Milan: Feltrinelli.

Levy, Jonah. 1988. "Four on the Floor: The Political Economy of Industrial Restructuring at Fiat, PSA, Renault, and BL." Unpublished paper, Department of Political Science, M.I.T.

——. 1994. "Tocqueville's Revenge: Dilemmas of Institutional Reform in Post-Dirigiste France." Diss., Department of Political Science, M.I.T.

Libertini, Lucio. 1973. *La Fiat negli anni settanta.* Rome: Editori Riuniti.

Lipset, Seymour M., and Stein Rokkan. 1967. *Party Systems and Voter Alignments.* New York: Free Press.

Locke, Richard M. 1990a. "The Resurgence of the Local Union: Industrial Restructuring and Industrial Relations in Italy." *Politics and Society* 18, no. 3, September: 347–80.

——. 1990b. "The Weakness of Strong Ties: The Changing Relationship between Intellectuals and Labor in Italy." Paper presented at the Workshop "Changing Relationships between Intellectuals and Labor," Center for European Studies, Harvard University, November 16–18.

——. 1994. "Eppure Si Tocca: The Abolition of the Scala Mobile." In Carol Mershon and Gianfranco Pasquino, eds., *Politica in Italia*, vol. 9. Bologna: Il Mulino.

Locke, Richard M., and Cristano Antonelli. 1990. "International Competitiveness, Technological Change and Organizational Innovation: Strategy and Structure of the Italian Apparel Industry in the 1980s." In Donald Lessard and Cristiano Antonelli, eds., *Managing the Globalization of Business.* Naples: Editoriale Scientifica.

Locke, Richard M., and Serafino Negrelli. 1989. "Il caso Fiat Auto." In Marino Regini and Charles Sabel, eds., *Strategic di riaggiustamento industriale.* Bologna: Il Mulino: 87–90.

Lombardi, Giancarlo. 1986. "Le prospettive del settore tessile-abbigliamento europeo nel confronto mondiale: Il ruolo dell'Italia." Paper presented at the "VI Convegno nazionale degli industriali tessili e dell'abbigliamento." Milan, September 29.

Lorenzoni, Gianni. 1980. *Lo sviluppo industriale di Prato*. Prato: Edizioni Cassa di Rirparmi e Depositi.

Lutz, Veza. 1962. *Italy: A Study in Economic Development*. New York: Oxford University Press.

Mack Smith, Denis. 1985. *Cavour*. New York: Knopf.

Magatti, Marco. 1991. "On the Social Embeddedness of Economic Life: A Comparative Analysis of Two Textile Districts, Britain and Italy, 1950s–1970s." Diss., Faculty of Social Sciences, University of Kent at Canterbury.

Malerba, Giorgio. 1986. "Innovazione e relazioni industriali." Paper presented at the "VI Convegno nazionale degli industriali tessili e dell'abbigliamento." Milan, September 29.

Mana, Franco, and Tino Valvo. 1985. *Fiat Auto anni '80: Organizzazione, professionalita e salario*. Milan: Franco Angeli.

Manghi, Bruno. 1985. "Cultura torinese e sindacata dell'autonomia." Internal Union Document, CISL Provincia di Torino, February 2.

——. 1986. "Professionalita: Le ragioni di una ambigua fortuna." Internal Union Document, CISL Provincia di Torino, October 3.

Manghi, Bruno, Gianprimo Cella, and Paola Piva. 1972. *Un sindacato italiano negli anni '60: La FIM CISL dall'associazione alla classe*. Bari: De Donato.

Mannheimer, Renato. 1991. *La Lega Lombarda*. Milan: Feltrinelli.

Mantelli, Bruno, and Marco Revelli. 1979. *Operai senza politica: Il caso Moro alla Fiat e il qualunquismo operaio*. Rome: Savelli.

Maraffi, Marco. 1990. *Politica ed economia in Italia: La vicenda dell'impresa pubblica dagli anni trenta agli anni cinquanta*. Bologna: Il Mulino.

Marcellino, Nella. 1981. "Sindacato e industria tessile." *Quaderni di rassegna sindacale* 88, January–February.

March, James G., and Johan P. Olsen. 1984. "The New Institutionalism: Organizational Factors in Political Life." *American Political Science Review* 78, No. 3, September: 734–49.

Marchese, Gino. 1986. "Nuovi modelli di relazioni con il sindacato." Paper presented at the "Convegno annuale dell'Unionmeccanica di Torino." Turin, November 22.

Marchesini, Enrico, and Attilio Masiero. 1975. *Il caso tessile: Ciclo produttivo e forza-lavoro: Lanerossi 1963–1974*. Milan: Gabriele Mazzotta.

Marchionatti, Roberto. 1987. "L'accordo Multifibre: Storia, bilancio critico e prospettive del protezionismo tessile." In CER-IRS, *L'europa delle industrie*. Bologna: Il Mulino.

Marconi, Mauro, and Fausto Vicarelli. 1980. "L'accumulazione di capitale nella visione della CISL." In Guido Baglioni, ed., *Analisi della CISL*, vol. 2. Rome: Lavoro.

Mariotti, Sergio. 1982. *Efficienza e struttura economica: Il caso tessile-abbigliamento*. Milan: Franco Angeli.

——. 1983. "I mutamenti organizzativi nel tessile–abbigliamento." *Fabbriche e idee* 16, November.

Marks, Gary. 1989. *Unions in Politics: Britain, Germany, and the United States in the Nineteenth and Early Twentieth Centuries.* Princeton: Princeton University Press.

Martin, Andrew. 1984. "Trade Unions in Sweden: Strategic Responses to Change and Crisis." In Peter Gourevitch, Andrew Martin, George Ross, Christopher Allen, Stephen Bornstein, and Andrei Markovits, *Unions and Economic Crisis: Britain, West Germany, and Sweden.* London: George Allen.

——. 1991. "Wage Bargaining and Swedish Politics: The Political Implications of the End of Central Negotiations." Unpublished manuscript. Cambridge, Mass. June.

Martinelli, Alberto. 1980. "Organized Business and Italian Politics: Confindustria and the Christian Democrats in the Postwar Period." In Peter Lange and Sidney Tarrow, eds., *Italy in Transition.* London: Frank Cass.

——. 1981. "The Italian Experience: A Historical Perspective." In Raymond Vernon and Yair Aharoni, eds., *State-Owned Enterprises in Western Economies.* New York: St. Martin's Press.

Martinotti, Guido, ed. 1982. *La citta difficile: Equilibri e diseguaglianze nel mercato urbano.* Milan: Franco Angeli.

Masiero, Antillo. 1973. "Ristrutturazione e scomposizione della forza lavoro alla Lanerossi." *Classe* 7: 247–56.

Massazza Gal Adriano. 1987. "Gil anni del cambiamento." In Marco Neiretti, et al., *L'altra storia: Sindacato e lotte nel biellese 1901–1986.* Rome: Ediesse.

Masucci, Ettore. 1985. "L'esperienza dei chimici sulle ristrutturazioni e le relazioni industriali per lo sviluppo." In Sandro Gloria and Gianni Caraussi, eds., *Il sindacato è protagonista?* Rome: Ediesse.

Maurice, Marc, François Sellier, and Jean-Jacques Silvestre. 1984. "The Search for a Societal Effect in the Production of Company Hierarchy: A Comparison of France and Germany." In Paul Osterman, ed., *Internal Labor Markets.* Cambridge: MIT Press.

——. 1986. *The Social Foundations of Industrial Power: A Comparison of France and Germany.* Cambridge: MIT Press.

McKay, David, and Wyn Grant. 1983. "Industrial Politics in OECD Countries: An Overview." *Journal of Public Policy* 3, no. 1, February: 1–12.

Medusa, Giuseppe. 1979. "Condizioni di impiego nella grande impresa: Il caso Alfa-Romeo-Arese." *Osservatorio sul mercato del lavoro e sulle professioni* 11–12.

——. 1983. *L'impresa tra produttività e consenso: Il caso Alfa Romeo.* Milan: ETAS Libri.

Melucci, Alberto. 1976. "Rischio, strategia, decisione nell'azione istitizionale del sindacato." In Tiziano Treu, ed., *Sindacato e magistratura nei conflitti di lavoro,* vol. 2. Bologna: Il Mulino: 17–62.

Mershon, Carol Anne. 1986. "The Micropolitics of Union Action: Industrial Conflict in Italian Factories." Diss., Department of Political Science, Yale University.

Michelsons, Angelo M. 1983. "La crisi del Fordismo e le possibilita di sviluppo di un'industria a 'specializzazione flessibile' a Torino negli anni settanta." *Annali della Fondazione Luigi Einaudi* 17: 545–90.

——. 1985. "La grande impresa tra sviluppo e crisi." In Angelo Michelsons, ed., *Tre incognite per lo sviluppo.* Milan: Franco Angeli.

——. 1986. "Turin between Fordism and Flexible Specialization: Industrial Structure and Social Change, 1970–85." Diss., Darwin College, Cambridge University.

Migone, Gian Giacomo. 1974. "Stati Uniti, Fiat e repressione antioperaia negli anni cinquanta." *Rivista di storia contemporanea* 2: 232–80.

MIT Commission on Industrial Productivity. 1989a. "The U.S. Textile Industry: Challenges and Opportunities." In *The Working Papers of the MIT Commission on Industrial Productivity*, vol. 2. Cambridge: MIT Press.

——. 1989b. "The U.S. Automobile Industry in an Era of International Competition: Performance and Prospects." In *The Working Papers of the MIT Commission on Industrial Productivity*, vol. 1. Cambridge: MIT Press.

——. 1989c. "The Transformation of the U.S. Chemicals Industry." In *The Working Papers of the MIT Commission on Industrial Productivity*, vol. 1. Cambridge: MIT Press.

Momigliano, Franco, ed. 1986. *Le leggi della politica industriale in Italia*. Bologna: Il Mulino.

Monicelli, Mino. 1981. *La follia Veneta: Come una regione bianca diviene culla del terrorismo*. Rome: Editori Riuniti.

Montini, Raffaela. 1986. "Il caso Alfa Romeo: Anni settanta." Unpublished manuscript. Milan.

Moranino, Luigi. 1987. "La Camera del lavoro di Biella dall'armistizio al patto di Palazzo Vidoni (1918–1925)." In Marco Neiretti, et al., *L'altra storia: Sindacato e lotte nel biellese 1901–1986*. Rome: Ediesse.

Morlino, Leonardo. 1984. "The Changing Relationship between Parties and Society in Italy." *West European Politics* 7, No. 4, October: 46–66.

Mortara, Alberto, ed. 1982. *Le associazioni italiane*. Milan: Franco Angeli.

Mosconi, Antonio, and Dario Velo. 1982. *Crisi e ristrutturazione del settore automobilistico*. Bologna: Il Mulino.

Moy, Joyanna. 1988. "An Analysis of Unemployment and Other Labor Market Indicators in 10 Countries." *Monthly Labor Review*. 111, no. 4, April: 39–50.

Nacamulli, Raul, Giovanni Costa, and Luigi Manzolini. 1986. *La razionalità contrattata*. Bologna: Il Mulino.

Nanetti, Raffaella Y. 1988. *Growth and Territorial Policies: The Italian Model of Social Capitalism*. London: Pinter.

Napoli, Mario. 1989. "Il quadro giuridico-istituzionale." In Gianprimo Cella and Tiziano Treu, eds., *Relazioni industriali*. Bologna: Il Mulino.

Nardin, Giuseppe. 1987. *La Benetton: Strategia e struttura di un'impresa di successo*. Rome: Lavoro.

Negrelli, Serafino. 1985. "FIAT: Sistema LAM di Mirafiori." *Relazioni industriali nell'impresa degli anni '80*, special issue of *Quaderni di formazione* 3, May–June.

——. 1988. "Il sindacato perduto nella foresta dei robot." *Politica ed economia* 1, January.

Neiretti, Marco. 1987. "Dalle origini alla fine della prima guerra mondiale." In Marco Neiretti, et al., *L'altra storia: Sindacato e lotte nel biellese 1901–1986*. Rome: Ediesse.

Nelson, Wayne Brooke. 1987. "Improving Competitiveness in Mature Industries: Lessons from the West German Textile Industry." M.A. Thesis, Department of Political Science, MIT.

Neufeld, Maurice F. 1960. *Italy: School for Awakening Nations*. Ithaca: Cornell University Press.

Novelli, Diego. 1970. *Dossier FIAT*. Rome: Editori Riuniti.

OECD. 1979. *Economic Surveys: Italy, 1978–1979*. Paris: OECD.

——. 1983. *Textile and Clothing Industries: Structural Problems and Policies in OECD Countries*. Paris: OECD.

——. 1984. *Economic Surveys: Italy, 1983–1984*. Paris: OECD.

——. 1988a. *Economic Surveys: Italy, 1987–1988*. Paris: OECD.

——. 1988b. *OECD Economic Indicators*. Paris: OECD.

——. 1990. *OECD Economic Outlook*. Paris: OECD.

Office of Technology Assessment. 1987. *The U.S. Textile and Apparel Industry: A Revolution in Progress—Special Report*. Washington, D.C.: U.S. Congress, Office of Technology Assessment.

Ortaggi, Simonetta. 1978. "Cottimo e produttiva nell'industria italiana del primo Novecento." *Rivista di Storia Contemporanea* 1: 15–58.

——. 1979. "Padronato e classe operaia a Torino negli anni 1906–11." *Rivista di Storia Contemporanea* 3.

Osservatorio Tessile Biellese. 1981. *Progresso tecnico e nuove forme organizzative nel comparto laniero biellese*. Turin: IRES Piemonte.

Paldman, Martin, and Peder H. Pedersen. 1982. "The Macroeconomic Strike Model: A Study of Seventeen Countries, 1948–1975." *Industrial and Labor Relations Review* 35, no. 4, July: 504–21.

Panara, Marco. 1987. "Montedison: Tutti i conti e le promesse di Foro Bonaparte." *La Repubblica*. March 6.

Pansa, Gianpaolo. 1988. "Quei trentacinque giorni che sconvolsero la Fiat: Romiti racconta la sfida di Mirafiori." *La Repubblica*. April 14.

Panzieri, Raniero. 1976. *Lotte operaie nello sviluppo capitalistico*. Turin: Einaudi.

Partito Comunista Italiano, Federazione di Torino. 1980. *La lotta alla Fiat: Il giudizio del PCI torinese*. Turin.

Pasquino, Gianfranco. 1983. "Partiti, societa civile, istituzioni e il caso italiano." *Stato mercato* 8, August.

——. 1986. "Party Government in Italy: Achievements and Prospects." In Richard S. Katz, ed., *The American and European Experiences of Party Government*. Berlin: De Gruyter.

——. 1989. "Strategia industriale e programmazione." In Franco A. Grassini and Carlo Scognamiglio, eds., *Stato e industria in Europa: L'Italia*. Bologna: Il Mulino.

Pasquino, Gianfranco, and Umberto Pecchini. 1975. "Italy." In Jack Hayward and Michael Watson, eds., *Planning, Politics, and Public Policy: The British, French, and Italian Experience*. London: Cambridge University Press.

Patriarca, Stefano. 1986. "Caratteristiche e risultati della politica dei·redditi 1983–1984." In Mimmo Carrieri and Paolo Perulli, eds., *Il teorema sindacale*. Bologna: Il Mulino: 55–63.

Peet, Richard, ed. 1987. *International Capitalism and Industrial Restructuring*. Boston: George Allen and Unwin.

Pennacchi, Laura, ed. 1981a. *Il sistema delle participazioni statali.* Bari: De Donato.

——. 1981b. *L'industria italiana: Trasformazioni strutturali e possibilita di governo politico.* Milan: Franco Angeli.

Pennisi, Giuseppe, and Eduardo M. Peterlini. 1987. *Spesa pubblica e bisogno di inefficienza: L'esperienza del Fondo Investimenti e Occupazione (1982–1986).* Bologna: Il Mulino

Perlmutter, Ted. 1988. "Urban Crisis and Union Response in Fordist Cities: Turin 1950–1975 and Detroit 1915–1945." Paper presented at the Center for European Studies, Harvard University. May 13.

Perona, Gianni. 1987. "Gli anni del fascismo." In Marco Neiretti, et al., *L'altra storia: Sindacato e lotte nel biellese 1901–1986.* Rome: Ediesse.

Perotti, Pietro, and Marco Revelli. *FIAT autunno 80: Per non dimenticare.* Turin: Centro di ricerca e iniziativa comunista.

Perulli, Paolo. 1984. "Conseguenze delle ristrutturazioni sulle relazioni industriali: Ipotesi e verifiche empiriche." *Economia e politica industriale* 43.

——. 1987. "Cercando Tecnocity." *Politica ed economia,* January.

Piattoni, Simona. 1986. "La politica di incentivazione agli investimenti in capitale fisso in Italia (1970–1985)." "Unpublished paper. Milan: Universita Commerciale Luigi Bocconi.

——. "Reinterpreting Clientalism: Local Economic Development in the Italian South." Diss. in progress, Department of Political Science, MIT.

Piore, Michael J. 1988. "Corporate Reform in American Manufacturing and the Challenge to Economic Theory." Unpublished paper. MIT.

——. 1990. "Response" to Ash Amin and Kevin Roberts. In Frank Pyke, Giacomo Beccatini, and Werner Sengenberger, eds., *Industrial Districts and Interfirm Cooperation in Italy.* Geneva: International Institute for Labor Studies.

Piore, Michael J., and Charles F. Sabel. 1983. "Italian Small Business Development: Lessons for U.S. Industrial Policy." In John Zysman and Laura Tyson, eds., *American Industry in International Competition.* Ithaca: Cornell University Press.

Piore, Michael J., and Charles F. Sabel. 1984. *The Second Industrial Divide.* New York: Basic Books.

Pizzorno, Alessandro, Emilio Reyneri, Marino Regini, and Ida Regalia. 1978. *Lotte operaie e sindacato: Il ciclo 1968–1972.* Bologna: Il Mulino.

Poggi, Gianfranco. 1978. *The Development of the Modern State.* Stanford: Stanford University Press.

Polanyi, Karl. 1944. *The Great Transformation.* Boston: Beacon Press.

Pontusson, Jonas, and Peter Swenson. 1992. "Markets, Production, Institutions, and Politics: Why Swedish Employers Have Abandoned the Swedish Model." Paper presented at the "Conference of Europeanists." Chicago. April.

Ponzellini, Angela. 1984. *I contratti di solidarieta.* Rome: CESOS.

Porter, Michael. 1990. *The Competitive Advantage of Nations.* New York: Free Press.

Posner, Alan R. 1978. "Italy: Dependence and Political Fragmentation." In

Peter J. Katzenstein, ed., *Between Power and Plenty*. Madison: University of Wisconsin Press.

Posner, Michael V., and Stuart J. Woolf. 1967. *Italian Public Enterprises*. Cambridge: Harvard University Press.

Prodi, Romano. 1974. "Italy." In Raymond Vernon, ed., *Big Business and the State—Changing Relations in Western Europe*. Cambridge: Harvard University Press.

——. 1981. "Le conseguenze economiche dei processi di decisione." In Emilio Gerelli and Giuseppe Bognetti, eds., *La crisi delle participazioni statati: Motivi e prospettive*. Milan: Franco Angeli.

Pugno, Emilio, and Sergio Garavini. 1974. *Gli anni duri alla Fiat: La resistenza sindacale e la ripresa*. Turin: Einaudi.

Putnam, Robert D. 1987. "Institutional Performance and Political Culture in Italy." *Center for European Studies Working Paper*, no. 8. Harvard University, Center for European Studies.

——. 1993. *Making Democracy Work: Civic Traditions in Modern Italy*. Princeton: Princeton University Press.

Putnam, Robert D., Robert Leonardi, Raffaella Y. Nanetti, and Franco Pavoncello. 1983. "Explaining Institutional Success: The Case of Italilan Regional Government." *American Political Science Review* 77, no. 1, March: 55–74.

Pyke, Frank, Giacomo Becatini, and Werner Sengenberger, eds. 1990. *Industrial Districts and Interfirm Cooperation in Italy*. Geneva: International Institute for Labor Studies.

Raffaele, Joseph A. 1962. *Labor Leadership in Italy and Denmark*. Madison: University of Wisconsin Press.

Ramella, Franco. 1983. *Terra e telai. Sistemi di parentela e manifattura nel Biellese dell'Ottocento*. Turin: Einaudi.

Ranci, Pippo. 1987. "Italy: The Weak State." In Francois Duchene and Geoffrey Shepherd, eds., *Managing Industrial Change in Western Europe*. London: Pinter.

Ranci, Pippo, and Sergio Vaccà, eds. 1979. *L'industria petrolchimica in Italia: Anatomia di una crisi*. Milan: Franco Angeli.

Ravasio, Bruno. 1984. "La manovra sugli orari nel settore tessile." *Quaderni di rassegna sindacale* 108–9, May–August.

——. 1987. "Ristrutturazione industriale e contrattazione degli orari nel settore tessile e abbigliamento." Paper presented at the Conference "Flessibilità degli Orari." Milan. April 9–10.

Regalia, Ida. 1984. *Eletti e abbandonati*. Bologna: Il Mulino.

——. 1985. "Sindacati e governi periferici." *Democrazia e diritto* 5.

——. 1986. "Centralization or Decentralization? An Analysis of Organizational Changes in the Italian Trade Union Movement at a Time of Crisis." In Otto Jacobi, et al., *Technical Change, Rationalization, and Industrial Relations*. London: Croom Helm.

Regini, Marino. 1981. *I dilemmi del sindacato*. Bologna: Il Mulino.

——. 1984. "The Conditions for Political Exchange: How Concertation Emerged and Collapsed in Italy and Great Britain." In John H. Goldthorpe, ed., *Order and Conflict in Contemporary Capitalism*. Oxford: Clarendon Press.

Regini, Marino, and Peter Lange. 1988. "Introduction: Italy from Rupture to Change." Paper presented at the Conference "Work and Politics in Italy: Twenty Years after the Hot Autumn." Center for European Studies, Harvard University. November 18–20.

Regini, Marino, and Charles Sabel, eds. 1989. *Strategie di riaggiustamento industriale.* Bologna: Il Mulino.

Regione Lombardia, Assessorato Industria e Artigianato. 1981. *Proposte di intervento per il settore della componentistica auto.* Milan: Regione Lombardia.

Reich, Robert. 1988. "Bailout: A Comparative Study in Law and Industrial Structure." In A. Michael Spence and Heather A. Hazard, eds., *International Competitiveness.* Cambridge, Mass.: Balinger.

———. 1991. *The Work of Nations.* New York: Alfred A. Knopf.

Renaux, Jean-Jacques. 1987. "Ghidella: An Auto Giant in Europe But Little Known in U.S." *Automotive News.* May 4.

Revelli, Marco. 1981a. "La bureaucratie syndicale et les militantes de base en Italie." In K. Armington, et al., *Les syndicates européens et la crise.* Grenoble: Presses Universitaires de Grenoble.

———. 1981b. "L'ultima Fiat: Appunti su un tempo perduto." *Quaderni Piacentini* 1.

Rey, Guido. 1982. "Italy." In Andrea Boltho, ed., *The European Economy: Growth and Crisis.* Oxford: Oxford University Press.

———. 1989. "Small Firms: Profile and Analysis, 1981–85." In Edward Goodman, Julia Bamford, and Peter Saynor, eds., *Small Firms and Industrial Districts in Italy.* London: Routledge.

Reyneri, Emilio. 1976. "Comportamento di classe e nuovo ciclo di lotte." In Aris Accornero, ed., *Problemi del movimento sindacale in Italia, 1943–1973,* special issue of *Annali della Fondazione Feltrinelli.* Milan: Feltrinelli.

———. 1987. "Il mercato del lavoro italiano tra controllo statale e regolazione sociale." In Peter Lange and Marino Regini, eds. *Stato e regolazione sociale.* Bologna: Il Mulino.

———. 1989. "The Italian Labor Market: Between State Control and Social Regulation." In Peter Lange and Marino Regini, eds., *State, Market, and Social Regulation.* New York: Cambridge University Press.

Reyneri, Emilio, and Renata Semenza. 1990. "Strategie di adattamento dei lavoratori espulsi dalle grandi imprese." In *Collana "Ricerche."* Milan: IRES Lombardia.

Ricci, Maurizio. 1988. "Sistema di relazioni industriali e contrattazione collettiva nell industria chimica privata." In Bruno Veneziani, ed., *Relazioni industriali e contrattazione collettiva in Italia.* Bari: Cacucci Editore.

Ricci, Maurizio, and Bruno Veneziani, eds. 1988. *Tra conflitto e partecipazione: Un'indagine empirica sul Protocollo IRI e sui diritti di informazione.* Bari: Cacucci Editore.

Richetti, Marco. 1987. "Le fasi del ciclo tessile laniero: Flussi di produzione e alcuni aspetti strutturali." Unpublished paper. Milan.

Rieser, Vittorio. 1981. "Come si riproduce un'avanguardia." In Aris Accornero and Vittorio Rieser, eds. *Il mestiere dell'avanguardia: Riedizione di "Fiat Confino" di Aris Accornero.* Bari: De Donato.

———. 1986. "Immagini del progresso tecnologico e del lavoro." *Ex machina* 2.

REFERENCES

Ritaine, Evelyne. 1990. "Prato: An Extreme Case of Diffuse Industrialization." In Giorgio Inzerilli, ed., *The Italian Alternative: Flexible Organization and Social Management*, special issue of *International Studies of Management and Organization* 20, no. 4, Winter: 61–76.

Rocella, Massimo. 1982. "La composizione dei conflitti di lavoro nella grande impresa: Il caso dell'Alfa Romeo di Arese." *Giornale di diritto del lavoro e di relazioni industriali* 14.

Rollier, Matteo. 1986. "Changes in Industrial Relations at Fiat." In Otto Jacobi, et al., *Technological Change, Rationalization, and Industrial Relations*. London: Croom Helm.

Romagnoli, Guido, ed. 1980. *La sindacalizzazione tra ideologia e pratica*, vol. 1. Rome: Lavoro: 55.

Romagnoli, Marco. 1983. "Tecnologie e organizzazione del lavoro nell'industria laniera." *Quaderni di rassegna sindacale* 105.

Romiti, Cesare. 1988. *Questi anni alla Fiat*. Milan: Rizzoli.

Ronchi, Rossella. 1986. "Protocollo IRI: Una indagine sullo stato di applicazione." *Collana Ricerche*, no. 11. Milan: IRES Lombardia.

Roverato, Giorgio. 1984. "La terza regione industriale." In *Storia d'Italia: Le regioni. il Veneto*. Turin: Einaudi.

——. 1986. *Una casa industriale: I Marzotto*. Milan: Franco Angeli.

——. 1988. "Metamorfosi del tessile-abbigliamento." Unpublished manuscript. Università di Padova.

Roveri, Alessandro. 1974. *Le origini del fascismo a Ferrara: 1918–1921*. Milan: Feltrinelli.

Ruffolo, Giorgio. 1973. *Rapporto sulla programmazione*. Bari: Laterza.

Rullani, Enzo. 1979. "La Riorganizzazione del ciclo etilenico in Italia: Elementi di valutazione sulle alternative strategiche in discussione." In Pippo Ranci and Sergio Vacca, eds., *L'industria petrolchimica in Italia: Anatomia di una crisi*. Milan: Franco Angeli.

Rullani, Enzo, and Sergio Vaccà. 1979. "Miti e realta della crisi petrolchimica italiana." In Pippo Ranci, Sergio Vaccà, eds., *L'industria petrolchimica in Italia: Anatomia di una crisi*. Milan: Franco Angeli.

Rullani, Enzo, and Antonello Zanfei. 1988. "Area Networks: Telematic Connections in a Traditional Textile District." In Cristiano Antonelli, ed., *New Information Technology and Industrial Change: The Italian Case*. Dordrecht: Kluwer.

Rusconi, Gian Enrico. 1993. *Se cessiamo di essere una nazione*. Bologna: Il Mulino.

Sabel, Charles. 1982. *Work and Politics*. New York: Cambridge University Press.

——. 1989. "Flexible Specialization and the Reemergence of Regional Economies." In Paul Q. Hirst and Jonathon Zeitlin, eds., *Reversing Industrial Decline*. London: Berg.

——. 1992. "Studied Trust: Building New Forms of Cooperation in a Volatile Economy." In Frank Pyke and Werner Sengenberger, eds., *Industrial Districts and Local Economic Regeneration*. Geneva: International Institute for Labor Studies.

Sabel, Charles, Gary Herrigel, Richard Kazis, and Richard Deeg. 1987. "How to Keep Mature Industries Innovative." *Technology Review* 90, No. 3, April: 26–35.

Sabel, Charles, and Jonathan Zeitlin. 1985. "Historical Alternatives to Mass Production." *Past and Present* 108, August.

Salerni, Dario. 1980. *Sindacato e forza lavoro all'AlfaSud: Un caso anomalo di conflittualità industriale.* Turin: Einaudi.

Salvati, Michele. 1975. *Il sistema economico italiano: analisi di una crisi.* Bologna: Il Mulino.

——. 1980. "Muddling Through: Economics and Politics in Italy 1969–1979." In Peter Lange and Sidney Tarrow, eds., *Italy in Transition: Conflict and Consensus.* London: Frank Cass.

——. 1984. *Economia e politica in Italia dal dopoguerra a oggi.* Milan: Garzanti Editore.

——. 1985. "The Italian Inflation." In Leon Lindberg and Charles S. Maier, eds., *The Politics of Inflation and Economic Stagnation.* Washington, D.C.: Brookings Institution.

Samuels, Richard J. 1984. "Public Energy Corporations in the Industrial Democracies: Japan in Comparative Perspective." *Journal of Comparative and Commonwealth Studies* 22, no. 1.

Santi, Ettore. 1977. "Formazione e organizzazione: Il caso del Centro Studi della CISL." *Studi organizzativi* 9: 95–127.

——. 1983. "L'evoluzione delle strutture di categoria: Il caso CISL." *Prospettiva sindacale* 48.

Santi, Paolo. 1982. "All'origine della crisi del sindacato." *Quaderni Piacentini* 4.

——. 1986. "I metalmaccanici milanesi negli anni '50 e '60." Paper presented at the seminar "Il movimento dei metalmeccanici a Milano anni cinquanta e sessanta." CERISS-FIOM: Milan. October 31.

Sapelli, Giulio. 1975. *Fascismo, grande industria, e sindacato. Il caso di Torino 1929/1935.* Milan: Feltrinelli.

——. 1978. *Organizzazione, lavoro e innovazione industriale nell'Italia tra le due guerre.* Turin: Rosenberg and Sellier.

——. 1987. "La cultura della produzione: 'Autorita tecnica' e 'autonomia morale.'" In Bruno Bottiglieri and Paolo Ceri, eds., *Le culture del lavoro: L'esperienza di Torino nel quadro europeo.* Bologna: Il Mulino.

Sapelli, Giulio, Emilio Pugno, Riccardo Gobbi, and Bruno Trentin. 1979. *Fiat e Stato.* Turin: Istituto Piemontese di Scienze Economiche e Sociali Antonio Gramsci.

Sartori, Giovanni. 1966. "European Political Parties: The Case of Polarized Pluralism." In Joseph La Palombara and Myron Weiner, eds., *Political Parties and Political Development.* Princeton: Princeton University Press.

Sateriale, Gaetano. 1985. "Le aree di lavoro integrate e i circoli di qualità: L'esperienza dei chimici." *Cds documentazione* 3–4.

Saville, Lloyd. 1967. *Regional Economic Development in Italy.* Durham: Duke University Press.

Saxenian, Annalee. 1994. *Regional Advantage.* Cambridge: Harvard University Press.

References

Scamuzzi, Sergio. 1982. "Operai e impiegati Fiat tra vecchi e nuovi radicalismi." *Politica ed economia* 6.

Scanziani, Sergio. 1986. "Profili di analisi del sistema tessile Biellese." Tesi di Laurea, Facoltà di Economia e Commercio, Università Commerciale Luigi Bocconi, Milan.

Scharpf, Fritz W. 1991. *Crisis and Choice in European Social Democracy.* Ithaca: Cornell University Press.

Padoa-Schioppa, Fiorella. 1990. *L'economia sotto tutela.* Bologna: Il Mulino.

Padoa-Schioppa, Tommaso. 1987. "Reshaping Monetary Policy." In Rudiger Dornbusch, Stanley Fischer, and John Bossons, eds., *Macroeconomics and Finance: Essays in Honor of Franco Modigliani.* Cambridge: MIT Press: 265–86.

Schmitter, Phillippe. 1981. "Interest Intermediation and Regime Governability in Contemporary Western Europe and North America." In Suzanne Berger, ed., *Organizing Interests in Western Europe.* New York: Cambridge University Press.

Sciarra, Silvana. 1980. "L'influenza del sindacalismo 'americano' sulla CISL." In Guido Baglioni, ed., *Analisi della CISL,* vol. 1. Rome: Lavoro.

Sclavi, Gastone. 1982. "La chimica in Italia: Da problema politico a scelte di sviluppo industriale nazionale: Necessità di una fasi di industrializzazione del mezzogiorno." In *Programmazione nazionale e territoriale, intervento pubblico, controllo sindacale.* Rome: FULC.

Scognamiglio, Carlo. 1979a. "Il finanziamento dell attivià industriali." In Franco A. Grassini and Carlo Scognamiglio, eds., *Stato e industria in Europa: L'Italia.* Bologna: Il Mulino.

——. 1979b. "Strategie industriale e programmazione." In Franco A. Grassini and Carlo Scognamiglio, eds., *Stato e industria in Europa: L'Italia.* Bologna: Il Mulino.

Secchia, Pietro. 1960. *Capitalismo e classe operaia nel centro laniero d'Italia.* Rome: Editori Riuniti.

Serafino, Adriano. 1986. "Omissis sulla CISL Torinese." *Il Manifesto,* September 29.

Serravalle, Giovanni. 1980. *L'industria chimica in Italia e in Europa.* Milan: CLUP.

Sewell, William H., Jr. 1980. *Work and Revolution in France.* New York: Cambridge University Press.

Sforzi, Fabio. 1990. "The Quantitative Importance of Marshallian Industrial Districts in the Italian Economy." In Frank Pyke, Giacomo Beccatini, and Werner Segenberger, eds., *Industrial Districts and Inter-firm Co-operation in Italy.* Geneva: International Institute for Labor Studies: 75–107.

Shalev, Michael. 1983. "Strikes and the Crisis: Industrial Conflict and Unemployment in the Western Nations." *Economic and Industrial Democracy* 4, November.

Sheriff, Anthony M. 1986. "Fiat: The Comeback of the 1980s and the Future with Alfa Romeo." Unpublished paper. Sloan School of Management, MIT.

Shonfield, Andrew. 1965. *Modern Capitalism.* Oxford: Oxford University Press.

Silvani, Marco. 1985. "Dipendenza energetica, struttura produttiva, e composizione del commercio estero." In Fabrizio Onida, ed., *Innovazione, competitività, e vincolo energetico*. Bologna: Il Mulino.

Soskice, David. 1990. "Reinterpreting Corporatism and Explaining Unemployment: Co-ordinated and Non-co-ordinated Market Economies." In Renato Brunetta and Carlo Dell'Aringa, eds., *Labour Relations and Economic Performance*. London: Macmillan.

Spriano, Paolo. 1964. *L'occupazione delle fabbriche: Settembre 1920*. Turin: Einaudi.

Squarzon, Corrado. 1990. "Sindacalizzazione e rappresentanza." In CESOS, *Le relazioni sindacali in Italia—Rapporto 1988/89*. Rome: Lavoro.

Stedman Jones, Gareth. 1983. *Languages of Class: Studies in English Working Class History. 1832–1982*. Cambridge: Cambridge University Press.

Stefani, Giorgio. 1988. "Privatizing Italian State Holdings." *Rivista internazionale di scienze economiche e commerciali* 35, nos. 10–11.

Stern, Alan. 1975. "Political Legitimacy in Local Politics: The Communist Party in Northeastern Italy." In Donald L. M. Blackmer and Sidney Tarrow, eds., *Communism in Italy and France*. Princeton: Princeton University Press.

Streeck, Wolfgang. 1985. "Introduction: Industrial Relations, Technical Change, and Economic Restructuring." In Wolfgang Streeck, ed., *Industrial Relations and Technical Change in the British, Italian, and German Automobile Industry: Three Case Studies*. Berlin: WZB Discussion Papers.

——. 1987a. "Industrial Relations and Industrial Change: The Restructuring of the World Automobile Industry in the 1970s and 1980s." *Economic and Industrial Democracy* 8, no. 4, November: 437–62.

——. 1987b. "Skills and the Limits of Neo-Liberalism: The Enterprise of the Future as a Place of Learning." Paper presented at the Conference "Muttamenti del lavoro e trasformazione sociale." Turin. November 27–28.

——. 1991. "On the Institutional Conditions of Diversified Quality Production." In Egon Matzner and Wolfgang Streeck, eds., *Beyond Keynesianism: The Socio-Economics of Production and Employment*. London: Edward Elgar.

——. 1992. *Social Institution and Economic Performance: Studies of Industrial Relations in Advanced Capitalist Economics*. London: Sage.

Swenson, Peter. 1989. *Fair Shares: Unions, Pay, and Politics in Sweden and West Germany*. Ithaca: Cornell University Press.

Tarrow, Sidney. 1976. *Peasant Communism in Southern Italy*. New Haven: Yale University Press.

——. 1977a. *Between Center and Periphery: Grassroots Politicians in Italy and France*. New Haven: Yale University Press.

——. 1977b. "The Italian Party System: Between Crisis and Transition." *American Journal of Political Science* 21, No. 2, May: 193–224.

Tarrow, Sidney, Peter Katzenstein, and Luigi Graziano, eds. 1976. *Territorial Politics in Industrial Nations*. New York: Praeger.

Tassinari, Giorgio. 1986. *Il sistema industriale dell'Emilia-Romagna*. Bologna: Il Mulino.

Templeman, Donald C. 1981. *The Italian Economy in the 1970s*. New York: Praeger.

REFERENCES

Textile Institute. 1985. *World Textile: Investment, Innovation, Invention.* London: Textile Institute.

Thelen, Kathleen. 1991. *Union of Parts: Labor Politics in Postwar Germany.* Ithaca: Cornell University Press.

Tilly, Charles. 1975. "Reflections on the History of European State-Making" In Charles Tilly, ed., *The Formation of National States in Western Europe.* Princeton: Princeton University Press.

Tolliday, Steven, and Jonathan Zeitlin, eds. 1985. *Shop Floor Bargaining and the State: Historical and Comparative Perspectives.* Cambridge: Cambridge University Press.

Tolliday, Steven, and Jonathan Zeitlin. 1986. "Introduction: Between Fordism and Flexibility." In Steven Tolliday and Jonathan Zeitlin, eds., *The Automobile Industry and Its Workers.* Cambridge: Polity Press.

Toyne, Brian, et al. 1983. *The U.S. Textile Mill Products Industry: Strategies for the 1980s and Beyond.* Columbia: University of South Carolina Press.

Toyne, Brian, et al. 1984. *The Global Textile Industry.* London: George Allen and Unwin.

Treu, Tiziano. 1973. "La CISL degli anni '50 e le ideologie giuridiche dominanti." In Giovanni Tarello, ed., *Materiali per una storia della cultura giuridica.* Bologna: Il Mulino.

———. 1984. "L'accordo del 22 gennaro: Implicazioni e aspetti giuridico-instituzionali." In CESOS, ed., *Le relazioni sindacali in Italia, Rapporto 1983–84.* Rome: Lavoro.

———. 1986a. "Italy." In Roger Blanpain, ed., *The International Encyclopedia of Labor Law and Industrial Relations.* 11th ed. Deventer, Netherlands: Kluwer.

———. 1986b. "Le relazioni industriali nella impresa: Il protcollo IRI." *Rivista italiana di diritto del lavoro* 5, no. 3, July–September.

———. 1987. "Accordo Alfa: Scambio Vincente." *Il Sole 24 Ore,* May 20.

———. 1991. *Lo Statuto dei lavoratori vent'anni dopo.* Unpublished manuscript. Milan.

Treu, Tiziano, and Serafino Negrelli. 1983. *I diritti di informazione nell'impresa.* Bologna: Il Mulino.

Trigilia, Carlo. 1986. *Grandi partiti e piccole imprese.* Bologna: Il Mulino.

———. 1987. "La regolazione localistica: Economia e politica nelle aree di piccola impresa." In Ugo Ascoli and Rainardo Catanzaro, eds., *La società italiana degli anni ottanta.* Rome: Laterza.

———. 1989. "Il distretto industriale di Prato." In Marino Regini and Charles F. Sabel, eds., *Strategie di riaggiustamento industriale.* Bologna: Il Mulino.

———. 1992. *Sviluppo senza autonomia: Effetti perversi delle politiche nel Mezzogiorno.* Bologna: Il Mulino.

Trombetta, Pino Luca. 1979. "Sviluppo tecnologico e organizzazione del lavoro nel ciclo tessile." *Economia e politica industriale* 22.

Tullio-Altan, Carlo. 1976. *La nostra Italia: Arretratezza socioculturale, clientelismo, trasformismo e ribellismo dall'Unità ad oggi.* Milan: Feltrinelli.

Turani, Giuseppe, ed. 1976. *Sull'industria tessile.* Milan: Feltrinelli.

Turner, Lowell. 1991. *Democracy at Work: Changing World Markets and the Future of Labor Unions.* Ithaca: Cornell University Press.

Turone, Sergio. 1976. *Storia del sindacato in Italia.* Bari: Laterza.

Uberto, Franco, and Luigi Cerato. 1984. *Tecnologie e organizzazione: Sfide aperte.* Rome: ENFAPI.

Ufficio Economico Filtea Nazionale. 1983. "Primi risultati dell'indagine Fulta sull'industria laniera." Rome: Filtea Nazionale.

———. 1984a. "Valore aggiunto, fatturato, investimenti nelle imprese industriali." Rome: Filtea Nazionale.

———. 1984b. "L'industria laniera tra i due censimenti (1971–1981): Unità locali e addetti nei dati nazionali, del Piemonte, Veneto, Toscana." Rome: Filtea Nazionale.

Unione Industriale Biellese. 1980. *Biella negli anni '80.* Biella: Unione Industriale Biellese.

———. 1981. *La pendolarità dei lavoratori dipendenti dell'industria biellese.* Biella: Unione Industriale Biellese.

———. 1983. *Scuola e industria.* Biella: Unione Industriale Biellese.

———. 1986. *Sistema tessile italiano e industria biellese nel commercio internazionale (1970–1984).* Biella: Unione Industriale Biellese.

———. 1987a. *Economia biellese: 1986.* Biella: Unione Industriale Biellese.

———. 1987b. *Il ruolo dell'Italia nel commercio mondiale di prodotti meccano-tessili, 1970–1986.* Biella: Unione Industriale Biellese.

———. 1987c. *La realtà Socio-economica biellese.* Biella: Unione Industriale Biellese.

U.S. Congress, Office of Technology Assessment. 1987. *The U.S. Textile and Apparel Industry: A Revolution in Progress—Special Report.* Washington, D.C.: U.S. Government Printing Office.

U.S. Department of Commerce, International Trade Administration. 1987. *A Competitive Assessment of the U.S. Textile Machinery Industry.* Washington, D.C.: U.S. Government Printing Office.

Utili, Gabriella. 1989. "Mutamenti organizzativi nei distretti industriali: Osservazioni su due casi." In Fabio Gobba, ed., *Distretti e sistemi produttivi alla soglia degli anni '90.* Milan: Franco Angeli: 61–90.

Vannicelli, Maurizio. 1984. "A Labor Movement in Search of a Role: The Evolution of the Strategy of the Italian Unions since 1943." Diss., Department of Government, Harvard University.

Vignoli, Italo. 1992. "Torino: La città-Fiat." In Riccardo Mainardi and Carlo Tombola, eds., *Grandi città e aree metropolitane,* vol. 1. Milan: Franco Angeli.

Visser, Jelle. 1987. "Trade Unionism in Western Europe: Present Situation and Prospects." Paper presented at the Symposium "The Future of Trade Unionism in Industrial Market Economies." Turin. December 9–11.

Volpato, Giuseppe. 1983. *L'industria automobilistica internazionale.* Padua: CEDAM.

———. 1986. "The Automobile Industry in Transition: Product Market Changes and Firm Strategies in the 1970s and 1980s." In Steven Tolliday and Jonathan Zeitlin, eds., *The Automobile Industry and Its Workers.* Cambridge, U.K.: Polity Press.

———. 1993. "Una strategia di rioganizzazione e di rilancio: La Fiat negli anni ottanta e novanta." Unpublished manuscript. Venice.

Volpato, Giuseppe, and Arnaldo Camuffo. 1992. "Past Patterns and Emerging Trends of Assembly Automation in the Italian Automobile Industry." Paper presented at the International Workshop "Assembly Automation and Work Organization in the Automobile Industry." Berlin: WZB. November 21.

von Hippel, Eric. 1987. "Cooperation between Rivals: Informal Know-How Trading." *Research Policy* 16, no. 6, December: 291–302.

———. 1988. *The Sources of Innovation*. New York: Oxford University Press.

Watkins, J. W. N. 1978. "Ideal Types and Historical Explanation." In Alan Ryan, ed., *The Philosophy of Social Explanation*. Oxford: Oxford University Press.

Weiss, Linda. 1988. *Creating Capitalism: The State and Small Business since 1945*. Oxford: Basil Blackwell.

Weitz, Peter R. 1975. "Labor and Politics in a Divided Movement: The Italian Case." *Industrial and Labor Relations Review* 28, No. 2, January: 226–42.

Welluz, Stanislow H. 1957. "The Coexistence of Large and Small Firms: A Study of the Italian Mechanical Industries." *Quarterly Journal of Economics* 71, February.

Wilentz, Sean. 1984. *Chants Democratic: New York City and the Rise of the American Working Class, 1788–1850*. New York: Oxford University Press.

Wollieb, Enrico, and Gugliemo Wollieb. 1991. *Divari regionali e dualismo economico*. Bologna: Il Mulino.

Womack, James, Daniel T. Jones, and Daniel Roos. 1990. *The Machine That Changed the World*. New York: Rawson Associates.

Woods, Dwayne. 1992. "The Centre No Longer Holds: The Rise of Regional Leagues in Italian Politics" *West European Politics* 15, no. 2, April: 56–76.

Zamagni, Vera. 1990. "L'industria chimica in Italia dalle origini agli anni '50." In Franco Amatori and Bruno Bezza, eds., *Montecatini 1886–1966*. Bologna: Il Mulino 1990: 69–148.

Zanetti, Giovanni. 1986. *La piccola impresa tra sviluppo e innovazione tecnologica: Una indagine condotto su 900 imprese dell'area torinese*. Turin: API.

Zanfei, Antonello. 1985. "Cambiamento tecnologico e strategie di internazionalizzazione delle imprese tessili italiane." *Economia e politica industriale* 46, 47.

Ziegler, Jonathan Nicholas. 1989. "The State and Technological Advance: Political Efforts for Industrial Change in France and the Federal Republic of Germany, 1972–1986." Diss., Department of Government, Harvard University.

Zoccatelli, Mario. 1991. "Esperienze partecipative nell'industria italiana: Il settore tessile-abbigliamento." Paper prepared for the Seminar "La Partecipazione nell'Impresa degli Anni '90: Indicazioni dalle Esperenze Francesi e Italiane." Rome: ENI-ISVET. April 23.

Zuckerman, Alan S. 1979. *The Politics of Faction: Christian Democratic Rule in Italy*. New Haven: Yale University Press.

Zysman, John. 1977. *Political Strategies for Industrial Order: State, Market, and Industry in France*. Berkeley: University of California Press.

———. 1983. *Governments, Markets, and Growth*. Ithaca: Cornell University Press.

Index

Cornell Studies in Political Economy

EDITED BY PETER J. KATZENSTEIN